AN HONOURABLE
DEFEAT

AN HONOURABLE
DEFEAT

A History of German
Resistance to Hitler, 1933–1945

Anton Gill

Henry Holt and Company
New York

Henry Holt and Company, Inc.
Publishers since 1866
115 West 18th Street
New York, New York 10011

Henry Holt® is a registered trademark
of Henry Holt and Company, Inc.

Library of Congress Cataloging-in-Publication Data
Gill, Anton
An honourable defeat : a history of German
resistance to Hitler, 1933–1945 / Anton Gill. — 1st ed.
p.   cm.
Includes bibliographical references and index.
1. Anti-Nazi movement—Germany.   2. Hitler, Adolf,
1889–1945—Assassination attempt, 1944 (July 20)
3. Germany—Politics and government—1933–1945.
I. Title.
DD256.3.G465   1994   94-14833
943.086—dc20   CIP

ISBN 0-8050-3514-1

Henry Holt books are available for special promotions
and premiums. For details contact: Director, Special Markets.

First American Edition—1994

Printed in the United States of America
All first editions are printed on acid-free paper.∞

1   3   5   7   9   10   8   6   4   2

Illustration acknowledgments appear on page 295.

This book is dedicated to
all those Germans who risked and gave their lives
for the sake of humanity and freedom, because
they would not accept the Nazi dictatorship,
and to all those who resist
dictatorship today.

ACKNOWLEDGEMENTS

There are not many survivors of the struggle within Germany against Hitler. After the failure of the famous assassination attempt by Graf Stauffenberg at Rastenburg on 20 July 1944, the Gestapo and the Security Service launched an enormous operation (known as 'Thunderstorm') in the course of which about 7000 people were arrested, of whom 4500 were executed. In their last orgy of summary justice and killing, the Nazis brought in many thousands who were innocent of any plot to kill the dictator, but who had long been under suspicion – however slight – of disloyalty to the regime. The authorities also found themselves with an excuse to execute many more dissidents who had been in prison or the concentration camps since before the 20 July attempt. Virtually all the leading players in the German Resistance died at the time. In finding witnesses of the period today there is another problem: this book describes events which took place half a century ago; since then natural mortality has thinned even further the ranks of those who took part.

I am very grateful to the relatives and friends of those who died for sharing their memories of them with me, and to the handful of people still alive who experienced the events themselves, as young Army officers, Communist activists, nurses, civil servants, priests and factory workers, to give only a few of their occupations. Several of the names I list below recur in the book in heroic contexts, and I am privileged to have met people capable of not only such physical bravery but also of moral courage. I thank everyone who has helped me in this difficult but rewarding task. Without them I could not have completed it.

For their interest in my work, for their time, expertise, hospitality and generosity I wish to thank: Inge Aicher-Scholl, Professor Theodor Bergmann, Christabel Bielenberg, Birgit Brandau, Major Nigel Browne, Franz Brückl, the late Axel Freiherr von dem Bussche, Clare Colvin, Professor David Dilks, Dr Klaus von Dohnanyi, Nicholas Elliott, Professor Dr Theodor Eschenburg, Eberhard Fechner, Joachim Fest, Professor Dr Ossip K. Flechtheim, Ann Fox, David Fox, George and Nikki Gill, Nicola Gill, Julius Goldstein, Alan Gunn, Ludwig Freiherr von Hammerstein-Equord, Zenta Herker, Victoria Huntingdon-Whiteley, Dominique Jubien, Ernst Kehler, Eugen Kessler, Dr Lothar Kettenacker of the German Historical Institute, London; Ewald Heinrich von Kleist, the late Professor Ulrich Klug, Wolfgang and Sabine Koch, Barbara von Krauss (*née* Oster), Dr A.E. Laurence, Mark Lucas, Sue Maconachy, Max Mannheimer, Kunigunda Messerschmitt, Jo Morley, Erna Nelki, Gertrud Neubaur (*née* Beck), David Neville, Kate Neville, Dr Traute Page (*née* Lafrenz), Dr Jochen Rasch, Emma Rhind-Tutt, Irmgard Roecken, Manfred Rommel, Connie and Edwin Rosenstiel, Hartmut Schickert, Adam and Elisabeth Schliefer, Fritz Graf von der Schulenburg, David Sincock, Franz Ludwig Graf Stauffenberg, Nina Gräfin Schenk von Stauffenberg, Otto-Philipp Graf Stauffenberg, Joe Steeples, John Stevenson, Klaus Täubert, Dr Clarita von Trott zu Solz, Dr Johannes Tuchel, Tom Weldon, the late Sir Dick White, Stephen White, Christa Wichmann, and Dr Jürgen Zarusky.
I also wish to acknowledge the help of the following institutions, their staffs and archivists: the British Library, London; Bundesarchiv Koblenz; Bundesarchiv Militärarchiv Freiburg i. Br.; Gedenkstätte Deutscher Widerstand, Berlin; Geheimes Staatsarchiv Preussischer Kulturbesitz; the Goethe Institute Library, London; Interessenverband ehemaliger Teilnehmer am antifaschistischen Widerstand, Verfolgter des Naziregimes und Hinterbliebener (IVVdN) e.V.; Institut für Zeitgeschichte, Munich; Landesarchiv Berlin; Maximilian-Kolbe-Werke; Preussische Staatsbibliothek; Vereinigung des Verfolgten des Naziregimes (VVN); the Wiener Library, London; and the Zentralverband Demokratischer Widerstandskämpfer (ZVDW).

There is a large amount of material available in Germany on the Resistance. It has been the subject of many and varied commentaries in the last fifty years, and some of what is published, in the absence of much written material from the conspirators themselves, is contradictory and hard to verify. Different periods of history since the war, responding to different political pressures, the most obvious of which was the Cold War, have handled the material in a variety of ways. Fresh sources are becoming available from the archives of the former German Democratic Republic (East Germany), and from Eastern Europe and the Commonwealth of Independent States generally, though, to judge from what I have seen, it will take many years to explore them fully. I have verified everything here to the best of my ability, and I take responsibility for any errors. All translations from German are my own, unless I have acknowledged them otherwise in the Notes.

CONTENTS

CHRONOLOGY

(Dates of meetings and conferences of more than one day's duration are those on which they began.)

1933

30 January	Hitler becomes Chancellor.
31 January	Communists and Social Democrats declare their opposition to Hitler.
27 February	Reichstag fire.
3 March	Wave of arrests of Communists. Many to exile. Those who remain begin underground work.
21 March	Potsdam Day.
23 March	Enabling Act passed.
1 April	Boycott Day (boycott of Jewish shops).
2 May	Dissolution of trade unions.
10 May	Book burning (burning of proscribed books).
June and July	All political parties officially disbanded. National Socialist and Democratic Workers' Party of Germany becomes only party.
3 June	Social Democratic Party in Exile founded in Prague.
20 July	Concordat with Vatican signed.
21 September	Niemöller forms Pastors' Emergency League.
14 October	Germany withdraws from League of Nations.

1934

16 February	Catholic Church places Rosenberg's *The Myth of the Twentieth Century* on the Index.

22 April	First meeting of Confessing Church at Ulm.
29 May	First synod of Confessing Church at Barmen.
17 June	Franz von Papen makes anti-Nazi speech at Marburg University.
30 June	Night of the Long Knives purge begins.
2 August	Death of Hindenburg. Hitler becomes President and Chancellor. Personal Oath of Loyalty demanded of Armed Forces.

1935

16 March	Conscription reintroduced.
May and June	Wave of Social Democrat Underground arrests.
18 June	Anglo-German naval agreement.
15 September	Nuremberg laws formalise measures already started against Jews.

1936

7 March	German troops enter the Rhineland.
August	Olympic Games held in Berlin.
9 September	Hitler announces Four Year Plan.
25 October	Treaty with Italy.
25 November	Treaty with Japan.
1 December	Membership of Hitler Youth and League of German Girls made compulsory.

1937

January and February	Wave of Communist underground arrests.
14 March	Encyclical 'With Deepest Anxiety' (*Mit brennender Sorge*) by Pope Pius XI.
June	Goerdeler travelling abroad.
1 July	Niemöller arrested.
26 November	Schacht resigns from Economics Ministry.

1938

4 February	Blomberg resigns. Fritsch compromised. Reorganisation of leadership of Armed Forces gives Hitler much wider power.
12 February	Austrian Chancellor Schuschnigg visits Hitler.
2 March	Niemöller sent to concentration camp.
12 March	Annexation of Austria.
20 May	Czech Army mobilises.

May–July	Beck submits memoranda to Brauchitsch opposing Hitler's war plans.
21 August	Beck's resignation accepted.
September	Chamberlain struggles to prevent war at all costs. Culmination of efforts at Munich torpedoes first planned coup against Hitler by the Resistance.
October	Sudetenland annexed.
9 November	*Kristallnacht*: national night of atrocities against Jews.

1939

20 January	Schacht dismissed from Presidency of State Bank.
15 March	Germany invades Bohemia and Moravia. Slovakia becomes a separate vassal state.
23 March	Germany annexes Memelland.
31 March	Britain and France make Treaty with Poland.
23 August	Germany and USSR sign Non-Aggression Pact.
1 September	Germany and USSR invade Poland.
3 September	Britain and France declare war on Germany.
October	Euthanasia programme secretly put in train.
2 October	Adam von Trott zu Solz arrives in New York.
6 October	Hitler makes veiled peace proposal to Allies.
5 November	Hitler outfaces Brauchitsch.
8 November	Elser's assassination attempt. Second planned coup fails to get airborne.
9 November	Venlo Incident.

1940

9 April	Germany invades Denmark and Norway.
10 May	Germany invades Holland, Belgium and Luxemburg. Churchill replaces Chamberlain as Prime Minister of Britain.
28 May	Dunkirk.
10 June	Italy enters war.
22 June	France occupied.
July–October	Battle of Britain.

1941

8 March	USA agrees officially to aid Britain.
10 May	Rudolf Hess flies to Scotland.

22 June	Germany invades USSR.
July and August	Galen's sermons against the euthanasia programme.
1 December	German Army halted before Moscow.
7 December	Japanese bomb Pearl Harbor.
11 December	Germany declares war on USA.
19 December	Brauchitsch retired. Hitler takes over command of the Army.

1942

20 January	Wannsee Conference decides on extermination programme for the Jews – the 'Final Solution'.
10 April	Moltke and Dietrich Bonhoeffer visit Norway.
22 May	First Kreisau Circle meeting at Moltke's estate.
26 May	Assassination of Gestapo leader Reinhard Heydrich. Anglo-Soviet Pact.
26 May	Schönfeld and later Dietrich Bonhoeffer meet Bishop George Bell in Sweden.
16 October	Second Kreisau meeting.
11 November	Germany occupies Vichy France. Allen Dulles opens OSS office in Berne.

1943

24 January	Casablanca Conference. Churchill and hawkish Roosevelt agree to demand Unconditional Surrender from Germany.
2 February	6th Army surrenders at Stalingrad.
18 February	Goebbels' 'Total War' speech at the Berlin Sports Palace.
13 March	Operation Flash – bomb attempt on Hitler in Smolensk.
21 March	Bomb attempt on Hitler in Berlin by Gersdorff.
5 April	Resistance within Abwehr broken up. Arrests of Hans von Dohnanyi, Dietrich Bonhoeffer and others.
12 June	Third Kreisau meeting.
19 July	National Committee for Free Germany founded.
25 July	Fall of Mussolini.

| August and September | Collapse of Red Orchestra organisation in Berlin. |
| 1 October | Stauffenberg becomes Chief of Staff to Olbricht. |

1944

19 January	Arrests of Solf Circle and Moltke. Collapse of Kreisau Circle.
6 June	D-Day.
1 July	Stauffenberg becomes Chief of Staff to Fromm.
2 July	Kluge becomes commander-in-chief on west front.
17 July	Rommel wounded.
20 July	Stauffenberg's bomb attempt on Hitler at the Wolf's Lair.
21 July	Operation Thunderstorm: massive wave of Gestapo arrests begins. Show trials and executions follow for rest of year and until end of war.
12 August	Arrest of Goerdeler.

1945

9 April	Dietrich Bonhoeffer, Canaris, Oster and others hanged at Flossenburg concentration camp.
22 April	SS murder Klaus Bonhoeffer, Guttenberg, Schleicher and others in Berlin.
30 April	Hitler commits suicide.
7 May	War ends.

THE RESISTANCE NETWORK

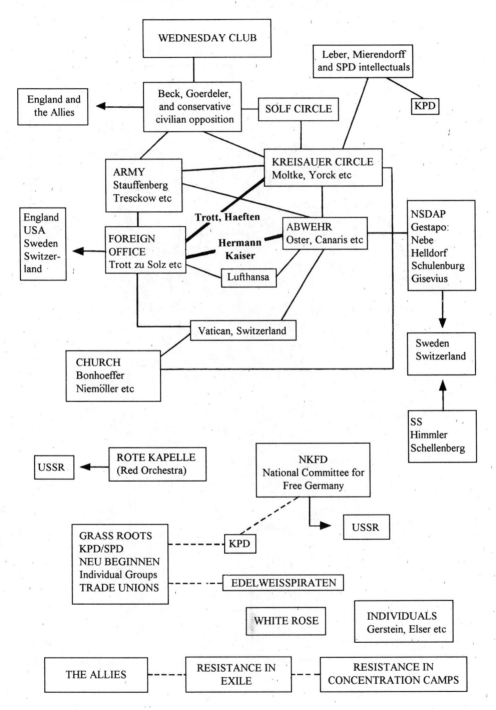

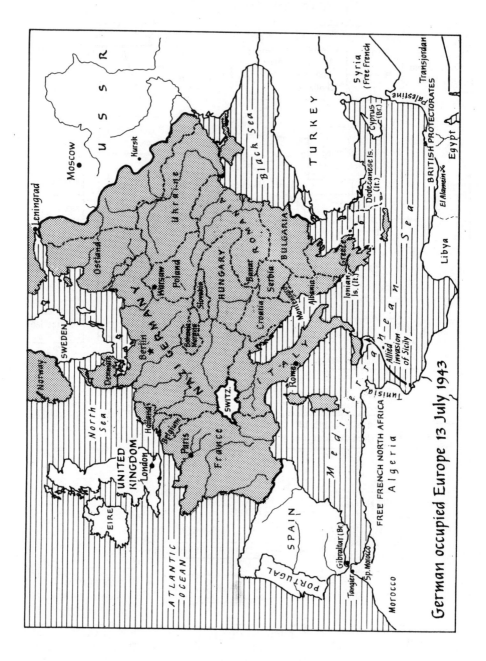

German occupied Europe 13 July, 1943

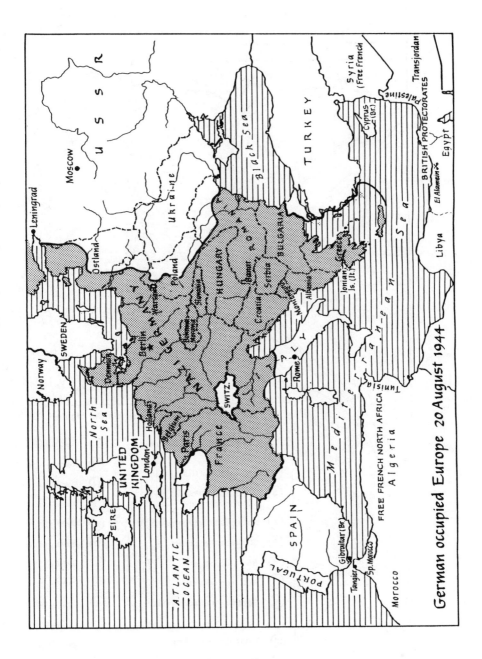

German occupied Europe 20 August 1944

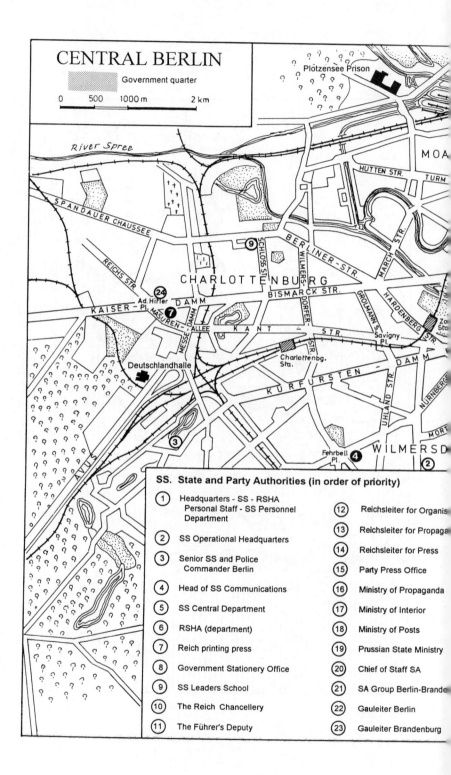

CENTRAL BERLIN

Government quarter

0   500   1000 m   2 km

Plötzensee Prison

River Spree

MOA

HUTTEN STR.

TURM

SPANDAUER CHAUSSEE

BERLINER - STR.

SCHLOSS STR.

WILMERS-DORFER STR.

MARCH STR.

REICHS STR.

CHARLOTTENBURG

BISMARCK STR.

GROLMANN STR.

HARDENBERG STR.

Ad. Hitler DAMM

KAISER - PL.

MASUREN- ALLEE

MESSE- DAMM

KANT — STR.

Savigny Pl.

Zo
Sta

Deutschlandhalle

Charlottenbg. Sta.

DAMM

KURFURSTEN - DAMM

UHLAND STR.

NÜRNBERGE

AVUS

STR.

MORT

Fehrbell Pl.

WILMERSD

SS. State and Party Authorities (in order of priority)

1. Headquarters - SS - RSHA
   Personal Staff - SS Personnel
   Department

2. SS Operational Headquarters

3. Senior SS and Police
   Commander Berlin

4. Head of SS Communications

5. SS Central Department

6. RSHA (department)

7. Reich printing press

8. Government Stationery Office

9. SS Leaders School

10. The Reich Chancellery

11. The Führer's Deputy

12. Reichsleiter for Organis

13. Reichsleiter for Propaga

14. Reichsleiter for Press

15. Party Press Office

16. Ministry of Propaganda

17. Ministry of Interior

18. Ministry of Posts

19. Prussian State Ministry

20. Chief of Staff SA

21. SA Group Berlin-Brande

22. Gauleiter Berlin

23. Gauleiter Brandenburg

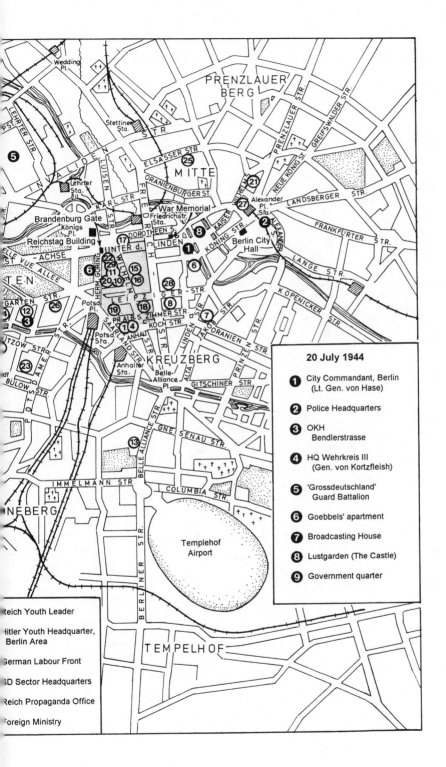

20 July 1944

1 City Commandant, Berlin
(Lt. Gen. von Hase)

2 Police Headquarters

3 OKH
Bendlerstrasse

4 HQ Wehrkreis III
(Gen. von Kortzfleish)

5 'Grossdeutschland'
Guard Battalion

6 Goebbels' apartment

7 Broadcasting House

8 Lustgarden (The Castle)

9 Government quarter

Reich Youth Leader

Hitler Youth Headquarter,
Berlin Area

German Labour Front

SD Sector Headquarters

Reich Propaganda Office

Foreign Ministry

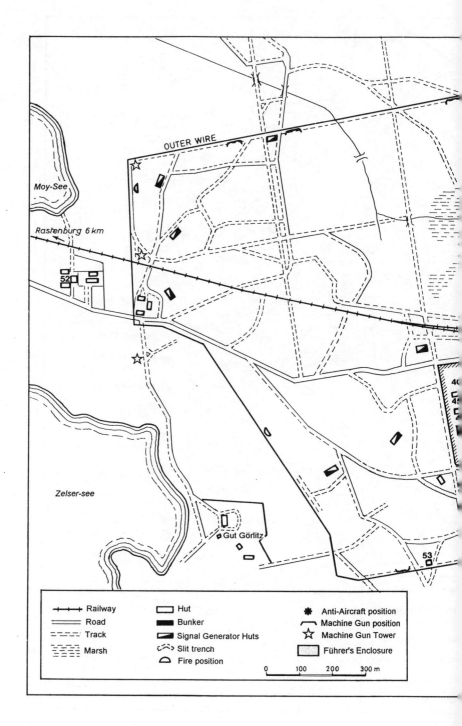

Moy-See

Rastenburg 6 km

OUTER WIRE

52

Zelser-see

Gut Görlitz

40
44

53

┼┼┼ Railway	▭ Hut		✳ Anti-Aircraft position
═══ Road	▬ Bunker		⌒ Machine Gun position
┄┄┄ Track	◼ Signal Generator Huts		☆ Machine Gun Tower
▨ Marsh	⌇ Slit trench		▦ Führer's Enclosure
	⌓ Fire position		

0   100   200   300 m

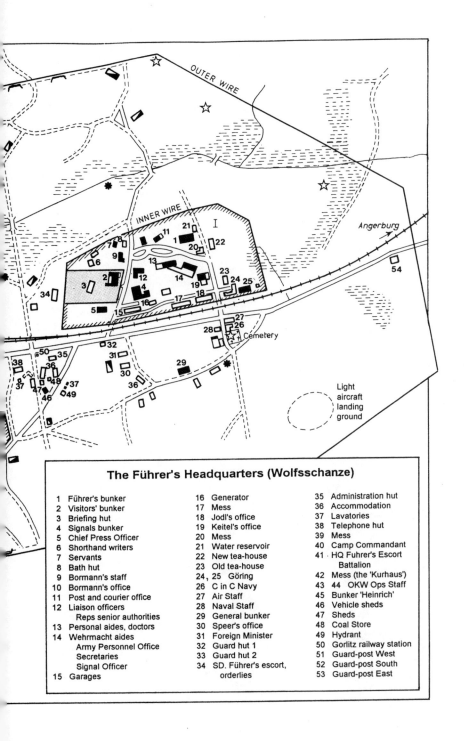

The Führer's Headquarters (Wolfsschanze)

1 Führer's bunker
2 Visitors' bunker
3 Briefing hut
4 Signals bunker
5 Chief Press Officer
6 Shorthand writers
7 Servants
8 Bath hut
9 Bormann's staff
10 Bormann's office
11 Post and courier office
12 Liaison officers
  Reps senior authorities
13 Personal aides, doctors
14 Wehrmacht aides
  Army Personnel Office
  Secretaries
  Signal Officer
15 Garages

16 Generator
17 Mess
18 Jodl's office
19 Keitel's office
20 Mess
21 Water reservoir
22 New tea-house
23 Old tea-house
24, 25 Göring
26 C in C Navy
27 Air Staff
28 Naval Staff
29 General bunker
30 Speer's office
31 Foreign Minister
32 Guard hut 1
33 Guard hut 2
34 SD. Führer's escort,
  orderlies

35 Administration hut
36 Accommodation
37 Lavatories
38 Telephone hut
39 Mess
40 Camp Commandant
41 HQ Fuhrer's Escort
  Battalion
42 Mess (the 'Kurhaus')
43 44 OKW Ops Staff
45 Bunker 'Heinrich'
46 Vehicle sheds
47 Sheds
48 Coal Store
49 Hydrant
50 Gorlitz railway station
51 Guard-post West
52 Guard-post South
53 Guard-post East

FOREWORD

Only a few Germans resisted the Nazi regime. But what is Resistance? Is it participating in a plan to overthrow a government and kill its leader, is it writing 'Down with Hitler' – or whoever the leader might be – in chalk or paint on a wall, or is it everything between those two extremes? In Germany under Hitler's regime, the penalty for the second offence, and less than that, was death. Under such circumstances, it is difficult to set a limit to what Resistance is. German historians are obsessed by the significance of the word, as well they might be in a country where those who conspired against Hitler are celebrated in street-names in liberal cities like Berlin, but ignored elsewhere. The biographer Wolfgang Venohr writes: 'The chief conspirator of 1944, Claus von Stauffenberg, isn't popular in his own country. Katarina Lazarova, a Slovak writer and anti-fascist fighter in those days, told me in an interview: "If he had been my countryman, we would have erected monuments to him, would have bound wreaths, written histories, poems, songs . . ."'[1]

Several relatives of conspirators whose names are famous told me that to carry such a surname was a disadvantage in postwar Germany – a fact which bears out the conspirators' fear at the time that by killing Hitler before the war was definitively lost they might create a myth around the monster, along the lines of: 'If only Hitler had been spared we might have won the war after all.' It is certain that at no stage could the conspirators, at whatever level they were working, count on the absolute support of the populace or even the Army. But we who have never lived in a police state, who can criticise the government in letters to the paper or on an open postcard to a

friend, who can speak our minds freely on the telephone, can have
no idea of what it is like to work against a regime whose hold on
power depends on fear and informers, on mistrust and deception,
on children reporting parents and parents denouncing children. We
have not even had the experience of living in a country occupied by
such a power – like France – and yet even there, where the patriotic
and political issues were clear cut, where every Axis soldier was an
enemy, only 2 per cent of the adult population were involved in the
Resistance at any level.

In Germany, the issues were never clear cut. Unlike the First
World War, there was no enthusiasm for the Second. Hitler ran the
country into massive debt very quickly, and rejoicing at his solution
of the unemployment problem was soon dampened by the straitened
circumstances – both physical and ethical – under which the Nazis
forced people to live. The depression of the late twenties and the
thirties was universal, yet other countries resolved their material
problems without becoming totalitarian states, and Germans were
aware of this. But even those who resisted Hitler still had to live
and work within German society. Those who had jobs in the Army,
the Intelligence Service and the Foreign Office had to do their duty
as Germans at the same time as they obeyed their consciences by
working against the evil government. They had to remind themselves that by betraying that government they were not betraying
their country. They had to accept that defeat was necessary and
desirable for Germany – a *sine qua non* of its moral rebirth. But
it was hard to accept. At the same time, they had to work under
the enormous pressure of the fear of denunciation, and to cope for
years with a Jekyll-and-Hyde existence. These pressures became
greater according to the degree of responsibility, executive power
and, therefore, effectiveness, of the conspirator; and the Resistance
to Hitler necessarily took the form of a revolution from above. The
Nazis were quick to stamp out or drive into exile their most powerful
political opponents, and the political underground lacked the means
of expressing itself other than through pamphleteering and limited
acts of sabotage. The Army, with its strongly forged infrastructure
and its practical power, was the only organisation with the potential
capacity to overthrow the government. But the Army was managed
traditionally by the ruling class.

Hitler found his fatal moment in German history. Germany was

– and still is – a very young democracy. It was only united as a federation of states in 1871, and military and monarchist traditions survived well after the defeat of 1918 and the departure of the Kaiser. The Weimar Republic's first politicians led the world in democratic principles but never developed enough stability of government for the Republic itself to survive. They were constantly attacked by conservative and popular elements for having 'stabbed the Army in the back' by surrendering (in fact it was the Army that surrendered), and for signing the Treaty of Versailles. The Treaty, designed to have the maximum humbling effect on Germany, demanded considerable loss of territory, the establishment of a Polish corridor to the Baltic coast which separated East Prussia from the body of the Fatherland, and required the Germans to have a standing army of no more than 100,000 men. The Imperial Army never got over this humiliation, and those who survived within it were no friends of the civilian Social Democrats who had taken power in 1919. Never mind that Germany had imposed far harsher terms on Russia by the Treaty of Brest-Litovsk, rearmament and the re-establishment of Germany as the central and leading power of Europe were at the forefront of conservative German minds. They looked back to Bismarck with nostalgia, and the succession of tottering coalitions which governed them between 1919 and 1933 gave them no reason to feel optimistic.

Nevertheless, it was from within the Army that the main Resistance to Hitler came, as a handful of determined officers perceived the evil towards which the Führer was leading the country. The German Air Force was a new service and more or less entirely a Nazi creation, though a word should be said in favour of Colonel-General Ernst Udet, a First World War ace and the Luftwaffe's administrative chief. Never a Nazi, he was forced to commit suicide in 1941, after it had been established that the Air Force could not maintain a war on multiple fronts, and that warplane production for such a fight was impossible. Udet became the scapegoat, carrying the blame for Göring's mismanagement.[2] The Navy, which had been the great revolutionary force at the end of the First World War, provided only a handful of men to the Resistance, and its commanders, first Raeder and later Dönitz, were completely loyal to Hitler. In any case, the problems posed by trying to present a unified front against Hitler were great enough in the Army; they would have been impossible to overcome in a service whose forces were spread across the world.

As Hitler imposed his own ideas of command on the Armed Forces, the department known as Oberkommando Wehrmacht (OKW) – Overall High Command of the Armed Forces – came into being. Under it were the three High Command Offices of the Army, Navy and Air Force – the OKH (Oberkommando des Heeres), the OKM (Oberkommando der Kriegsmarine) and the OKL (Oberkommando der Luftwaffe). Only the first of these plays a significant part in this story. Within it were the Army General Staff Office, concerned with operations, intelligence, administration and so on; and the Allgemeines Heeresamt (AHA) – the General Army Office, concerned with supplies, publications and budgets. From the ranks of these two offices, whose members, crucially, had no direct command of troops, the majority of the members of the military Resistance came.[3]

The two other official organisations which were of central importance to the Resistance were the Foreign Office and the Abwehr. Nazi administration was extraordinarily complicated – it seemed to grow organically, almost whimsically, reflecting the various individual ambitions and intrigues of the leaders – Himmler, Heydrich, Göring and Goebbels. At the centre of the web sat Hitler, using his demonic criminal genius to divide and rule. Thus it was that the foreign minister, Ribbentrop, established his own office, 'the Ribbentrop Bureau', which was run independently of the Foreign Office under its Secretary of State, Ernst von Weizsäcker, a courageous man who fought the Party from within, and under whose aegis contacts abroad were maintained and developed.

The Abwehr was made up of several departments dealing with military intelligence and counter-espionage, among other duties. It reported to the OKW and was responsible for liaison between the OKW and the Foreign Office. It was not a Party organisation, and until spring 1943 and even for some time thereafter it was a vital centre of Resistance.

Towards the end of the war, the Abwehr was integrated into the vast secret intelligence and police organisation called the Reichssicherheitshauptamt (RSHA) – the Chief Office of State Security, among whose many branches (there were seven departments comprising 180 sub-departments) were the Sicherheitsdienst (SD) – the Security Service – and its most notorious executive arm, the Geheime Staatspolizei (Gestapo) – the Secret State Police. The other main organ of the Nazi terror system was the SS, Hitler's 'private army', led by Himmler.

This in turn had two main divisions: the Waffen SS, or fighting units; and the Totenkopfverbände – the Death's Head Brigades, which ran the concentration camps.

These then were the principal battle lines for one of the most difficult and dangerous struggles in modern history. However, the validity and even the existence of the Resistance have been disputed. Bad luck dogged the conspirators' attempts to remove Hitler, and on three occasions nothing but a perverse Fate saved his life. For a variety of reasons, some inexcusable but others perfectly understandable, the Allies refused to help them. As the war dragged on they became increasingly isolated, and at the end they knew that they would fail – if not to kill Hitler, then to destroy his regime and thereby save Germany and Germany's honour. But for the sake of that honour they persisted.

In reading their history it is important to understand the conspirators and their political aspirations in the context of their period. Few of them survived their failure; if they had, they would have seen a postwar world and a postwar Germany quite different from the one they had imagined and planned. But the wheel has turned again since 1945. Germany is reunified and powerful; Europe is unstable and in economic disarray; nationalism has raised its head once more. Humanity never learns the lessons of history, and so perhaps the conspirators' ideas are not as remote as all that. I think Schopenhauer has written truly: 'However much the plays and the masks on the world's stage may change, it is always the same actors who appear. We sit together and talk and grow excited, and our eyes glitter and our voices grow shriller: just so did *others* sit and talk a thousand years ago: it was the same thing, and it was the *same people*: and it will be just so a thousand years hence. The contrivance which prevents us from perceiving this is *time*.'[4]

Part One

1933–1938

A Nazi bigwig on holiday in Switzerland asked
what a certain official building was. 'That's our
Admiralty,' his Swiss companion told him. The
Nazi laughed mockingly. 'You mean to say you
have an Admiralty – you, with your two or three
ships?' The Swiss gave him a straight look and
said, 'In that case you'd better tell me what you
Germans want with a Ministry of Justice.'

ONE

The End of the Republic

On 30 January 1933 Paul von Hindenburg made Adolf Hitler Chancellor of Germany. Hindenburg was in his eighty-sixth year, a hero of the First World War who had come out of retirement to take on the Presidency of the ailing Weimar Republic in obedience to his sense of duty. He was a confirmed monarchist himself, and had even asked the exiled former Kaiser's permission to assume the office. The old soldier had been at his post for eight years now, having defeated Hitler in the presidential elections of 1932, and he was tired. His was not a political temperament, and now his mind was giving way to old age. It is hard to imagine with what feelings he conferred the Chancellorship on Hitler, a man whom only four days earlier he had referred to contemptuously as 'the Austrian corporal', and declared that he would never give him even the Ministry of Posts. But his advisers, his own son among them, had told him that this peevish and insecure forty-three-year-old, with his rasping peasant accent and uncouth manners, who only very recently had become a naturalised German, was the only hope for his country. The quick succession of shaky coalition governments which had marked the last few years had brought the country to the brink of economic collapse, and Germany was in danger of coming apart at the seams: above all, there loomed the spectre of Bolshevism. A strong hand was needed on the wheel of state.

For Hitler, quiet and reserved for once, his brown uniform exchanged for a morning coat, the day marked the culmination of a decade of struggle. His first attempt to seize power, in November 1923, had misfired disastrously, but the German government had neither repatriated him to Austria nor imposed a long prison sentence on him. He turned the twelve months in Landsberg fortress to good effect, living in relative comfort, writing *Mein Kampf*, and, by his own account, collecting and ordering his thoughts and emotions. On his release, he returned to his work with a will, and found Germany not at all an unsympathetic place to be. He developed the small political party he had joined and then taken over with great speed and remorseless energy. At the same time, he was careful to remain within the bounds of the law, earning him the nickname among his opponents of Adolphe Légalité. Even after his assumption of power he paid lip service to the Constitution, though he never subsequently pretended to be curbed or controlled by it. Others, particularly the Social Democrats, found it comfortable, for the short time left to them, to believe that he was.

The truth was that Hitler was a brutal powermonger who disposed of anything he disagreed with, and anyone who got in his way, with utter ruthlessness. His very crudeness and his disregard for any accepted political or diplomatic rules caught his opponents, both at home and abroad, wrong-footed. His initial successes blinded people to his immorality, and his criminal megalomania was mistaken for strength of purpose. Above all, his supporters on the conservative right in Germany, and those who were to become his opponents in the Army, thought they could control him. By the time they realised they could not, it was too late. His chief political rivals, the Social Democrats and the Communists, made the mistake of regarding each other, and not the Nazis, as the most dangerous enemy. Instead of banding together against the threat of National Socialism, they dissipated their energy in fighting each other; and though violent street battles between Communists and Nazis typified the Berlin of the early thirties, the two parties were briefly allied during a public transport strike in the capital in 1932.

Not that Germany wasn't forewarned. The thuggishness of the National Socialist Party's private army, the Sturmabteilung (SA), or brownshirts,[1] was well-known before Hitler came to power. Once he had power, he barely troubled to camouflage his intentions. Thousands of brownshirts marched throughout Berlin in triumphant torchlit processions on the night Hitler was declared Chancellor.

One reaction to him was simple disbelief; another, that such a man could not possibly last a year. Part of Hitler's initial success was due to the fact that enough powerful people did not take him seriously, and part was due to the related fact that they did not see him for what he really was. One man under no illusions was the eminent painter Max Liebermann, born in the same year as Hindenburg. When he saw the torchlight processions cross Pariser Platz under the Brandenburg Gate, he closed the shutters of his flat windows. 'There comes a time when you can't eat as much as you want to throw up,' he remarked to journalists. He died two years later. He had never reopened his shutters.

Hitler was also a brilliant opportunist, with a famous sixth sense for personal danger which helped preserve him more than any of his considerable security measures. His indecisiveness, his habit of changing his plans at the last minute, and of not attending a given meeting or function at the appointed time, also hamstrung attempts to kill him. It is not hard to imagine Hitler living out his life as a kind of dream – a fantasy-fulfilment which even he could hardly have imagined possible. At each new step he may have asked himself, 'Am I going to be able to carry this one off too?' And as time progressed, and his success continued, so he might well have come to believe in his own infallibility. He never so far lost his grip of reality, however, as to neglect matters regarding his own safety.

Hitler was under no illusions about the dissident elements in the Army, especially in the General Staff, and always regarded the Army with suspicion, even after he had 'tamed' it. In 1933 the Army, traditionally above politics, was prepared to go along with what it perceived as a strong new leader who was committed to rearmament (in the interests of defence) and the re-establishment of Germany's place in the world. They were prepared to turn a blind eye to the bully-boy tactics of his minions; but in any case senior officers had no love or respect for the democratic tradition as demonstrated by the Weimar Republic, and they feared the influence of Bolshevism in a country where the Communist Party had always been extremely powerful. This is not to say that some senior members of the Army were not opposed to Hitler from the very first. There was even a plot to topple Hitler on the eve of his appointment to the Chancellorship; but this, headed by the last Chancellor of the Weimar Republic, Major-General Kurt von Schleicher, a career soldier with political ambitions who had managed to hold on to his position for only a matter of months, had more to do with a power struggle between the National Socialists and the old-guard conservatives than with disapproval of Hitler's policies. Indeed, the worst of these were yet to emerge, although he had made no secret of his plans in *Mein Kampf*.

For his part, Hitler was not yet secure enough in his position to attempt to muzzle or otherwise curb the Army's power. True, the SA, under his long-time comrade-in-arms, Ernst Röhm, was a powerful force itself. With several million members it far outnumbered the Army; but the SA, despite Röhm's ambitions for it, was not a disciplined force, and in the course of the next year Röhm would fly fatally close to the sun. When the chips were down, it didn't matter that Röhm was Hitler's oldest friend, the only man he was on the familiar 'Du' terms with;[2] when the Führer felt threatened, he struck hard – and his accurate political instincts ensured that he never missed his mark.

The Nazis had yet to build up their organisation of terror, too. The dreaded secret police network which was to spread all over Germany and the countries it conquered, which was to employ six million agents, was still in its infancy. This is not a history of Nazi administration,[3] but it is worth pointing out that the complexity already alluded to did not lead to efficiency. The Gestapo was never subtle in its methods and its field agents were not always intelligent, though of course the system threw up evil geniuses in the upper ranks like Reinhard Heydrich and Walter Schellenberg. They relied on a system of informers and on denunciation, not detection, to make their arrests. They tapped telephones and infiltrated suspect groups as fifth columnists and *agents provocateurs*. Once arrested, a victim might well have information tortured out of him – increasingly so as the regime progressed – or he might be thrown into a concentration camp for a few years. Dachau was opened as early as March 1933 for political undesirables.

Those arrested in the early days by the regular courts might find themselves acquitted or sent to an ordinary prison for a short term, only to be picked up by the Gestapo on their release and summarily 'disappeared' into the camps. One lawyer was arrested because his name – he was located by the Gestapo through the expedient of looking him up in the telephone book – was the same as that given to the man they were really after in a recently published *roman-à-clef*.

Another example of early Gestapo methods, which borders on black farce (as do many matters in the history of the Third Reich), is given by Hans Bernd Gisevius, the civil servant who joined the Gestapo as a lawyer as part of his normal career structure, but who became one of the earliest and most dedicated members of the Resistance. It deals with the fate of a petty criminal, Rall, who was implicated in the murder of the notorious early Nazi, Horst Wessel, himself a pimp and small-time crook, who was elevated to the Nazi pantheon by Goebbels after his death:

After it [the hearing] was over, the prisoner was taken out of the police lock-up by night, stripped of all his clothes except his shirt, and driven out of the city. The car stopped at what seemed to be a favourable spot. The rest of the story was eloquently told to me by one of the murderers, a man named Reineking, who later ended in a concentration camp for knowing too much and talking too loosely. Near a small forest they saw an open field, and nearby there was a bench. They forced Rall to sit down on this bench, and then they choked him to death. According to Reineking's story, it took ages before their victim died; at any rate, the murderers felt that each minute was an hour.

Then they left the body sitting on the bench and set about digging a grave in the field. But imagine their horror when they suddenly heard a noise, turned around, and saw their 'corpse' running away. The sight of this dead man racing along in the bright moonlight, his shirt fluttering behind him, was terrifying even to these hard-boiled SA [sic – the two men have previously been referred to as Gestapo] killers.

But the murderers' dread that they would be discovered outweighed their terror. They rushed after the corpse, and this time really choked him to death. Then they hastily buried him. We can easily believe Reineking when he reported that he and his accomplice were very uneasy when they were called to account about the matter by the following noon.

There are certain impressions one never forgets. This description of Rall's murder is one of those for me. Although, in later days, I heard thousands of more horrible tales, this ghostly scene repeatedly rises before my eyes: the automobile roaring through the countryside, the moonlit night, the man in the shirt . . . the ghastliness of the whole story is so vivid that I feel it a chronicler's duty to recount it . . .'[4]

The SA barely bothered to arrest people, though they had their own system of barracks and semi-official prisons, where brutal torture of opponents took place, usually Communists and other left-wingers in the very early days. One infamous incident occurred in the Silesian village of Potempa in August 1932. Konrad Pietzuch was a Communist sympathiser, and when five of his workmates who were members of the SA took exception to this, they kicked him to death in front of his mother. The perpetrators were variously sentenced to death and to life imprisonment, but Hitler sent them a personal telegram expressing his solidarity with them, and the Nazi Party newspaper, the *Völkischer Beobachter*, echoed his support. These were violent times, but this endorsement of lawlessness and the callous murder of a political opponent opened the eyes of some Germans at least to what they might expect if the Nazis came to power. Unfortunately Hitler's early success brought him popular support which never absolutely deserted him; and on the other hand the various elements of the Resistance could never show a united front. In the case of the Army, which had the only real means of toppling the regime, the number of people recruited to the conspiracy had to remain relatively small for reasons of security. Within the Army, too, there was disunity, and very few generals with real executive power could be persuaded to join the Resistance. Nevertheless, given the frankness with which Army conspirators made approaches to their colleagues, there was remarkably little betrayal.

Hitler never wholly liked or trusted the Army. To him the generals were a bunch of monocled snobs who embodied old Prussian values and traditions, which he, coming from a lower-middle-class Austrian background, feared, resented and failed to understand. Hitler himself was an inverted snob of the worst kind, and it is central to his character that he hated what he longed to be part of, but which rejected him, from art school to German high society, and consequently wished to destroy it. He surrounded himself with kindred spirits – all the leading Nazis were, in their way, malcontents from petty bourgeois or lower-middle-class backgrounds – backgrounds in which resentment and prejudice flourished in those days like maggots in an apple. Only a small percentage of German aristocrats joined the SS or the SA – a notable and prominent example being the old Kaiser's fourth son, August-Wilhelm.

Nazis disliked universities (which, curiously, supported the Party on the whole), intellectuals, the Church – both Evangelical and Roman Catholic; indeed the long-term plan was to de-Christianise Germany after the 'final victory' – and the old ruling class. The key word for Hitler was *Gleichschaltung* – one of many German words that took on a special significance in Nazi-speak. *Gleichschaltung* meant the conformity and subservience of everything to the Party line. There was to be no law but Hitler, and ultimately no god but Hitler. The identities of the country and the Führer were to be fused. This led to reckless iconoclasm, part of the reason for which may be sought in the relative youth of the Nazis. In 1933, Hitler celebrated his forty-fourth birthday, but Göring was forty, and Goebbels only thirty-six. Himmler was born in 1900, and Heydrich in 1904. By the time war broke out in 1939, the young soldiers going to fight had reached maturity knowing only Nazi rule. The police state was the norm.

Hitler was Chancellor, but the National Socialist Party did not hold a majority of Cabinet posts. The National Conservatives, who had helped Hitler to power, thus thought they could direct this 'new broom' with which they hoped to sweep away the debris of the Weimar Republic (though still acting constitutionally). Their plans to replace it varied – ranging from, in its most liberal aspect, a restored but constitutional monarchy, through benign oligarchy, to military dictatorship. At the back of their minds was the old German ideal of the father figure and leader – Bismarck, Wilhelm I, even the deposed Kaiser. President Hindenburg, a link with Imperial Germany, filled the role; but he was old, and gave no leadership any more. And Hitler, with all the warped romanticism that coloured his view of 'Germania', the old empire of the German-speaking peoples which he saw as the cradle of civilisation and the natural source of world leadership, aspired to the part. With far less excuse than the Kaiser, he did not perceive that power had passed from Central Europe, from Berlin, London and Paris, to Washington and Moscow. He was an anachronism, a nineteenth-century throwback disastrously active out of his time.

But he was still – just – Adolphe Légalité. Though fierce enemies, the Social Democrats (SPD) and the Communists held a total percentage of the vote which outstripped that of the National Socialists. The gap had narrowed steadily since 1930, but in the elections of November 1932 the Nazis had dropped 4 per cent. They had only 33.1 per cent of the vote when Hitler became Chancellor, against the Communists' 16.9 per cent and the SPD's 20.4 per cent. Despite its smaller showing, the Communist Party was far more vociferous than the SPD, which was largely discredited as the leading spirit behind the Weimar Republic, and in such volatile times, with unemployment spiralling and the economy in chaos, the people's support was polarising. It was one of the triumphs of the Nazi Party, whose full name was the National Socialist German Workers' Party, that it managed to capture the imagination, the hopes and the loyalty of the masses; though it never had a clear majority of the vote, despite hugely energetic electioneering and heavy funding from industry.

Hitler badly needed to hang on to the power he had gained, to crush the Communists and to make his power absolute. Already the SA was employing brutal terror tactics – in the face of a supine (when not actively sympathetic) police force and legal system[5] – and coercing those who disagreed with the Nazi government to toe the line. The Social Democrats continued to delude themselves that Hitler could be combated by legal means, but the Communists, who bore the brunt of the SA's attack, saw early on which way the wind was blowing, though they were hampered in their reactions by having to obey directives from Moscow. In any case they were shortly to be outlawed. The way Hitler chose to do this was both drastic and simple.

On the night of 27 February 1933 the Reichstag – the German parliament building – burnt down. The fire was started deliberately, and it was patently the work of the Nazis themselves, but a scapegoat was found in the shape of a young Dutch Communist drifter called Marinus van der Lubbe. As it was clear that a fire of such size could not have been planned and carried out by one man alone, four others were implicated: Ernst Torgler, the Communist Party's parliamentary leader, and three Bulgarian Communist emigrés, Vassil Taneff, Blagoy Poppoff and Georgi Dimitroff.[6] It was put about that van der Lubbe was simple-minded, but the apathy and lethargy he displayed at the show trial in September of the same year were more likely to have been induced by drugs and beatings. Of the other defendants, Torgler proved to be a man of straw. He was acquitted, and later became a Nazi henchman. Dimitroff was the only one of the Bulgarians who could speak German, and as he was able to prove beyond the shadow of a doubt that he had been in Munich at the time of the fire-setting, he used the trial as a soap-box, despite the efforts of the presiding judge to gag him. The future Bulgarian leader was even able to make a fool of Göring in court, goading him into making wild statements about Russia's inability to pay her debts – statements for which the humiliated Prussian Interior Minister (as he then was) was obliged to apologise in the press the following day. Nevertheless, Fabian von Schlabrendorff, a young officer and lawyer who became a leading figure in the military Resistance and survived by a miracle, remembers witnessing Göring slapping his thigh and laughing with triumph as he told Hitler of the success of the Reichstag fire.[7]

A parade of witnesses was produced and, through a new law specially introduced and having retroactive effect, van der Lubbe – the only one of the five to be convicted – was condemned to death on 23 December 1933 and executed immediately after Christmas.

But there was another victim of the Nazi cover-up. Walter Gempp, head of the Berlin Fire Department, refused to prevaricate. He stated publicly that the Fire Brigade had arrived in good time, that they had encountered SA men at the scene, and furthermore that Göring had expressly forbidden Gempp from giving the fire the highest level of priority and from calling in all available fire engines. He also stated that after the fire enough incendiary material was found in undamaged rooms within the Reichstag to fill a lorry, suggesting a degree of organisation which the Communists would not have had the means to set up. As a result, Gempp was dismissed from his post. At that time, the Nazis had not yet muzzled the press. A major Berlin liberal newspaper, the *Vossische Zeitung*, reported his sacking on 25 March 1933 in the following terms: 'We are in ignorance of the circumstances under which the State Commissar [Göring] has found it necessary to give notice to the respected head of the Berlin Fire Department, who has been in the service of the city for twenty-seven years. We can however state that Gempp, who is in his fifty-fifth year, has made the Fire Brigade into the protector of the city's population. Many thousands of foreigners have visited our city to study and envy the firefighting techniques Gempp has developed.'

Walter Gempp was arrested in 1937 and found strangled in his cell on 2 May 1939. He was among the first to pay the price of personal integrity, and one of tens of thousands of good men and women whose service was of value to Germany to be liquidated because they spoke out.

The Reichstag fire enabled Hitler to conjure up the bogeyman of Foreign Bolshevism at Work in the Fatherland. As was his habit, he moved quickly. The following day an Emergency Measure was enacted in the interests of State and Public Security, forbidding rallies and marches by the Communist and Social Democratic Parties. By this action the Nazis clearly hoped to stifle the opposition expected at the national elections due to take place on 5 March. Yet, despite the Emergency Measure, despite the continuing enmity between the Communists and the Social Democrats, and despite further intimidation of opponents by the SA, the election results (the last a united Germany was to see for nearly sixty years) were 18.3 per cent to the Social Democrats, 12.1 per cent to the Communists, and 43.9 per cent to the National Socialists. The Nazis could not have been very confident of success, for Fabian von Schlabrendorff learnt of confidential plans to falsify the polls if necessary.[8] Ninety per cent of the electorate turned out to vote, but Hitler was not going to be dislodged now. His first move to consolidate his position was to woo the Army. In doing so he showed a cynical, contemptuous, but accurate, knowledge of what can only be called his victim. Very few of the High Command were not taken in.

The new parliament was inaugurated on 21 March at a ceremony in Potsdam. Potsdam, a little town just to the south-west of Berlin, was the heart of Old Prussia, with its long military tradition and its connection with Frederick the Great, the enlightened eighteenth-century monarch affectionately known as 'Old Fritz' who is the father of modern Germany and its greatest hero. The Garrison Church at Potsdam is the *sanctum sanctorum* of these associations, and it was here, once again modestly garbed in a morning coat, that Hitler paid court to the Army. The ceremony was the first and last of the Third Reich to be presided over by a Christian priest, and at it the Chancellor – still officially the twenty-first Chancellor of the Weimar Republic – strove to identify National Socialism with the Prussian tradition, and to present himself as the true heir of Frederick. President Hindenburg, resplendent in his uniform, was present to add the right touch of gravitas to the occasion. A symbolic empty chair was placed for Kaiser Wilhelm II.

It was a highly successful *coup de théâtre*, and though Hitler's physical appearance cuts a ridiculous figure to us today, we should not forget that the toothbrush moustache and the famous forelock were not stock images then, nor that he clearly had great personal charisma, and the ability to instil fear and respect in those around him. It is also worth remembering that, although he had an uncontrollable temper, Hitler was not the carpet-chewing maniac sometimes presented to us. The reactions of Germans to their new rulers were crucial. There were those who were active supporters of Nazism; there was a very small number who actively opposed the regime; but the vast majority simply accepted the status quo. The most popular way of letting off steam against the regime was the joke; Goebbels even sanctioned certain cabarets critical of National Socialism until the mid-thirties – though some of the most famous comics ended up in the concentration camps. Christabel Bielenberg, an Englishwoman married to a German with strong Resistance contacts, who lived in Germany throughout the Third Reich, remembers one such joke:

> The story goes that at Hitler's birth three good fairies came to give him their good wishes, and the first wished for him that every German should be honest, the second that every German should be intelligent, and the third that every German should be a National Socialist. An uplifting thought. But then came the bad fairy, and she stipulated that every German could only possess two of those attributes. She left the Führer then with intelligent Nazis who were not honest, honest Nazis who had no brains, and intelligent, honest citizens who were not Nazis. A funny little story, perhaps, but one not too far from the truth; for it seemed to me that those three categories of Germans did indeed live and work together side by side, unable, because of the nature of the regime, to maintain more than the most superficial contact with each other.[9]

Two days after Potsdam, at a session of parliament held in the Kroll Opera House, which was standing in for the damaged Reichstag, Hitler struck his first serious official blow against democratic freedom. The Communists had been banned soon after the elections of 5 March, and could do nothing to oppose it. The opera house was filled with SS and SA men, the swastika flag – at that time only the Party flag, not yet the National flag – dominated the auditorium. The atmosphere was that of a Nazi mass meeting, not a parliamentary session. The subject under debate was the Enabling Act, which, if passed, would give Hitler complete power in the question of making laws. He was still within the law – just. Rule by decree was permissible under Article 48 of the Weimar Constitution in times of national emergency and for a limited number of years. In fact, the Nazi government even bothered to renew the Enabling Act twice during its lifetime, although effectively, once passed, it had served its purpose and Hitler treated its true legal sense with as little respect as he treated anything which had served its purpose. Only seven laws were passed by the Reichstag

during the twelve years of the Third Reich. In 1933 alone under the
Enabling Act, Hitler issued 218 decrees. No one objected. Franz
Gürtner, the Minister of Justice, and not himself a Party member,
expressed satisfaction when Göring stated that 'justice and the will
of the Führer are one and the same thing'. The *Juridical Review*
published in an editorial the view that 'the Führer cannot work
against the law, for he is the supreme lawgiver . . .' Between 1933
and 1939 the ordinary courts sentenced 225,000 people to a total
of 600,000 years' imprisonment for political offences. Between 1933
and 1945 three million Germans were held at one time or another
in prison or in the concentration camps on political grounds, or for
active Resistance.[10] Further comment is superfluous.

Of the other parties still with a notional say in the Reichstag,
only the Social Democrats raised their voice against the Enabling
Act. Loudly supported by his followers, and just as loudly shouted
down by the Nazis, the stocky moustachioed figure of Otto Wels,
the SPD leader, spoke strongly and eloquently:

> No Enabling Act gives you the power to destroy ideas which
> are invincible and everlasting. You yourselves [the Nazis] have
> demonstrated your recognition of the principles of Socialism . . .
> Social Democracy will not be beaten by persecution, but draw new
> strength from it. We greet those of our colleagues who have already
> been persecuted and oppressed. We salute our friends in the Reich.
> Your steadfastness and loyalty deserve our admiration. Your courage
> and your unshakeable confidence [National Socialist laughter; Social
> Democrat cheers] guarantee a brighter future.

But early in June the SPD was banned. Otto Wels was among those
who set up the SPD in exile (SOPADE), initially in Prague. By the
end of July there was only one Party in Germany, and that was the
ruling National Socialist German Workers' Party: the Nazis.

It was not long after this that Hitler turned his attention to
the Jews. Anti-Semitism was nothing new in Germany, or indeed
in Europe, nor was it uncommon, although no one in 1933 had
an inkling of the horror the Nazis would soon unleash. The Jews
made up a small proportion of Germany's population, but their
contribution to the country was very high in proportion to their
numbers. Pro rata, there were more leading Jewish doctors, lawyers
and bankers than from any other group. In the First World War, again

pro rata, more Jews had given their lives for Germany and received high decorations for bravery. The contribution of Jewish Germans to twentieth-century art and science is famous. Most Jewish Germans were assimilated, saw themselves as Germans first and Jews second, and were deeply patriotic. Their sense of patriotism proved fatal for many, because they would not try to leave until it was too late.

Resentment of the Jews persisted and thrived in periods of economic stress and high unemployment. No matter that the Jews in Germany suffered just as much from poverty and unemployment as their fellow countrymen; this, too, was nothing new. In the fourteenth century people believed that the Jews were responsible for the Black Death, though just as many Jews died from it as did others. But the nine-teenth century had seen a fresh spawning of anti-Semitic literature, and the young Hitler had fed on this greedily. Out of the ruin of the First World War, in which he had fought bravely as a corporal (earning the Iron Cross, First Class – a rare honour for an NCO), and the collapse of Imperial Germany, he spun the myth of a world Marxist-Jewish conspiracy, a myth in which he believed passionately and relentlessly right up until his final hour.

It was still too early for him to root the Jews out of Germany. At first he had no plans to kill them: he would have been content to expel them, if any other country had been prepared to take them, and for a time a plan to convert the island of Madagascar, which would have been conquered for the purpose, into a vast Jewish ghetto, was on the Nazi table. In the early thirties he still needed the infrastruc-ture of business the Jews ran. Jewish factories made SA uniforms and swastika flags; Jewish investment aided the German economy – and rearmament cost money. Even so, the Führer evidently needed to make an early stand, and his ability to recognise and exploit the worst aspects of human nature led him to the conclusion that the Germans needed a scapegoat, convenient and recognisable, for their woes. His own obsessive hatred, coupled with his confused ideas of racial 'purity', led him immediately to the Jews.[11]

The first of April 1933 was declared National Boycott Day. SA men, their uniforms still in these early days looking pretty home-made, stood on guard outside Jewish businesses bearing placards, often, curiously, in English as well as German: 'Germans! Protect Yourselves! Don't Buy At Jewish Shops!' It was not a huge success from the Nazi point of view. Most of the major department stores in Berlin were Jewish owned, and among those who ignored the boycott, shopping as she always did at the Kaufhaus des Westens, was Julia Tafel Bonhoeffer, the ninety-year-old grandmother of Klaus and Dietrich Bonhoeffer, who were to become pillars of the civilian and church Resistance respectively.

The next significant single action Hitler took was to destroy the trade unions. These had been living an uneasy existence since the outlawing of the Communist Party. There were several Social Democrat and Christian Unions, among which were some which hoped to survive by coming to an accommodation with National Socialism. But the policy of *Gleichschaltung* allowed no exceptions. The Nazis inaugurated a German Labour Front under one of Hitler's more repulsive henchmen, Dr Robert Ley, an alcoholic wife-beater who finally dispatched his wretched spouse with a revolver. The Front's function was to replace the unions. On 1 May, Hitler supplanted the traditional left-wing and labour celebrations with his own Nazi version of them. The following day, SA brigades seized all trade union property and newspapers. Another potential source of Resistance had been crushed. Thousands of trade unionists now joined Communist leaders already in the concentration camps. By the end of the year their ranks would be swollen by fresh waves of political prisoners.

Intellectual opposition and freedom of thought were the Nazis' next targets: throughout Germany on 10 May town squares bore witness to a spectacle not seen since the Middle Ages: the burning of prohibited books. All Jewish and Communist writers were banned, including the works of such great contemporary writers as Brecht, Thomas and Heinrich Mann, Franz Kafka, Stefan Zweig and Erich Kästner. Artists and scientists were similarly persecuted – a Nazi School of Physics sprang up to disprove Einstein's Theory of Relativity (for Einstein was a Jew) – and, though some remained in Germany in 'internal exile', this action heralded the start of the great exodus of intellectuals which was to impoverish Europe and enrich America.

Not that all this went unchallenged. The outlawed and exiled Communist and Social Democratic Parties established an illegal underground press and pamphleteering network which continued vigorously until 1939 and even in a reduced form during the war, although conditions after 1940 and the improved efficiency of the

Gestapo made such actions as, for example, smuggling material into Germany far more difficult then.

I have mentioned the vexed question of what actually constitutes Resistance, and it may be worth adding here that the smallest act against the Nazi government required enormous bravery. As time passed, so more savage did the punishments for transgression become. At Plötzensee, the Berlin prison which was the Calvary of so many of those involved in the 20 July Plot of 1944, many others, no less brave than the conspirators, were guillotined or hanged by executioner Friedrich Wilhelm Röttger. The accounts of their trials, their pleas for clemency and the record of their deaths may still be seen:

> Emmi Zehden, executed at 1p.m. on 9 June 1944, aged forty-four. A member of the Jehovah's Witnesses. She helped three young men avoid their call-up. Her punishment was death by the guillotine. Sentence took seven seconds to carry out. Like everyone sentenced by the Nazi courts of crimes against the state, she had to bear the cost of her own trial and execution.
>
> Karl Robert Kreiden from Düsseldorf. A musician. While lodging in Berlin during a concert tour he tried to persuade his land-lady, one Frau Ott-Monecke, to join the Resistance. He described Hitler as a brute, and told Frau Ott-Monecke, a convinced National Socialist, that she had better change her ideas. She informed on him and he was tried on 3 September 1943, executed on 7 September, aged twenty-seven.
>
> Otto Bauer, a fifty-six-year-old businessman, unguardedly said on a train in June 1942 that Germans only had two alternatives: to kill Hitler or be killed by him. He was overheard by a married couple who reported him. He was beheaded on Thursday, 16 September 1943 for fomenting discontent and unrest.
>
> Erich Deibel. On 29 April 1940 he drew the symbol of the SPD – three arrows – on the wall of the lavatory in his factory, adding the words: 'Hail Freedom!' On 22 July the following year he chalked up: 'Workers! Help Russia! Strike! Up With the Communist Party of Germany!' and drew the red star and the hammer and sickle. He also allegedly listened to broadcasts from the BBC. Accused of sabotage and treason, he was executed on 15 August 1942.

All the reports of these trials are cold, factual, official and peppered with outraged exclamation marks – a feature of Nazi documents. They are sobering reading.

Yet despite the threat of summary trial and certain execution, many hundreds of thousands of Germans continued to listen to foreign broadcasts, read and distribute dissident literature, meet and discuss forbidden political questions, shelter Jews and political outlaws. They may represent a tiny minority in a population of seventy million, but these acts of individual courage demonstrate, as much as the organised military Resistance to Hitler, that the Nazis never fully crushed the spirit of freedom in Germany, nor wholly seduced the German people.

The most common and widespread opposition to Hitler from the beginning took the form of illegal pamphleteering, though no one was under any illusions for long that this would be a means of bringing the Nazis down. It was rather an attempt to keep hope alive, together with protecting the principles of free speech and thought. The most important early disseminators of such literature belonged to the Leninist group Neu Beginnen, which took its name – 'A Fresh Start' – from its principal pamphlet, and to the Roter Stosstrupp, or Red Shock Troop.

Neu Beginnen was founded by Walter Löwenheim, who wrote under the pseudonym 'Miles'. It started life in 1929 as a breakaway SPD group which also recruited members from the Communist Party. Aware from a very early stage of the danger posed by the rise of National Socialism, the new group organised itself in secrecy, and by 1932 had built up an extensive network within Germany. It thus had a great advantage over all other organised Resistance in that it already had experience of working under cover. Its manifesto was printed in Karlsbad in 1933 and distributed – as most illegal literature was – under the guise of a permitted work. Masquerading as *Schopenhauer: On Religion* the manifesto managed a distribution of 5000 copies in Germany and also attracted attention abroad by virtue of American, British and French editions.[12] Initially supported by the SPD in Exile, Neu Beginnen fell victim to internal political wrangling and, when the SPD withdrew subsidy, the pamphlet campaign dried up. German left-wing politicians in the West had little room to manoeuvre and could only sit out the Nazi storm.

The Roter Stosstrupp was a Berlin-based group which produced a newspaper carrying the same name from early in 1933. The group had its origins in the uniformed wing of the SPD, the Reichsbanner Black-Red-Gold, named after the colours of the flag of the Weimar Republic. The change of name to 'red' indicated a strongly leftward shift in the illegal organisation. It operated effectively only until the end of 1933, and was never under any illusions about its ability to overthrow the government.

A third early publication which managed to sidestep Nazi censorship was *Blick in die Zeit* – 'A Look at the Times' – which appeared from June 1933 to August 1935. It sought to protect freedom of speech and to counteract the blanket effect of the official Nazi newspaper, the *Völkischer Beobachter*, by printing not only edited reports of a given event by all the German papers, but by the foreign press as well. It was closed down by the Gestapo in 1935. At about the same time any latitude still allowed to the German press in general was withdrawn, and foreign newspapers would soon cease to be available even in Berlin. 1935 saw the end of the period of massive anti-Nazi pamphleteering as a wave of arrests mopped up the underground organisations of the Communist Party, the Social Democrats and the trade unions. But by then the first stirrings were coming from the one organisation which would ever have a real chance of performing a successful *coup d'état* – the Army.

TWO

The Big Battalions

The Army and the Civil Service were the two pillars of the community in Germany. While the Civil Service remained generally loyal to Hitler – or rather, to the new regime, which it served without regard to what it represented ethically or morally – the Army's attitude to Nazism, and especially to its leader, was more complex.

The Army had always been the mainstay of Germany. A long Prussian tradition of militarism, and the military successes of the late nineteenth century which had led to the unification of the country, made the Army into a kind of state within the state. A small incident – hardly that – which occurred in the very early thirties illustrates well how deeply Army values had penetrated German thinking (though the old clichés about German love of order and uniforms are evident, and also worth bearing in mind). At a film studio where a war film was being made the 'extras' canteen presented the following sight at the end of the first morning's shooting: officers and NCOs at the head of each table, with other ranks below the salt.[1] Respect for the Army and its pecking order lasted well into the Nazi era. Many are the stories of a German aristocrat or senior officer in the power of the Gestapo who managed to extricate him- or herself by 'pulling rank'.

The Army had sustained a severe blow when the Treaty of Versailles had reduced it to a fraction of its former self, but it had managed to keep all its traditions and essential strengths intact. Most important of these was the Officer Corps – a kind of freemasonry of soldiers who shared the same background, interests and politics – which ensured that whatever happened the Army would look after its own. Part of the tragedy of the German Army taken as a whole is that it put itself and its future before that of its country, not realising that one was dependent on the other; or perhaps believing that, after all, there would always be a moment when the Army could step in and restore order by taking temporary control until a new civilian government could be arranged under the Army's benevolent protection. Nineteenth-century thinking thrust a long spur into twentieth-century Germany.

The hundreds of thousands of unemployed soldiers and, more importantly, officers – that is, career soldiers – who sought a living in Germany after 1918 formed a dangerous core of right-wingers who felt betrayed by the country they had served. They elicited much public sympathy, especially from the upper and middle classes and the government could not control the large private armies, or Freikorps, which grew up. Nor did the Allied signatories of the Treaty of Versailles, having their own postwar troubles, have the power or the inclination to enforce it with regard to Germany's internal affairs. In any case Germany, with its heavy burden of reparation, seemed set to be preoccupied with its own problems for a very long time to come. Furthermore, since the Rhineland, Germany's major industrial area, was occupied by the French, there seemed little chance of the German werewolf re-emerging.

Among the masses of drifting soldiery was Hitler himself, a man who had responded positively and romantically to the military life, and who spent the last weeks of the 1914–18 war in a military hospital having been half-blinded during a British gas-attack. He experienced the collapse of Imperial Germany with a terrible intensity. Having believed at first that the revolution was a flash in the pan, he had the truth brought home to him on 10 November 1918 as 'the most terrible moment of my life':

> Summoned to a meeting by the hospital pastor, the patients learned that a revolution had broken out, that the House of Hohenzollern had fallen and a republic had been proclaimed in Germany. Sobbing gently to himself – thus Hitler described the 'old gentleman' – the pastor recalled the merits of the ruling house, and 'not an eye was able to restrain its tears'. But when the pastor began to tell them that the war was now lost and that the Reich was throwing itself unconditionally upon the mercy of its previous enemies – 'I could stand it no longer. It became impossible for me to sit still one minute more. Again everything went black before my eyes: I tottered and groped my way back to the dormitory, threw myself on my bunk,

and dug my burning head into my blanket and pillow. Since the
day I had stood at my mother's grave I had not wept . . . But now
I could not help it.'[2]

Though they would not have expressed themselves so extravagantly,
most of the German High Command would have sympathised with
this view. When Hitler came to power they welcomed his policies –
especially when it came to rebuilding the Army. Several of the most
prominent members of the Resistance – Carl Goerdeler, Artur Nebe,
Graf Helldorf, Fritz-Dietlof Graf von der Schulenburg – either joined
the Party or worked for it. There was scarcely an officer at Potsdam
on that raw March day in 1933 who did not invest his unreserved
hope in the new Chancellor. True, he was not a Prussian – nor even
a German. True, he was not from the right class – but then scarcely
a Chancellor among Hitler's twenty predecessors had been: the first
President of the Weimar Republic had been a saddler! But Hitler
had the Army's interests at heart, and it was prepared to give him a
chance.

One officer not taken in however was Colonel-General Kurt
Freiherr von Hammerstein-Equord, Commander-in-Chief and a close
friend of the Chancellor Hitler had succeeded, Kurt von Schleicher.
Hammerstein, who held liberal political views, may have acted from
motives of personal loyalty and friendship when he sought to prevent
Hitler's seizure of power at the eleventh hour early in January. But
those cannot have been the only reasons, and Hammerstein must stand
as the first Establishment figure to express Resistance sympathies by
action. He must certainly have cast a cold eye on the proceedings in
Potsdam two months later. In his memoir of the events, Fabian von
Schlabrendorff contends that only the consideration that Hindenburg
stood behind Hitler, and that Hindenburg still commanded enormous
esteem in Germany and the outside world, prevented him from pressing his action home. It is possible that Hammerstein placed too much
trust in his old commander's political integrity to act. Hammerstein's
son Ludwig, however, says that his father and Schleicher were
deeply disappointed at Hindenburg's behaviour in 1933, and that
later he regretted privately not taking the risk of a coup. But it
would have been next to impossible to undertake anything against
Hitler immediately after 30 January 1933, for the simple reason that
no Resistance had formed. Hammerstein would have had to have a

very convincing reason for ordering the Army to take control of the country, and Hitler might not have hesitated, in the event, to use his millions-strong SA to protect his position.

Hitler was well aware of being an outsider, and attempted to provide himself with at least some of the social graces.

We children never met Hitler,

says Ludwig von Hammerstein,

> but he came to visit my father at home early on – in 1928, I think, when we were living in Hardenberg Strasse. They sat on the balcony and talked. The connection with Hitler came through the piano makers, Bechstein. Bechstein had been a friend of my father's since before the First World War. Frau Bechstein was a great admirer of Hitler, and she taught him how to behave in society, when to kiss a lady's hand, how to address people, the proper way to hold a knife and fork, and which cutlery to use for what food. She was always giving dinner parties for Hitler to meet her influential conservative friends. My father's opinion of the man was that 'he talks too much and too confusedly', and he gave him the cold shoulder.

Still, Hitler wanted Army contacts, and Army support. He wooed General von Hammerstein, going so far as to give him a free subscription to the Nazi newspaper, and standing next to him at Bechstein's funeral a few years later. Hammerstein remained an active supporter of the Resistance until his death, though his view gradually changed to the more fatalistic one that Germany would have to be completely defeated to ensure Hitler's fall and the complete extirpation of National Socialism in the country. Events have proved that not even the crushing defeat of 1945 has sufficed to kill the weed completely.

Ultimately, control of the Army was Hitler's aim, but he was astute enough to know that he could not just go in and take it. In the early days, he was not secure enough in his power, either in the country or within his own Party. Gregor Strasser, his chief rival and a man who believed more sincerely than Hitler in the 'socialist' element of the Party's manifesto, had his own supporters among the German Establishment; and the old National Conservatives, among them Schleicher, still dreamt of destroying the National Socialists by splitting them in two. Then there was the question of the SA.

Under his old comrade Ernst Röhm, the SA had grown into a vast and well-organised national force with the potential to fulfil Röhm's ambition for it of becoming a People's Army, which would absorb the old Reichswehr. At the same time Heinrich Himmler, another long-time Nazi, was developing various secret police organisations, including the black-uniformed SS, or Schutz-Staffel – the Protection Brigade – formed as another private army but owing direct loyalty and allegiance to Hitler personally. Röhm's ideas were old-style Nazi, concerning a cultural revolution affecting life in Germany at every level. Hitler had moved beyond that stage and was thinking now in more imperial terms – for himself as much as for the country he had adopted and taken over. The Führer may never have trusted the Army, but he did not want to see the SA swamp it and thus put him in the position of losing the initiative to Röhm – as the SS was still a relatively small force. Hitler also already had plans for war and he needed experienced officers to fight for him.

For its part, the Army viewed the rise of the SA with a mixture of disdain and dismay. However, though it strove to maintain its traditional position above politics, the time was approaching when it would have to declare some sort of stance. Since it could not possibly be for the SA, it had to be either for Hitler or against him. This Hitler knew. No less influenced by traditional thinking than any other of his conservative contemporaries (Hitler did not have one original thought), he was impressed by the Army and feared it. It was because of this that he worked hard to make it his own. By 1939 he had increased its size to 1,400,000. The Officer Corps grew from 4000 in 1935 to 24,000 in 1939. In the early days it was less easy for Hitler to feed National Socialists into such a diehard conservative body of men, but as time went on, and as Hitler Youth members grew to manhood, he was able to dilute the old guard so effectively as to make the former Imperial Army into an Army of the Third Reich after his own plan. This Army had more senior officers – generals and field marshals – than Germany had ever had before, and an even higher percentage of them came from the Nazi fold as the Third Reich progressed. Hitler was liberal with decorations – he awarded so many Iron Crosses that by 1944 almost one third of the Wehrmacht had been decorated – but equally he hired and fired his officers with no reference to Army administration, traditions, or to the General Staff. By then, though, the Army had no room to manoeuvre against the man who had made himself its absolute master.

As we shall see, the Army, with a few notable exceptions, did not possess a High Command that was very capable – either in terms of political astuteness or moral courage – of withstanding Hitler. Steeped in military tradition and often coming from families who had provided soldiers for centuries, they had a hidebound outlook, and, at best, even if their patriotism was not in doubt, even if they occasionally dared to question Hitler's decisions on military matters, they could be self-serving. The Führer's ability to suborn the top brass with bribes is an example of this, and it was a policy he continued with a high degree of success throughout his rule. Not all his generals were corrupt, many fought bravely – incredibly bravely – and well for their country, and some simply chose not to enter the political debate at all, restricting themselves to their soldierly duty. In this they were not unlike the majority of their countrymen, who allowed Hitler to succeed by not daring to protest; and in this they were no different from human beings under any dictatorship. But those in key positions at the outset – when Hitler could have been stopped most effectively – proved to have feet of clay.

The Minister of Defence from 1933 to 1938, succeeding to the post left vacant by Schleicher, was Colonel-General Werner von Blomberg. A man possessed of Wagnerian good looks, though not of mighty intellect, his courage was undisputed; but his record as Hitler's War Minister (as he was called officially from 1935) was such as to earn him the nickname of 'Rubber Lion'. Blomberg's chief fault was to believe that Hitler would restore to the Army all its former power and glory. Once he had given his loyalty to Hitler, he was able, by virtue of his position, to block any influence the anti-Nazi Kurt von Hammerstein had enjoyed through his friend. Hammerstein resigned at the end of 1933 and was followed by Blomberg's appointee, Colonel-General Werner Freiherr von Fritsch, who assumed his duties February 1934.

Fritsch was a Prussian nobleman and came from a military family. He had kept his hands clean of National Socialism, but he had not criticised it either. For the present, everyone felt safe with him as Commander-in-Chief. For Hitler, he was an improvement on the unsympathetic Hammerstein, and Hitler still had to move cautiously in his plans to take over control of the Army. Fritsch was not devious, nor was he interested in politics. He would carry out his orders unquestioningly. Those on the Right who opposed Hitler (the

National Conservatives and the Schleicher faction) felt that at least Fritsch was not a Nazi either, and could be 'turned' if the moment to overthrow Hitler presented itself.

Von Schleicher had not been idle since Hitler had taken over the reins of power, and gathered about him was a small number of generals prepared to move their troops against the SA, arrest Hitler and have Hindenburg declare a state of emergency. The excuse for this was the coup anticipated from the SA in view of the mounting tension between them and the Army. This tension had been growing throughout 1933 and had reached snapping point by the late spring of 1934, when the power of the SA was alarming the most lugubrious conservative opposition. By now, of course, Hitler had neutralised any other opposition in Germany, and it is of interest to remember that Blomberg and Fritsch had accepted their appointments from a man whom they knew to have unconstitutionally outlawed the Communist Party and the Social Democratic Party, to have dissolved trade unions and all other political parties, and to have taken oppressive measures against the Jews.

From the beginning, the Resistance (and at this stage it could barely be called that yet) had to be one stemming from the Establishment. The present plan was a desperate one.

Events seemed to be moving too fast even for Hitler, who, as he often did when overtaxed by the occasion, dithered. He did not feel confident enough to throw in his lot with the Army against the SA, much as he wanted to; on the other hand, the longer he delayed, the greater became the perceived threat from Röhm. Once again, Germany was in political turmoil. This time, a blood-letting was inevitable.

It was triggered on 17 June 1934. At the University of Marburg Franz von Papen, a vain Prussian aristocrat and a favourite of Hindenburg, who had been Chancellor briefly and disastrously in the dying days of the Weimar Republic and was now Hitler's Vice-Chancellor, gave a speech to the students. The speech was an attack on the National Socialists in general and Goebbels in particular, but it took the form of an appeal to Hitler's conscience. By now everyone knew that Hindenburg's days were numbered (he was in his eighty-seventh year), and that when he died Germany would be bereft of the father figure which was all that was holding it together. By now the National Conservatives were aware that they were well in sight of their last chance of controlling Hitler, and that the SA had to be neutralised at all costs.

The speech was written by Papen's assistant, the young lawyer Edgar Jung, who was shortly to pay with his life for putting too much faith in the power of his chief. At the time Papen was making the speech, Hitler was at a Nazi conference in Gera, a small town to the south of Leipzig. When news of the Marburg speech reached him, he rushed to Berlin in a panic, to find that Röhm had retreated to Munich, his stronghold since the old days of the Party, and that Blomberg had gone to Neudeck, Hindenburg's estate in East Prussia. Goebbels meanwhile had made every effort to suppress the text of Papen's speech, and was pouring out a torrent of invective against the Establishment Right, and Papen especially. Papen, together with his political kindred spirits the Foreign Minister and the Finance Minister, offered their resignations to Hitler, but he refused to accept them. He was not yet so powerful as to be able to defy the outside world, and he still needed the cloak of respectability provided by the Army and the Government. The SA was three million strong. It was a Party organisation, not national; but Hitler was not confident of his control over it. His own leadership was not yet absolutely secure, and the head of the SA, Ernst Röhm, might have turned out to be a powerful rival.

Only by the sacrifice of the SA could Hitler survive, and once he had decided on his course of action, he moved with characteristic speed and ruthlessness.

But not immediately. The SA was very powerful, and would have to be taken by surprise. In the ten days of planning with Göring and Himmler which followed, the plot to remove all the SA leaders from the board at a stroke was extended to include other enemies of the NS State, from religious troublemakers to dissident Nazis and National Conservatives.

On 30 June the SS, secretly drilled and organised, struck. There were three days of intense slaughter. Röhm and his principal henchmen were gunned down immediately, in circumstances which showed that they, at least, were not on the verge of launching a coup against the government – Röhm himself was pulled squealing from the bed of his latest SA boyfriend. In the slaughter that followed – the 'Night of the Long Knives' – many members of the early opposition learned what it meant to cross Hitler. Gregor Strasser was arrested, taken to

Gestapo cells, shot in the lungs and left to bleed to death. General Schleicher, answering his doorbell, was shot dead together with his wife. His housekeeper, unable to live with the memory, later committed suicide. General von Bredow, Schleicher's loyal assistant, met the same fate as his master on the evening of the same day.

Now for the first time no clear-sighted person could pretend that the new regime in Germany was not a criminal one. This was still an internal affair, and foreign reactions could be managed as the government wished. Foreign correspondents were concentrated in Berlin, a city where Nazism deliberately kept a low profile in its early years: Hitler had no wish to start alarm bells ringing abroad until he was good and ready. Intelligence gathering was rudimentary and espionage was still an unsophisticated science. But at home, the Army had mortgaged its good name for the sake of losing an unworthy rival.

The Army saw itself as the guardian of German security at home and abroad, and of German honour. Hypocritical as it may have been in the past, nevertheless it had remained true to this function. It had suffered emasculation and humiliation, but it had kept its integrity until now. It had seen a dangerous and criminal rival removed in the shape of the SA, but it had done so not only by connivance, but by actively aiding the SS – an organisation more akin to the Army than the SA in its structure and physical appearance, but none the less a Party organisation. The SS was still relatively small, and lacked its own full complement of *matériel*. It had carried out the butchery; but the Army had provided the transport. This was the first, but very far from the last time that the Army would stand by and/or provide the arena for the SS to do its dirty work. Admittedly, it did not always do this without protest; but the protests were few and went unheard.

The cynical postscript to Hitler's illegal purging of his enemies with the Army's help – Stalinist techniques which Prussian officers ought to have been appalled at, but who really perceives himself? – was the obtaining of Hindenburg's imprimatur. Hindenburg was by now a sick man, whose mind had almost completely decayed. He did not have a completely unblemished record himself, but he was at core an honourable man who, if he had been in full possession of his faculties, would have condemned such actions. But his son and his secretary were in the Nazis' pocket. It is to his credit that the one appeal which reached him did not fail completely.

The landowner Elard Kammerherr von Oldenburg-Januschau was as old as Hindenburg. He was a neighbour, and a political and personal friend. It was to him that Hindenburg had confided that he would never make Hitler Chancellor, a decision which Januschau approved. Since the Nazis had come to power nevertheless, Januschau had tried to maintain his influence with his old friend. During the June 1934 purge, Hitler intended to eliminate Franz von Papen along with his assistants. To this end the SS surrounded the Vice-Chancellery on 30 June; but one of Papen's men, Wilhelm von Ketteler, managed to escape, and drove hell for leather from Berlin to East Prussia, where he intended to appeal to Hindenburg, who was in semi-retirement on his Neudeck estate there. Ketteler managed to avoid all SS road-blocks, but found Hindenburg's grounds cordoned off. In desperation he drove on to Januschau, and told him what was going on. Papen was a great favourite and protégé of the President.

The eighty-year-old former cavalry officer listened carefully to what Ketteler had to say, and made his decision fast. Calling for his horse to be saddled, he was soon mounted and riding across country to Neudeck, able to avoid SS patrols because he had been born and brought up in the country and knew it like the back of his hand. He arrived at Hindenburg's front door unchallenged, but there stood a guard. Before he could challenge Januschau, however, the old man dismounted, throwing the reins to him and shouting authoritatively: 'Just hold her, would you?' before springing up the steps into the house. Moments later he stood at Hindenburg's bedside. The President was too far gone to be wholly effective against Hitler any more, but Januschau's intervention did succeed in getting the President to order the release of several of those held in custody.[3] The pliant von Papen himself, extricating himself from his show of bravery at Marburg, survived, and later became German Ambassador to Turkey. Edgar Jung, the writer of the Marburg speech, was murdered during the purge. The Gestapo killed von Ketteler in 1938.

By 2 July the seal of approval sought from Hindenburg had been obtained. He sent a telegram to Hitler saying: 'From the reports placed before me, I learn that you, by your determined action and gallant personal intervention, have nipped treason in the bud. You have saved the German nation from serious danger. For this I express to you my most profound thanks and sincere appreciation.' Thus the action of 30 June was publicly and internationally justified and exonerated. As for the deaths of two of its own generals, Schleicher and von Bredow, the Army maintained a diplomatic silence about them. If the Nazis declared them to have been traitors, then that was justification enough.

Hitler was later to describe the Army contemptuously as a mastiff which he found he had to egg on to attack, but he could never bring himself to trust it. He knew he could rely on the Navy, though he feared the superiority of the British at sea, and the Air Force, which was a new and unfamiliar engine of war – at the outset the Germans saw it principally as a supporting arm of the Army. True, Göring had been a fighter ace in the First World War, but he failed to turn the Luftwaffe into an adequate means either of defence or attack.

The Army was the cornerstone. Hitler's mistrust of it persisted despite the fact that even by this early date he must have been feeling confident that he could control it by appointing weak, bribable or complaisant men to its top posts, and despite having seen that there was no unified Resistance to him within its ranks. It was clear from the outset that the war Hitler had in mind would be principally a land war, but the Army was never given the *matériel* allocated to the other two services. It is one of the great but obvious paradoxes of the Resistance that those who opposed Hitler were also among those who fought most bravely for Germany and sought to redress the deficiencies of the Nazi military administration.

The only thing that stood between Hitler and absolute power now was Hindenburg. Events had long since overtaken the old man and, fading fast, he died on 2 August. Once again, Hitler went into action quickly – this time so quickly that the entire affair must have been prepared well in advance, and with Blomberg's active assistance. On the very day of Hindenburg's death Hitler ordered the entire Armed Forces to be sworn in afresh, according to the words of a new Oath of Loyalty. 'I swear by Almighty God this sacred oath: I will render unconditional obedience to the Führer of the German Reich and people, Adolf Hitler, Supreme Commander of the Wehrmacht, and, as a brave soldier, I will be ready to stake my life for this oath at any time.' By the wording of the oath, Hitler had taken to himself the office of Supreme Commander which had been held until earlier that day by Hindenburg, as an office attached to the presidency. Hitler also took over the presidency, officially adopting the title of Führer – 'Leader' – which covered all three high offices. The last Weimar Chancellor had become Germany's first dictator, and not an official voice was raised in protest.

This oath was to become notorious. Viewed objectively, it was unconstitutional; but under what constitution? That of Weimar? But that had been superseded because Hitler had declared that the law was now embodied in his person. The oath was one more clever psychological ploy by the Führer. It was de facto invalid: if such solemn undertakings are to be given they presuppose a degree of moral and political obligation on the part of the individual to whom they are given. Luther had defined and stated this, and so had Hitler himself, in *Mein Kampf*. But to men used to a set form, breaking the oath was not so simple, especially when Hitler blurred the line between loyalty to him and loyalty to Germany. There were cases of soldiers who either killed themselves or deliberately sought death in battle because they could not resolve the problem.[4] For many of the generals, however, the oath provided a convenient excuse not to join the Resistance.

Who were the men responsible for the Army's connivance? Blomberg and Fritsch, of course; but also Fritsch's Chief of the General Staff, Lieutenant-General (as he then was) Ludwig Beck. Blomberg and Fritsch had only a short time to go before they too fell under the wheels of Hitler's chariot; but Beck was to become one of the seven most important leaders of the Resistance. Why did he, at least, support Hitler at this stage?

The Army was prepared to negotiate with Hitler, a foreign upstart it could easily have crushed if it had shown a united front, even to the extent of letting pass the murder of two of its most senior officers, for a variety of cogent reasons. German military expansion, cautiously permitted by the Allies at a Disarmament Conference in 1932 in the interest of security for all, was welcomed by the Army. When he came to power Hitler accelerated the process, leaving the League of Nations in order to avoid too many inhibiting negotiations and international undertakings. This, too, the Army approved. The revitalisation of the armaments industry created badly needed employment, and so did the national motorway construction programme. The Nazis, true to the socialist part of their programme, introduced a popular radio, to be available to all. A popular car was designed by Hitler's friend Dr Ferdinand Porsche, initially called the Strength-Through-Joy Car after the programme of which it formed part, but later simply known as the Volkswagen (People's Car). It did not go into production during the Nazi era, but all this activity helped restore German self-esteem, and not everything the Nazis did was either bad or mismanaged.

The patrician Army approved; and although conscription could not be reintroduced yet, it was very much on the cards. Despite the fact that it was still forbidden, 280,000 men had joined the Army by the spring of 1935, many of them from the ranks of the SA. The more Hitler defied the Treaty of Versailles, and the more the Allies let him get away with it, the greater the glow that surrounded him. His early successes were a severe hindrance to the Resistance. No one yet knew that Hitler planned to make war, though many may have made an intelligent guess at his intentions; but a strong Germany might have negotiated its way out of the rest of the Treaty of Versailles, and even got some of its former territory back. There were those who thought Hitler was undesirable, but a means to an end who could be got rid of once that end had been attained. There were those who thought Nazism so unspeakable that it would burn itself out; Germany simply would not support such a regime for more than a year or two.

Nevertheless a Resistance to Nazism had been formed among those various groups which had either already suffered for their dissident views, or which (like elements within the Church) perceived the immoral and unethical dynamic behind the Nazi philosophy. Certain individuals, like Fritz von der Schulenburg, an aristocratic career official who had joined the Nazi Party because he believed in its socialist aims, had quickly become disaffected. For many more, the Night of the Long Knives was the moment of disabuse. Among them was a man who became a key player in the Resistance. He was confronted by decisions which demanded the very highest courage because they involved the lives of thousands of his countrymen. The full story did not emerge until after the war, and then for many years even those sympathetic to the Resistance branded him a traitor to Germany. His name was Hans Oster.

Like his fellow conspirator Ludwig Beck, Oster was a career officer who came neither from an aristocratic nor a Prussian family. He was the son of a Saxony parson, born in Dresden in 1887. The family had a liberal, humanistic outlook and Oster was devoted to his cultivated mother, who died when he was seventeen. Oster grew up a keen horseman and a good cellist. (In passing it is interesting to note just how many of the conspirators were musically gifted. Beck was an accomplished violinist, for example; and Stauffenberg, also a cellist, whose story dominates the latter half of this account, was gifted enough to consider a musical career.)

Oster joined the newly formed 48 Artillery Regiment in March 1907 and thus started a solid military career which was aided by his own self-confident and optimistic personality. In 1912 he made an advantageous marriage to Gertrud Knoop, the daughter of a lawyer, with whom he had three children. The middle son, Harald, was to commit suicide aged twenty-five in the wake of the disaster at Stalingrad, though Oster never learnt the truth of this.

In the First World War he saw action at Yser and in Champagne, earning the Iron Cross First and Second Class and the Knight's Cross with Swords. He joined the Imperial General Staff in 1917, and was fortunate enough to keep his place in the Army after the defeat. Like most professional soldiers, he was no friend of the Weimar Republic, though he served it loyally. Unlike most of his colleagues, he was a bit of a maverick. It was unusual for a Captain of the General Staff to speculate on the Stock Exchange before work, for example, or to ride a bicycle to the office.

His peacetime career advanced steadily, bringing him into contact with many other officers who would later find their comradeship put to the test under Hitler. He also came into contact with the Nazis, but regarded their politics and their chances of success with scepticism. Nevertheless, in common with most professional soldiers, he accepted Hitler when he came to power.

Oster was slightly built, with an intelligently humorous face. He is by far the least military-looking of all the German generals. His daughter remembers him as a strict father, but also one who was never remote. Those who served with him and worked for him also remember a man who was easy-going without ever losing his authority. His chief pleasure remained riding – he was passionate about it – and the walls of his daughter's drawing room today are covered with his hunting trophies.

He was stationed in Münster in the early thirties when his career as a staff officer suffered a fatal blow. By now a major, he had been having an affair with a senior officer's wife. When this was discovered, Oster offered the wronged husband a duel, but this was refused and Oster had to leave active service in the winter of 1932–33. Fortunately there were no domestic or material repercussions for him; his wife was rich and stood by him, and they were able to keep their flat on in Münster. Nevertheless early in 1933 he was in Berlin seeking new employment. In Potsdam for 21 March, he was one of the few not taken in by Hitler's masquerade. He was, however, sceptical of the new regime rather than opposed to it.

Oster was unsuccessful in finding a fresh opening in active service, though he was still permitted the right to wear his uniform. However he was offered a job in Göring's so-called 'Research Department' (a kind of proto-secret police organisation), where he stayed for a short time, listening in to telephone conversations. He was approached by the SS, but turned them down, as he was becoming increasingly suspicious of Nazi ideology. In October 1933, he accepted a job in the Abwehr, then under the command of Conrad Patzig. This brought him into contact with the Gestapo (which Göring had founded in April 1933 and which Himmler would take over almost exactly a year later), the regular police and the SS. Hans Bernd Gisevius, the enormously tall lawyer who was one of the few survivors of the Resistance, met Oster at about this time and was able, as an employee of the Gestapo who was already working against the regime, to provide him with documentation on Nazi Security Service crimes as Oster began his own work against Hitler.

The Resistance, of course, was still barely an idea – a few pockets of like-minded individuals collecting information here and there, doing what they could without an overall plan, perhaps trying to build up files on the Nazis to be used in trials against them after the collapse of the regime. At this stage Oster could have had no idea how long his crusade was going to be. Like everyone else involved in the Resistance, he would spend long years under the terrible pressure of playing a double game, having to fulfil his official duties and at the same time – or rather, in what would otherwise have been his leisure hours – work in the interests of the enemy for the sake of long-term stability and the rehabilitation of Germany. 'My father was fully aware of what he was doing,' his daughter says. 'His decisions were based on logic and ultimately on humane considerations. Few people were in a better position to alter the course of events, and my father was a man of action. Once he had decided on a course of action he would stay on it. The risk of drawing the odium of treachery upon himself didn't seem too high a price to pay.' She also remembers how the years of stress took their toll, that he became grimmer and moodier.

An additional pressure on the conspirators was secrecy. They could share their feelings and confidence with virtually no one else. In the case of their families, it was for their own protection. Few Germans were unaware of the methods of the Gestapo.

Despite the need for discretion, Oster could be very careless. He had to involve his wife because she could speak English and he needed her to translate the BBC broadcasts for him, but he often voiced his opinion of the regime very clearly and in untested company. He would argue the state of things so loudly with Gisevius when the latter visited the Osters' Berlin flat that Gertrud had to beg them to lower their voices lest the neighbours hear. On another occasion, travelling by car with Gisevius to visit a senior Army officer involved in the conspiracy, Oster casually took a file of secret coup plans with him. When the Field Marshal learned of this, he was outraged: what did Oster imagine would have happened if he had had a car crash, for example? And yet the same man was able to build up his own anti-Nazi intelligence unit within the Abwehr and run it successfully for ten years. It was a quirk of fate that finally brought him down.

It was Oster's single-minded dedication to the Resistance that finally converted General Ludwig Beck to their cause. Given the contrast in Beck's and Oster's temperaments it is not surprising that Beck's conversion was effected as late as 1938. Oster had seen early how valuable an addition Beck would be to the Resistance group: his long experience and the high regard in which he was held would give the opposition movement great kudos. The Chief of the Abwehr Admiral Canaris had already tried to sway the hesitant Beck in January and February 1938, but it was Oster and his bravery that made a strong personal impression on the general. Both Oster and Beck were passionate riders, and the shared interest provided an excuse for several excursions into the Grünewald, where the horsemen could discuss Resistance matters undisturbed. Oster worked hard on Beck in his pragmatic way, and it is regrettable if not tragic that Beck became the spiritual head of the Military Opposition only after his retirement from Army service – something he himself acknowledged almost immediately, as he continued to believe for a long time that Hitler could be dissuaded rather than forced from his course of action. But as a retired officer, Beck had no executive power in official circles at all. The friendship with Oster continued and deepened, however, creating one of the strongest links in the chain of the senior Resistance.

Beck was given to lengthy consideration and reflection, a soldier who spent thirty-two of his forty years' Army service in the General Staff, a man whose manner and appearance were far more those of an academic than an officer. Never a National Socialist, he had a certain sympathy for Hitler's military and territorial aims, and his conversion to the anti-Nazi camp was a gradual process, built as much on practical as moral considerations.

He was born in 1880, the son of a Rhineland engineer who on account of bad eyesight had been the first to break the military tradition of the family. Beck grew up in a cultured household, a reserved and sensitive child whose favourite subjects were literature, history and mathematics. He always intended to join the Army, and was a captain in the General Staff by the time he was thirty-three.

He married in the spring of 1916, and his only child, a daughter, was born the following January. In November of that year, his wife died of tuberculosis. Beck was given the news on the West Front. His reaction throws an interesting light on his character. He was a talented musician, yet now he laid down his violin for ever. He never remarried, or had any relationship with another woman. Wherever he moved in the course of his subsequent military career, one room was designated as his wife's, and decorated and furnished precisely as her room had been during their brief marriage.

His daughter, who was brought up by relatives but who joined him at the age of fourteen, remembers that the Army was his life. He was an ascetic man – his pleasures taking the form of an occasional glass of wine and the odd cigar, though he liked thoroughbred horses, the interest which formed the basis for his friendship with Oster.

Beck certainly did not react to the rise of Nazism with antipathy. Like Oster he regretted the fall of Imperial Germany, though he had served the Republic conscientiously. He was depressed by the impo-sition of the Oath of Loyalty to Hitler, but although his secretary at the time, Luise Benda (later married to the Nazi general, Alfred Jodl), remembers his referring to 2 August as 'the blackest day of my life', he did take the oath, and there is every indication that he still believed at that stage that Hitler would uphold the German military tradition and even be its saviour. Only later did he express to his brother Wilhelm his regret at not having obeyed his initial instinct to resign over the matter.

Hitler as defender of the Army was certainly the gist of his speech to the War Academy on its 125th anniversary in October 1935, and it is also significant that he wholeheartedly approved of General Ludendorff, giving a radio broadcast loud in his praise on his seventieth birthday in April 1935. Ludendorff was one of the most prominent generals of the First World War, and a vigorous and active supporter of Hitler's abortive putsch in 1923. Beck had no second thoughts about Germany's moral right to have waged the Great War. He shared this attitude with most officers of his age and conservative outlook.

Such views did not preclude opposition to Hitler, especially as the Führer's ambitions and demands became increasingly outrageous, branding him unbalanced. Many secret discussion groups sprang up in Nazi Germany which contributed to the Resistance cause in keeping the spirit of free thinking alive. Among these was the Wednesday Club. It was composed of sixteen distinguished scientists, including the eminent surgeon Ferdinand Sauerbruch, Johannes Popitz – the only member of the Resistance to hold a post in Hitler's Cabinet, as Finance Minister of Prussia – and the conservative academic Professor Jens Jessen. Two specialist members were invited to join, as political and military experts. One was the Ambassador to Rome, Ulrich von Hassell; the other was Ludwig Beck. All were to be involved in the Resistance; many of them died as a result.

Beck was no pacifist, but he was convinced of France's military superiority, and, in his attitude to war, he mirrored the great early nineteenth-century German strategist and military thinker, General von Clausewitz, whose central premise was that war is a continuation of politics, to be used only when all other means of resolving a problem have failed. That this view is in direct contrast to Hitler's need hardly be stressed.

Beck's career was exemplary. By 1930 he was a Major-General,[5] but in that year came a crisis: two of the young officers under his command in 5 Artillery Regiment, Fulda, were accused of distributing Nazi propaganda. This was in contravention of Army regulations, which decreed that no soldier should have any political affiliation. Beck accepted the accusation, but, angry at not having been advised of it in advance, offered his resignation. It was refused, and Beck resumed his career. He became a Lieutenant-General in 1932, and joined Army Command, Berlin, under Kurt von Hammerstein, in October 1933. He was pleased to see the SA crushed during the action of the Night of the Long Knives, but he may well have genuinely believed that the method of the SA's destruction posed a threat to national security. Certainly he was disturbed at the deaths of Schleicher and von Bredow, and this probably marked the beginning of his disquietude at the Nazi regime. A stickler for order himself, he would not have liked such flagrant flouting of the law. Further, he was distressed at Blomberg's refusal to stand up to Hitler over the killings of his brother officers. Blomberg once more actively supported Hitler in this case, arguing that, as Hitler was the supreme lawgiver, it was his right to dispose of traitors as he saw fit. The Army Establishment would have argued that the two generals at least had the right to a hearing before a court martial.

Whatever Beck's personal views, he kept them to himself. In July 1935 he accepted the post of Chief of the General Staff, which represented the zenith of his career. In October he was promoted again, and three years later he retired with the rank of Colonel-General, one step below Field Marshal. But by then he had become a disillusioned man.

Oster and Beck were the two lynchpins of the early Resistance to Hitler, the driving force behind all efforts to remove him in the years immediately before and after the outbreak of war. Neither of them, however, was in command of troops. In the meantime came the reaction to Hitler of another big battalion – far greater in size and potential power than the Army, the Nazi Party, or the SA – the Church.

THREE

A Fortress Strong

In 1931, the Evangelical parish of St Ann's, Dahlem, in south-west Berlin, welcomed a new pastor. Martin Niemöller, handsome and humorous, was popular from the word go. Now just a year short of forty, he had been one of the most successful submarine commanders of the First World War, but after a brief period as a farmhand after its conclusion, he had entered the Church, and was ordained in 1924. Politically he leant to the Right, and was one of those prominent members of the Resistance who initially supported National Socialism.

Dahlem was the richest parish in Germany. Among his parishioners, Niemöller counted Kurt von Hammerstein, Hans Oster and other members of the future Resistance. It is a feature of the Resistance that many of its members were, or became, devout Christians – and it has been argued that faith was a form of 'inner emigration' for some of them,[1] though equally it may have been an attestation of their right to think independently. In the latter case, they could not have chosen a better champion than Niemöller.

But Resistance within the Church was not a simple matter; when Niemöller raised his voice against the Nazis, it was not against all aspects of their rule. Nazi anti-Semitism, for example, was no more singled out for initial criticism by the Church than it was by the Army. The Church's first consideration was its own independent right to exist. Its Resistance, therefore, was against *Gleichschaltung*. For his part, Hitler naturally wanted to bring the Church into line with everything else in his scheme of things. He knew he dare not simply eradicate it: that would not have been possible with such an international organisation, and he would have lost many Christian supporters had he tried to. His principal aim was to unify the German Evangelical Church under a pro-Nazi banner, and to come to an accommodation with the Catholics.

At the time there were three Protestants to every two Catholics in Germany, but the Church was more than a house divided against itself along the main sectarian line, and this was to the Nazis' advantage.

To take the Evangelical Church first. Every state in post-Reformation Germany had its own sect. In 1919 there were thirty-eight different Calvinist, Lutheran and United Churches under the domination of the Old Prussian Union, though this number was reduced by ten under an amalgamation move in 1922. Although the Church was seen – and saw itself – as apolitical, not interfering in the affairs of state, German Church leaders were conservative at heart and had watched some of the liberal and pro-secular developments of the Weimar Republic with dismay. The new authority, representing as it seemed the solid old values of Imperial Germany, was seen by some as a great opportunity – under *Gleichschaltung* – to unify the disparate sects. Hitler knew this, and exploited it. In doing so he caused the lines of division within the Evangelical Church to be redrawn along political rather than sectarian lines. But also he thus indirectly obliged the Church to look at its own meaning afresh.

Hitler's supporters within the Church formed the movement of German Christians, which upheld the idea of a Reich bishop and the unification of all sects under him. The movement also sought the nazification of the Church in that the Church would accept all the totalitarian and racist aspects of National Socialist policy. Hitler's candidate for the bishopric was Ludwig Müller, an Army chaplain whose chief claim to fame (and this is how Hitler must have heard of him) was that he had converted Blomberg to the idea of Nazism. Müller was not a forceful or convincing character, however, and once it was realised that he was a political tool rather than a spiritual leader, many of those who might have supported him in the interests of Church unity withdrew their support despite his Nazi backing. In the elections for Reich bishop, which took place in the spring of 1933, another candidate was elected: Friedrich von Bodelschwingh, a pious and respected churchman from the famous community of Bethel.

The victory was short-lived, for Hitler was not about to let the Church get its own way. To begin with, he tried to put pressure on it through political control. Bodelschwingh, unable to muster wholehearted support in protest at this, resigned, but still the Prussian Church would not accept the commissioner appointed to bring it into line. Hindenburg had to intervene, and Hitler again had to retreat. But not for long. In July 1933 there were fresh elections. This time, with the full force of the Nazi propaganda machine behind him, Ludwig Müller got the job, and the German Christians gained power in terms of important administrative posts. Few leading prelates spoke up against these bulldozer techniques. Among those who did was Bishop Theophil Wurm of Württemberg, who also objected to measures against non-Aryans. He was put under house arrest for a time, but the Nazis never dared move too drastically against dissident Church leaders because they were aware of the power of religion. During the early years of the Third Reich mass protests against the regime often took the form of enormous religious gatherings.

Nevertheless, with Müller's election Hitler might have thought the battle won. In reality it was only just joined. Two months later, Martin Niemöller and several like-minded clergy men founded the Pastors' Emergency League. This organisation, though not joined by many Church leaders, was hugely successful: by the beginning of 1934 it had 7036 members – more than one third of all the Protestant pastors in Germany – and though its membership dropped during the following decade, it never went below 3933. Its programme was to abide by the letter of the Christian law as expressed in Christ's teaching and the Confession of Faith. In this it represented a step forward for the Church. No longer would the Church simply be seeking the right of self-determination, it would be reaching out its hand in true Christianity to support other victims of Nazism. As the regime grew more draconian, so did the Church increase its humanitarian opposition.

Those days, however, were still some time away. Niemöller did object publicly at the end of the year to those 'Aryan paragraphs' – measures against the Jews – which had already been ushered in, but for the present there was no active questioning of Hitler's right to rule as secular head of state. Niemöller even sent him a telegram of congratulation on leaving the League of Nations.

Here one can clearly sense the difficulty and paradox attending the birth of a rebellion stemming from the Establishment, and understand why it was so slow to begin. Niemöller perceived that certain areas of National Socialism were wrong, but he could not see the whole picture, because he was a conservative German patriot and war hero. There is even a story that later, in 1941, when he had already been a prisoner of the Reich for four years, he volunteered for naval service. But he was also a convinced Christian who could not stand by and see the ethical and moral values of his Faith brushed aside. In a confrontation with Niemöller at the beginning of 1934, the Führer said, 'You confine yourself to the Church, I'll take care of the German people.' Niemöller replied, 'We too, as Christians and churchmen, have a responsibility to the German people which was entrusted to us by God. Neither you nor anyone else in the world has the power to take it from us.'[2] This retort earned him Hitler's personal animosity and shortly afterwards he was suspended, but with the backing of his parishioners he was able to continue his work.

Meanwhile, the German Christians had created problems for themselves by being too outspoken in their virulent anti-Semitism and thereby alienating a large number of people who now withdrew their support. The so-called 'Brown Synod' of September 1933 had called for the expulsion of all churchmen of impure Aryan origin, together with those married to non-Aryans. In November, at a mass meeting in the Sportpalast in Berlin, there had been a call to abolish the Old Testament as a 'Jewish script'. Gustav Heinemann, one of the most powerful German industrialists, wrote an outraged personal letter of protest to Hitler.

The Church, as an international organisation with deep roots and commanding profound loyalty, was a dangerous opponent. Further attempts to muzzle the dissident elements misfired, resulting in huge meetings in Ulm in April 1934, and a month later in Barmen. The Barmen Synod resulted in a Declaration, six points defining the articles of Faith: in sum it asserted that Jesus Christ is the ultimate authority and revealer of God's mystery; and that the Christian owes his duty first and foremost to God, and his obedience to God's laws. At the same time the Declaration refuted the doctrines of the German Christians. Its flavour may be sampled by this section of Article 5:

The Scriptures tell us that the State, by divine decree, is given the task in the as yet unredeemed world, where the Church also has her place, of concerning itself, to the limit of human understanding and human ability, with justice and peace when under the threat and pressure of force . . . We reject the false doctrine that the State, over and above its special charge, should become the single and totalitarian order of human life, thus fulfilling the Church's mission as well.[3]

It was the work of the great Swiss theologian Karl Barth, then a professor at Bonn University, but he spoke with the voice of thousands, and out of the Ulm and Barmen meetings was born the Confessing Church,[4] which united all the dissident Evangelical elements in Germany in a brotherhood dedicated to combating Nazi extremism. It did not stop Hitler's attempts to take over the Church, but it did permanently frustrate them.

With the death of Hindenburg, the Church lost a degree of protection. Ludwig Müller, having failed to serve his purpose, was dismissed in July 1935, and replaced by a Minister for Ecclesiastical Affairs – Hitler's aim being to secularise any Party offices that had to do with the Church and thus push it out into the cold. 1935 also saw increased measures against the Jews, and against dissident churchmen, who were at best deprived of their right to work and at worst thrown into the concentration camps. On the eve of a planned condemnation of Nazi ideology from all the pulpits of the Confessing Church, 715 pastors were arrested in Prussia alone. Hitler, impatient as always, wanted to pull out this thorn in his flesh regardless of the impression he might make abroad, and, as with the Army, having cautiously tested the opposition, he continued to push as far as he dared. Karl Barth, who in the autumn of 1934 had made a personal protest in refusing to take the new Oath of Loyalty for Officials unless he could add the rider: 'Insofar as I can answer for it as an Evangelical Christian', was expelled from Germany and returned to his native Basle.

The Confessing Church kept up its fight throughout 1936. In the spring, a memorandum addressed to the Führer and sharply critical of State anti-Semitism was leaked to the foreign press, and reported in the *Basler Nachrichten* and the *Morning Post*. As a result the head of the Provisional Central Office of the Confessing Church, Friedrich Weissler, was arrested and flung into Sachsenhausen concentration camp, where he was murdered early the following year. Undeterred,

the Church also raised strong objections to the illegal methods of the
Security Service, to an Oath of Loyalty introduced for children, and
to the thinly disguised deification of Hitler through Goebbels' Propaganda Ministry.

After the Olympic Games Hitler had even less reason to put up a
front for the benefit of foreign opinion. Progressively, youth organisations connected with churches were banned, and on 1 December
membership of the Hitler Youth (or State Youth) became compul-
sory for girls up to twenty-one and boys up to eighteen. Dissident
pastors and (by now) Catholic priests and monks were arraigned
on trumped-up charges ranging from embezzlement to paedophilia.
Many hundreds were sent to the concentration camps wearing the pink
triangle designating homosexuality. Conscription and, subsequently,
the war itself, cut great swathes through the ranks of those clergymen
who remained consistently opposed to Nazism. Even when they could
no longer present a united front, even when they were in a tiny minority, they continued their individual protest. Niemöller recognised that
this stance was not enough. Immediately after the war, he convened a
meeting at Stuttgart to formulate a Declaration of Guilt by the Church
for not having opposed Hitler sooner and more strenuously; but he
was being unrealistically harsh.

His own arrest was not far off, and he could no longer rely on
his fame and popularity to protect him from it. On the morning
of 1 July 1937 he had a meeting at his house in Dahlem with a
group of colleagues.[5] Barely had the meeting begun than one of
their number saw a column of black Mercedes cars approach and
draw up – unmistakably the Gestapo. The whole group, including
Frau Niemöller, was placed under house arrest and had to endure an
eight-hour-long search of the building, and especially of Niemöller's
study. At the end of it, all save Niemöller himself were free to go.
He was not tried until the following year, and then committed to the
concentration camp at Sachsenhausen as the 'personal prisoner of the
Führer'. He was later transferred to Dachau, and was liberated by
American forces in 1945. Niemöller lived to a great age, dying in
1984 after a distinguished postwar career in the course of which he
was no less outspoken than he had been against Hitler.

On the evening of her husband's arrest, alone in the house, Frau
Niemöller heard singing outside her window. The women's choir of
St Ann's had heard of their pastor's arrest and had come to comfort

his wife. Two days later, *The Times* in London published a letter by the Bishop of Chichester, a friend of the Confessing Church, in which he sounded one of the earliest unequivocal warnings from abroad about the Nazis: 'This is a critical hour. This is not a question just of the fate of a single vicar; it is a question concerning the whole attitude of the German state to Christianity.'

In early August, a service of intercession for Niemöller took place, and, when the police tried to stop it, a spontaneous demonstration occurred which resulted in 250 arrests. One of those taken was the pastor Franz Hildebrandt. He was now in great danger, in view of his Jewish ancestry; but by dint of the enormous exertions of a friend and colleague who had also been present with Hildebrandt at Niemöller's arrest, he was able to secure his release and escape to England. That friend was Dietrich Bonhoeffer.

Bonhoeffer and his twin sister Sabine were born in 1906. They were two of eight children in a remarkable family. The father, Karl Bonhoeffer, was chief psychiatrist at Berlin's main hospital, the Charité. He was later involved in the 1938 plot against Hitler to the extent of preparing a paper which demonstrated that the dictator was clinically insane. The mother, Paula, was the sister of General Paul von Hase, who was closely involved in the 20 July 1944 Plot. Sabine later married Gerhard Leibholz, a Jewish lawyer, and was thus obliged to leave Germany with him, spending the war in London. An older sister, Ursula, married another lawyer, Rüdiger Schleicher, who was also involved in the Resistance and killed by the SS in April 1945. Another older sister, Christine, married Hans von Dohnanyi, an important member of the Resistance who worked for the Abwehr. Dietrich's older brother Klaus, a senior lawyer with Lufthansa who also worked for the Resistance, married Emmi Delbrück, whose brother Justus was on Oster's staff and equally involved in the Resistance. The Bonhoeffer children were, moreover, distant cousins of Peter Graf Yorck von Wartenburg, another leading figure in the Resistance.

But it is Dietrich's story which must be told here.[6] A tall, blond young man, whose fine hair showed early signs of thinning, his chubby face and round, gold-rimmed spectacles belied a serious, rather lonely nature and a formidable intellect. He was also an excellent pianist and guitarist. Studies at Berlin led to his first thesis – on the nature of the identity and function of the Church – following which he took the

curacy of the German Lutherans in Barcelona, where he stayed for
one year from February 1928. This was the first time he had spent
away from his family, which had provided all the society he had
needed up until then, and his strong sermons, which reflected his
view of Man's dependence on God's grace, breathed new life into
the sleepy community.

That he had a profound need to define the meaning of God
led him, with the encouragement of his extraordinary grandmother
(she who defied the Nazis on National Boycott Day), to look beyond
the Christian Church to Buddhism and Hinduism. For five years he
dreamt of travelling to India, but he never got there. (He had, however, been very impressed by Gandhi's acolyte Mira Bai – Madeline
Slade – when he met her in London in the summer of 1934, and he
had exchanged letters with Gandhi himself.)

Dietrich returned to Berlin early in 1929 and resumed his studies, but by the autumn he had departed for the Union Theological
Seminary in New York City, where he was to spend the next year.
At home, the Weimar Republic was tottering and shortly after his
departure the number of Nazi seats in the Reichstag leapt from
12 to 107. He barely reacted to this, being too much taken up with
his impressions of the New World, which were not all good. He was
critical of what he perceived as American indiscipline and mental
flab, but he became very interested in black American life. When a
black fellow student, Frank Fisher, introduced him to it, he took an
active part in the Christian life of the Harlem community.

For the first and last time in his life he travelled extensively,
visiting Mexico and Cuba, and when he returned to Germany his
outlook was more international than it had been. He took the
job of chaplain at the Technical University, Berlin, but he was
unhappy, and for once his sense of humour deserted him. The
state of his homeland depressed him profoundly. Positive youth
work among underprivileged working-class boys in the Communist
district of Wedding during the winter of 1932–33 re-energised him,
but he could not ignore political developments. At the end of January
– the day after Hitler became Chancellor – he gave a radio broadcast on
'The Concept of Leadership'. This was moderate in tone, but it was
still cut off before he reached the end. Soon afterwards, the complete
talk was published and Dietrich circulated it, together with an angry
note, to his friends.

His father was suspicious of Hitler from the first, seeing right through to the power-hungry demagogue behind the traditionalist bluster. As a liberal with a Jewish son-in-law, he was quickly sensitive to the laws the Nazis introduced banning Jews from the Civil Service, and the more terrible ones that followed as the thirties progressed. Dietrich himself was among the first to argue that the Church should raise its voice against oppression, and he took a very public stance against State attempts to take over the Church. After the infamous Brown Synod, he was one of those who with Niemöller formed the Young Reformers in protest, from which the Confessing Church would soon stem. But for a time Dietrich would have to help in the fight from a distance. It was not an easy decision to take, but he accepted the post of pastor to a German community in Sydenham, a district in south London.

He was there from the summer of 1933 and remained throughout 1934, but there is no doubt that watching the battle from the sidelines was a painful and frustrating experience for him. Such was the telephone bill he ran up to Germany on one occasion that the British Post Office, in a kinder, pre-computerised age, took pity on him and cancelled it. He united the German clergymen of London in a repudiation of the German Christian movement, but he could not keep himself away from the centre of action, and soon returned to Germany to organise and run a seminary set up by the Confessing Church at Finkenwalde, in the depths of Pomerania, near Stettin. His optimism was high, but his confidence in the invincibility of the Confessing Church against Nazi attack was too great.

Dietrich ran Finkenwalde in a spirit of asceticism and comradeship designed to instil a sense of personal integrity and self-discipline in the seminarists. They would need it, because on qualification they would find it a cold world. As the Nazis tightened their grip on the Confessing Church, eroded its power, and enticed its weaker members away, they would find it impossible to find a normal pastoral job with a fixed salary and a home available. Finkenwalde alumni kept in touch by newsletter and managed to maintain a certain *esprit de corps*, but the Nazis kept up their body-blows and, under the provisions of a new Act of September 1935 'For the Settlement of the German Evangelical Church', all the seminaries of the Confessing Church were declared illegal.

Hidden as they were deep in the country, the seminarists did not feel the force of this law immediately. Dietrich's typical reaction to the fresh oppression was to organise and carry out an entirely 'illegal' tour of Scandinavian churches for his seminarists early in 1936, and he kept Finkenwalde going, though this was a rearguard action now and graduates would be lucky to escape arrest, let alone find a job. But Dietrich's personality was still a lodestone, and there were still enough young men whom conscription or the Nazis had not claimed. The seminary continued its work until the end of 1937, when the authorities finally closed it.

Still undeterred, Dietrich became involved in setting up new, secret theological colleges even deeper in the Pomeranian country-side, at Köslin and Gross-Schlönwitz. But he was in an embattled position, and the seminarist who wrote to him wondering if, after all, the Confessing Church was at the end of the road, was not alone.[7] Berlin was far away, and Dietrich was banned from visiting it on any form of Church business, but he did go to see his family often. He found comfort also in a great friendship with his disciple and future biographer, Eberhard Bethge, and in the company of a local landowning family. At their house he made the acquaintance of a little girl called Maria von Wedemeyer. In 1942, on a return visit to Pomerania after many years of struggle, he met her again, and fell in love with the beautiful eighteen-year-old woman she had become. They got engaged, an action which showed that Dietrich had by no means given up hope of the future.

In Berlin he began to involve himself with the Resistance work which already occupied his brother Klaus and his brother-in-law, Hans von Dohnanyi. By this time it was clear that war was imminent, and that everything possible had to be done to avert it. Dietrich made the contacts now that would help him in his own contribution to the fight against Hitler after 1939, but, before that, he had one more journey to make.

He left Germany for New York again in June 1939. His decision to do so was based on a refusal to serve a criminal government in any capacity in a time of war, but he came to it only with great difficulty. His friends in America hoped that by persuading him to come over they would have saved him from Nazi imprisonment; but Dietrich had by no means decided yet to make the move a permanent one. He was leaving his family and friends behind, and he was never a man to turn his back on a fight. He had barely arrived in New York before he knew he would have to return. On 15 June he wrote in his diary:

> Since yesterday evening I can hardly tear my thoughts away from Germany . . . I found a drive to visit a friend in the hills, in itself delightful, almost unendurable. We sat for an hour and chatted, not all that stupidly, but about matters to which I was entirely indifferent . . . and I thought how usefully I might have employed this hour in Germany. I should have liked best to board the next ship home.[8]

He caught the ship home on 7 July. He wrote: 'Last day. Paul [Lehmann – a young theologian] tries to make me stay. No longer possible . . . Packing . . . 11.30 farewell. 12.30 departure. Manhattan by night. The moon riding above the skyscrapers. It is very hot. The journey is finished.'

He was already committed to the Resistance and he knew it. On arrival, he returned to his work in Pomerania, but these were feverish years of transition, of coming to terms with what he had to do. He spent his time between conspiratorial work and absorption in theological reflection – periods of intense activity and relaxation. He became a passionate bridge player, and went to chamber music concerts when he stayed at his parents' house – which became his permanent base – in Berlin. The Catholic diplomat and conspirator Josef Müller arranged for him to take retreat over the winter of 1940–41 to the monastery of Ettal near Munich, whose monks were involved in helping those persecuted by the regime and in disseminating 'illegal' political literature. At about this time he wrote his most famous theological work, *The Ethics*, in which he strove to accommodate Christian ethics with the need to fight evil by force:

> Today there are once more villains and saints, and they are not hidden from the public view. Instead of the uniform greyness of the rainy day we now have the black storm cloud and the brilliant lightning flash. The outlines stand out with exaggerated sharpness. Reality lays itself bare. Shakespeare's characters walk in our midst. But the villain and the saint have little or nothing to do with systematic ethical studies. They emerge from primeval depths and by their appearance they tear open the infernal or the divine abyss from which they come and enable us to see for a moment into mysteries of which we had never dreamed.

The Confessing Church was dying. Its members were being called up, dispersed by the war. Dietrich applied for permission to become an Army chaplain. It was refused. He undertook his first mission for the Resistance on 24 February 1941. The course of the last four years of his life was fixed.

Hitler had to approach the Roman Catholic Church with greater caution than the nationally based Lutherans and Unionists, though when he had one of the Catholics' leading lay figures, Erich Klausener, shot dead during the purge of 30 June 1934, not one German cardinal or bishop protested. But the Roman Church did not approve of the Führer, nor was it ignorant of his moves against Christianity. However Eugenio Pacelli, who became Pope Pius XII in 1939, had before his elevation been the Vatican's not unsympathetic expert on Germany – indeed had spent much of his career there (since 1917 in fact). Furthermore his successor as Nuncio in Berlin, Diego Cesare Orsenigo, was an all but open supporter of the Nazis.

Perhaps the greatest hindrance to any co-ordinated opposition within the Catholic Church was deference to Rome. Even considering the potential problem of being a tiny neutral state in the middle of a fascist dictatorship allied to Hitler, the Vatican – particularly after the accession of Pacelli – gave vent to very little criticism of the regime. However Rome never approved of it, and provided a forum for discussions between representatives of the Resistance and the Allies. Characteristically, the ancient and international Catholic Church took a long-term view: the German problem was a local one, and clearly the Nazi form of government would neither dominate the world nor last a thousand years. On the other hand, if it were left to the Russians to destroy Nazism, that might throw Eastern Europe open to secularism and Communism.

Encouraged by Pacelli, but also for the sake of harmony and in order to protect its own interests, Rome promptly signed a Concordat with Hitler on 20 July 1933. This agreement was so hurried through that it was signed before all the details of its terms were defined, especially (and crucially) those protecting the rights of Catholic organisations. Pope Pius XI asked Hitler to give him his word of honour that the New Germany would continue to base its constitution on Christianity. This Hitler gladly did – he was always happy to make promises if they would get him his way and people were naive enough to believe he would keep them. In fact, his government had just promulgated its first Sterilisation Law, something which was not made public until the Concordat was signed, on the advice of the oily von Papen.

The advantage for the Catholic Church was that, under the terms of the agreement, the State would leave it alone. The advantage for Hitler was that he gained the support of the Catholic political parties (for the brief period that he needed it – ironically the Concordat was signed just after the abolition of all parties in Germany save the National Socialists). With his usual irresistible bullying technique, Hitler then proceeded to take a mile where he had been given an inch. Exploiting the imprecisions in the agreement, he proceeded to close down all Catholic organisations whose functions were not strictly religious, and it quickly became clear that he intended to imprison the Catholics, as it were, in their own churches. They could celebrate mass and retain their ritual as much as they liked, but they could have nothing at all to do with German society otherwise. Catholic schools and newspapers were closed, and a propaganda campaign against the Catholics was launched.

Naturally the Catholic Church objected. Cardinal Michael Faulhaber of Munich, one of the most prominent opponents of the regime, spoke out from his pulpit late in 1933 in a series of sermons in which he also defended the Old Testament against its attack from the Brown Synod. Early in 1934 the Vatican placed *The Myth of the Twentieth Century* on the Index. (A pseudo-scientific/philosophical work by the Nazis' 'spiritual ideologue' Alfred Rosenberg, the book sought to prove the racial purity and cultural superiority of the Nordic races.) Faulhaber was left alone because Hitler was never strong enough to remove senior clerics – though as we have seen he imprisoned priests, monks and nuns in their hundreds. As for the reproof to Rosenberg, it did not hurt the Führer: Rosenberg was already losing ground in the internal Nazi political dogfight, and his book had never been officially sanctioned by the Party. Among the few other Catholic voices raised in protest were those of the Mayor of Cologne, Konrad Adenauer (shortly afterwards dismissed and imprisoned), and the Catholic trade union leader Bernhard Letterhaus. A leading member of the Resistance, Letterhaus later used his position as a captain in the Oberkommando Wehrmacht to gather information. He was arrested in the purge following the failure of the 20 July 1944 Plot and was executed later that year.

Hitler gave ground a little, but essentially pressed on with his programme. Early opponents wavered. Cardinal Bertram of Breslau even came to an accommodation with the Nazis. The National Boycott Day aimed at the Jews evoked no unanimous Catholic condemnation, though as the year progressed consistent critics and opponents of the regime emerged.

The first martyr was Erich Klausener, a middle-aged civil servant who ran the police affairs department in the Prussian Interior Ministry and was also leader of Berlin's Catholic Action movement. Klausener organised the Catholic conventions in Berlin in both 1933 and 1934. The second, held at the Hoppegarten racecourse, attracted 60,000 people. They celebrated mass together, and Klausener spoke against political oppression. Not a swastika was to be seen. Six days later Klausener was shot dead in his office.

As I have said, no major voice was raised at this outrage, but the Catholic masses were not cowed. More than anyone else the Catholics showed their disapproval of the regime by huge gatherings, and this was the only collective Resistance the Catholics showed. Every seven years a pilgrimage centred on Aachen. In 1937, at least 800,000 people attended – a massive demonstration by the standards of the day. In the same year in Bamberg, a conservative Catholic town in Franconia, 60,000 people gathered in the cathedral square to celebrate the 700th anniversary of the founding of the bishopric there. Sixty thousand was about equal to the city's entire population.

1937 also saw a firm reaction to Hitler's activities from Rome. On Passion Sunday, 14 March, Pius XI issued an encyclical 'With Great Anxiety' ('*Mit Brennender Sorge*') on the state of the Catholic Church in the German Reich. It expressed the Pope's deep concern at Hitler's flouting of the terms of the Concordat, at his treatment of Catholics and his abuse of Christian values. While not mentioning the fate of the Jews specifically, it asserts the inviolability of basic human rights, makes a specific appeal to youth, and ends with a call for constancy and loyalty. The text was smuggled into Germany and secretly printed and distributed. Hitler was beside himself with rage. Twelve presses were seized, and hundreds of people sent either to prison or the camps. It is significant that these events took place before the demonstrations I have already described.

Among the Catholic bishops who took a firm and consistent stance against Hitler, two stand out. Konrad Graf von Preysing became Bishop of Berlin in 1935. Never a friend of the Nazis, he sought to work against them through every means at his disposal,

from sermons to argument at bishops' conferences. He worked closely
with the civilian conspirators Carl Goerdeler and Helmuth James Graf
von Moltke. He was an adviser on the 1937 Papal Encyclical, opposed
to the closure of Catholic schools, and tried to thwart the arrest
of Church officials on trumped-up charges. He opposed Cardinal
Bertram's appeasing, even servile, approach to Hiltler. His Pastoral
Letters for Advent of 1942 (on the nature of human rights) and 1943
reflect the spirit of the Barmen Declaration. The text of the first was
leaked to the BBC (British Broadcasting Corporation) which broadcast
it in their German Service. Preysing's reaction to hearing that they
had done so was to remark, 'That will make them build my gallows
even higher,' though Hitler never dared touch him. In spring 1944
he met and gave his personal blessing to Claus von Stauffenberg, the
man who made the last and most famous attempt on Hitler's life
soon afterwards. Naturally Preysing had not been made party to the
plans, but he had talked with Stauffenberg about whether the need
for radical change to the benefit of all could justify tyrannicide, and
he knew perfectly well what was afoot.

In one among the constant flow of letters to his wife, dated
6 September 1941, von Moltke wrote:

> I asked him [Preysing] about Galen. He assured me that Galen was
> a perfectly average type with little spiritual depth, who had
> therefore only very recently perceived how things were going and
> hence had always been prepared to compromise. So it is all the more
> impressive that the Holy Ghost has now filled and enlightened him.

Clemens August Graf von Galen was Preysing's cousin, and Bishop
of Münster. He was a member of one of Germany's oldest families;
one with a tradition of sending its sons into the Church. Preysing's
view of his cousin is not absolutely fair, as Galen had been aware of
the totalitarian nature of the regime, and its injustices, from the first.
Though he had pledged his loyalty to Hitler early, he too had worked
on the Encyclical. He had criticised Nazi racial policy in a sermon
given in January 1934. He objected to unquestioning obedience to
the Reich in another, calling it 'slavery', and he spoke out against
Hitler's theory of the 'purity' of German blood. His own line went
back to the beginning of the thirteenth century, so he was able to
dispute Hitler's personal claim that 'German blood spoke from him'
with some authority.

But it took the discovery of Nazi atrocities on his doorstep – in his own diocese – to spur him into his most famous action. Then, he earned his nickname of 'The Lion of Münster'.

On 14 and 21 July, and 3 August 1941, he delivered three powerful sermons – the third is the most important – attacking the Nazi euthanasia programme. Killing-centres disguised as sanatoria had been set up for the disposal – usually at this period by lethal injection, though gas chambers were in the experimental stage – of all those whom the Reich deemed useless to society: the mentally disabled and ill, epileptics, cripples, children with Down's Syndrome, the senile, and others similarly afflicted. The Evangelical Bishop Theophil Wurm had already protested vigorously about them, but Galen used his condemnation of this appalling policy to draw wider conclusions about the nature of the Nazi state. He also attacked the Gestapo habit of seizing Church buildings and converting them to their own uses – which included cinemas and even brothels. The sermons were illegally printed and distributed throughout Germany and also abroad for years after he had preached them.

So blistering was the assault that Hitler considered Galen's removal, but Goebbels dissuaded him, telling him that if he arrested the Bishop, he could write off the loyalty of all of Westphalia. Yet remarkably, after this tremendous warning, the Lion did not roar again. He had not stopped the euthanasia programme, though he did succeed in halting it in its tracks. Later it continued in conditions of greater secrecy. It is possible that Galen considered that he had done enough; yet in view of his outrage it seems extraordinary that within a month of his sermons he stated publicly that 'We Christians do not make revolution'. Perhaps again we are dealing with someone who was too much the prisoner of his traditions and his upbringing. Even Ludwig Beck, as late as 1938, observed that 'Mutiny and revolution are words not to be found in a German officer's vocabulary'. In 1938 Beck was fifty-eight. In 1941 Galen was sixty-three. It is hard to break the habits of a lifetime.

Men like Preysing and Galen, however courageous, were protected from Nazi retaliation by their position. Bernhard Lichtenberg, priest at St Hedwig's cathedral in Berlin, was a confidant of Bishop Preysing, but that was not enough to save him in the end. His story must serve for many brave individuals.

Lichtenberg came to St Hedwig's in 1932, and was well-enough known to the Gestapo to have his flat searched as early as 1933. He ran the aid unit of the diocesan authority for Preysing – an organisation which clandestinely gave help and advice to those persecuted by the regime – and from 1938 conducted public prayers of intercession for the Jews, 'the poor inmates of the concentration camps, and my fellow priests there'. He preached consistently against official Party propaganda, and wrote a courageous letter to the State Medical Director, Dr Conti, on 28 August 1941, endorsing the sentiments of Galen's sermons, pointing out the precise laws under the Constitution in which euthanasia was unequivocally defined as an act of murder. By that action he finally pushed the authorities too far. He was arrested and tried by a special court which sentenced him to two years' penal servitude. When these were completed he was rearrested by the Gestapo (a not uncommon occurrence) and sent to Dachau. Already ill, he died on the way there, at Hof, in November 1943, aged sixty-eight.

'*Ein' feste Burg ist unser Gott,*' wrote Luther: a fortress strong is God our Lord. Despite the great bravery of such individuals as Lichtenberg, Niemöller, Galen, Preysing and Bonhoeffer, the Church in Germany was no such fortress in the face of the Nazi menace. But then the Church is human. Bonhoeffer wrote: 'The exceptional necessity calls for freedom of responsibility. There is no law here behind which personal responsibility can seek shelter. Hence there is no law to compel the person responsible . . .' The loneliness implicit in that conclusion was something which every member of the Resistance had to accept.

FOUR

Lost Illusions

As the Nazis built up their strength, so the illusion that their regime would not last long faded. Once political opposition was gone, and with Hitler applauded abroad – despite the loud protests of Germans already in exile – the Party dug in and the task of dislodging it became much harder. The Party swastika flag became the National flag; the greeting 'Heil Hitler' became obligatory, not only as the way of signing off a letter, but also replacing 'Good day'. The salute spread – there was even a Nazi etiquette booklet which instructed one when and how far to stretch out one's arm, and when it was permissible to use the left arm. The salute spread everywhere: only a handful of Army officers didn't use it. Although the brownshirts of the SA became less common (the SA was relegated to the position of an auxiliary political police force), the black uniforms of the SS were seen more and more frequently. SS units were garrisoned all over Germany, as ready to protect Hitler against his own people as against foreign attackers. It became less and less possible to ignore the threat of war.

Still nothing happened. The question why is hard to answer. The Nazis had made no secret of their plans. Even before Hitler became Chancellor there had been the Potempa incident, and a year before that secret Nazi documents were discovered at Boxheim, which gave details of an administration that proposed the death sentence for practically every offence against the State, and rationing measures that effectively deprived the Jews of food. They had been drawn up by Werner Best, later Hitler's Commissioner for Occupied Denmark. They presented the State with a *prima facie* case for high treason.

Nothing was done. The mood of the period – indeed of any similar period, before, since or to come – is perfectly expressed in Martin Niemöller's bitter poem:

> When the Nazis came for the Communists
> I was silent.
> I wasn't a Communist.
> When the Nazis came for the Social Democrats
> I was silent.
> I wasn't a Social Democrat.
> When the Nazis came for the Trade Unionists
> I was silent.
> I wasn't a Trade Unionist.
> When the Nazis came for the Jews
> I was silent.
> I wasn't a Jew.
> When the Nazis came for me
> There was no one left
> To protest.

Hitler took advantage of chaos and uncertainty, and by encapsulating the hopes and fears of the little man – and all his resultant and attendant prejudices – by exploiting and personifying them, and by making as much noise as possible of any political success he had, he bullied and pushed his way to power. True, the soil he grew in was fertile, but he would never have succeeded if he had not been allowed to. He gives us the impression of being an irresistible force: but he was not. He was on thin enough ice in the early thirties not to have withstood Resistance from within Germany, and up until 1938 from outside. He was a terrible accident of history: the wrong man at the right time; if there is no unified protest against such people, they win. In the case of Germany, a combined Social Democrat/Communist stand would have crushed him; but that could not happen. The Weimar Republic governments, heavily chained by the terms of the Treaty of Versailles, were usually liberal and usually weak. The few strong statesmen they threw up died young. Meanwhile Imperial Germany cast a long shadow, and Hitler stepped out of it.

But one must not present Hitler merely as a demon who somehow seduced the German people into mass insanity. The working classes found themselves briefly with a better standard of living and greater possibilities for work. What they did not realise was that Hitler was building an economic miracle on sand: it was a short-term device. Ordinary people were in any case more concerned with their jobs and families than with politics, and they were pleased to see Germany's status raised among the nations again. If they were not Jewish and could prove that back as far as all their grandparents, if they were not married to Jews, if they closed their minds to the racist and warmongering aspects of Party propaganda, they could relax. There would be nothing in the newspapers or on the new, widely available and carefully controlled wireless to disturb them.[1]

At the outset virtually all those who joined the Regular Army during its development were loyal to Hitler. The reintroduction of conscription in March 1935 was popular with the Army top brass. In September of that year, the infamous Nuremberg Laws directed against the Jews were promulgated in the face of very little protest within Germany. As always, the Nazis introduced the new measures gradually, but most were in place within two years, and they covered everything from various degrees of 'Jewishness' – dependent on how many Jewish grandparents one had – to control of work (Jewish doctors were demoted to 'medical practitioners', for example, and only allowed to treat fellow Jews), restriction of shopping hours, use of parks, swimming pools, cinemas and other public places, the banning of wireless sets and, most cruelly, the forbidding of pets to Jews. In November there were mass trials of Communists and Social Democrats, just as the Communists and Social Democrats in exile in Paris were discussing the possibility of working together.

Hitler was on the crest of a wave and he was not going to pause at this point. In March 1936 he sent the Army into the demilitarised Rhineland. This was a crucial action, and definitive proof of Hitler's gambler tactics. In ordering the occupation, he went against his military advisers, who feared a confrontation with France at which Germany would have to step down. This would have been the case in fact, and the German Forces' commanders had sealed orders to do so if it came to it. But the French government was weak and about to fall, and it lost precious time by consulting Britain. For its part, Britain, under its Prime Minister Stanley Baldwin, was inclined to be sympathetic to Germany's right to 'go into her own back garden'.

In Germany, it was a hugely popular move, particularly among those industrialists who had backed Hitler and now saw their investment paid off. A plebiscite three weeks later gave Hitler (officially at least) 99 per cent of the public's backing. Meanwhile, sales of *Mein Kampf* had outstripped those of any other book and made him a rich man. By 1940, nine million copies had been printed.

In August, the Olympic Games were held in Berlin – a venue decided on before Hitler came to power. The capital was redecorated for the occasion, and except for huge swastika banners everywhere the Nazis kept the profiles of their military and racist ambitions low. The red glass-fronted boxes in which copies of the violently anti-Semitic magazine *Der Stürmer* were displayed disappeared from street corners, as did all public notices directed against Jews. No country boycotted the Games, though there were mutterings on the American Olympic Committee, and, as they were magnificently organised, they were a great success and provided another feather in Hitler's cap. His famous show of ill-temper at Jesse Owens' success raised fewer eyebrows then than it would now, and any protestors (for there were some) who attempted to convey the truth of what was really going on to the foreign athletes or the press were quickly tidied up by the Gestapo.

The last athlete had barely boarded his train home before the anti-Semitic laws were back in force. In September, Hitler concluded his Axis Treaty with Italy, and a month later the Anti-Comintern Pact was signed with Japan.

There was a strike at the Auto Union works in Berlin during the Games, which, though it was quickly suppressed by the authorities, showed that there was more than a spark of Resistance still in the parties of the far Left. Various cells were set up, mainly to write and distribute anti-Fascist propaganda, and though their average life was three months, there were always new ones to replace those exposed by the Gestapo. Gradually political bickering between the Social Democrats and the Communists petered out, at least within Germany, but it never disappeared completely, and rarely did the two groups mingle and work as one. Finance was another problem, solved partially by the revenue from vegetarian restaurants run by the underground. The table-legs of one in Frankfurt were hollow, to contain secret distribution lists. Newspapers and magazines produced to a professional standard, like *The Young Guard* and *The Workers' Illustrated* – the latter frequently carrying the anti-Fascist collages of the Communist artist and illustrator John Heartfield – were smuggled in successfully until the war closed the frontiers. Railway workers made especially good smugglers of illegal material, but were susceptible to infiltration by the Security Service.

Meeting places had to be chosen carefully – graveyards and the lobbies of good, busy hotels were preferred. Organisation was something which plagued the Resistance at all levels, since telephones and the post could not be trusted. Nevertheless, the working-class Resistance continued to carry out graffiti, leaflet and poster campaigns well into wartime. Although the official Communist Party was hamstrung by Moscow directives, particularly during the period of the Russian-German alliance between 1939 and 1941, splinter groups working primarily for their country and secondarily for the good of the international workers' cause had no such inhibition. The KPO – the Opposition Communists – were even opposed to Stalinism and social Fascism.

The principal problem facing Communist and Social Democrat Resistance cells was lack of leadership. The most prominent functionaries of both parties were either in exile or in prison, and those who were released and returned to underground work were quickly picked up again, for the Gestapo never let them out of their sight. Small, isolated groups could do little that was effective, and were always a prey to prying neighbours, police infiltration and the part-time informer. Most superintendents of blocks of flats, for example, were paid stool-pigeons. In political terms, whether the Resistance was inspired by right- or left-wing politics, only courageous lonely voices loudly raised were heard – and then not widely or for long.

On the Left, the earliest such opponent was the lifelong Communist Ernst Niekisch, who founded his magazine *Resistance* in 1926 as a 'journal for socialist and national-revolutionary ideology'. He campaigned against Hitler vigorously well after the Nazi takeover, and yet his magazine was not closed down until November 1934. Niekisch was not arrested until 1937. He remained in prison until 1945.

Resistance made for strange bedfellows. Niekisch had engaged the services, as an intermediary between himself and the official Communist Party, of Josef 'Beppo' Römer, a former member of the right-wing Freikorps who had subsequently become a Communist. Römer himself was later involved in a plot to kill Hitler planned

by the lawyer and industrialist Nikolaus von Halem and the Legation Secretary Herbert Mumm von Schwarzenstein – all three were
executed by the Gestapo as a result.

As the Nazi net closed round him, Niekisch sought contacts
beyond his own political associates, and as he was interested in the
particular problems of the agrarian eastern part of the country he
made the acquaintance of Ewald von Kleist-Schmenzin[2]. Politically,
Kleist was as far to the Right as Niekisch was to the Left. He was
a monarchist and a landowner. But he was a fellow magazine editor
– of the *Information Journal of the Central Conservative Association*, a
periodical banned by the Nazis in 1933. Kleist and Niekisch became
early if unlikely allies in the fight against Hitler, and Kleist visited
Niekisch whenever he came to Berlin. They also became friends,
respecting each other's views and learning from them, for neither
was a bigot. Both independently published booklets that warned
against and condemned Nazism; and even the titles were similar:
Niekisch's was called 'Hitler: a German Fate', and Kleist's 'National
Socialism: a Danger'. Kleist was outspoken in his condemnation of
the spinelessness of the military leadership, and wrote: 'In future the
word will be: "As characterless as a German official, as godless as a
Protestant pastor, as unprincipled as a Prussian officer".'[3]

Von Kleist had refused to fly the swastika flag from the roof
of his country house, and he had refused to give a penny to Party
funds. Many aristocrats and landowners paid up for the sake of peace
and quiet – some even joined the Party – but Kleist would not even
compromise to the extent of paying a token ten pfennigs, which the
local Party leader had suggested as a means of satisfying everyone
without losing face. The Security Service put his name on the list
of those to be liquidated on 30 June 1934, but friends forewarned
him, and he fled to Berlin, where Niekisch sheltered and protected
him. For a time they shared a flat, and each invited his own political
friends for discussions, sometimes at the same time, the 'Right' and
'Left' meetings being held in different rooms.

This friendship demonstrates that National Socialism was not a
political party like any other. It was a danger to all free expression,
and, further, a threat to humanity. Those who perceived this menace
closed ranks; but there was never enough unity to defeat it from
within: the Nazi system itself made sure of that. In the meantime,
Niekisch's humane act meant that Kleist survived to fight another

day – a fight which he continued until he, too, was executed.

By the end of 1937 Hitler felt himself to be in a strong enough position to reveal his wider ambitions to the Armed Forces. Accordingly
he called a meeting on 5 November in the Reich Chancellery in Berlin.
Present were Blomberg and Fritsch, together with the commander of
the fleet, Erich Raeder, and Göring for the Luftwaffe. The minutes
were taken by Colonel Friedrich Hossbach, one of the Führer's aides
and also a representative of the General Staff. Ludwig Beck was not
in attendance.

The forgathered military experts were in for a shock. In the
course of the meeting, which lasted for over four hours, Hitler
peremptorily presented them with nothing less than his plans for
a war. He expatiated on the need for 'living space' for the German
masses; this should be found in the lands adjoining Germany, which
meant 'breaking the resistance' of those who happened to be living
there at present. The ideal time to strike would be when the Reich's
principal potential enemies – Britain and France – were preoccupied
with internal problems. In any case Austria and Czechoslovakia should
be taken as quickly as possible and consolidated so that France – the
most immediate enemy – could be faced in time. Germany should
not wait later than 1943 – certainly not later than 1945 – to strike.
Hitler implied that Poland, Russia and Britain would be unlikely to
involve themselves – at any rate not until after Germany had armed
itself sufficiently to deal with them too.

It is hard to imagine the immediate reaction of those present
to this proposal. Göring, hitherto a moderate, certainly sided with
Hitler. Those most nearly affected, however, those who would have
to plan the details and implement them, order troop movements
and take responsibility, were Blomberg and Fritsch. They raised
objections, technical and political. Germany was not strong enough
to oppose Britain or France and the risk of their not standing idly
by while fellow European nations were invaded was too great.
Czechoslovakia had a strong armaments industry and solid forti-
fications along its frontier with Germany. Hitler listened to the
objections without losing his temper, although the argument became
sharp at times. Neither Blomberg nor Fritsch actually refused to
carry out the plans, neither man offered his resignation or expressed
the slightest objection on the grounds of violating international law.
Nevertheless they had shown that they were not wholeheartedly with

the Führer, and Hitler did not want such men in charge of the Army.

The fall of Blomberg and Fritsch marked the change within the services able to do anything practical about toppling the regime – the Abwehr, the Foreign Office and the Army – from information gathering and discussion to concerted action. The storm clouds were gathering with a speed no one would have imagined possible.

Beck, when he learned of the matter from Hossbach, was appalled, and, as was his habit, committed his thoughts and objections lengthily to paper, pointing out the dangers of making enemies out of France and Britain, and also the long-term impossibility of running Germany as an autarchy, which was another of Hitler's proposals. Like most of the men who were to become conspirators against the regime, Beck was a European, not a Nationalist, and he accurately foresaw a future in which states would depend increasingly on trade with each other. He regarded the idea of an unprovoked war with Czechoslovakia with particular distress.

In the meantime, Hitler was making plans to get rid of Blomberg and Fritsch, and it so happened that the possibility to do so – with a little engineering of events – was quickly available in both cases. At the beginning of 1938, on 12 January, Göring's birthday, the widowed Blomberg had married a girl called Erna Gruhn. In the old days this would have been a problem, because Fräulein Gruhn was a member of the working classes. The various accounts that exist suggest that Blomberg had met her in a nightclub. He must have been besotted with her, but he did consult Hitler and Göring about the marriage before embarking on it. They had no objections – indeed, it accorded with Nazi ideology for someone in Blomberg's position to feel free to marry 'a girl of the people' – and even acted as witnesses. Unfortunately, soon after the marriage a routine vice squad check turned up some pornographic photographs of the War Minister's new wife, and a discreet follow-up revealed that Erna had worked at least part-time in a Berlin brothel. This information, which quickly leaked to various members of the High Command in the form of rumours, threatened to cause a major scandal. The Chief of Police of Berlin, Graf von Helldorf, an old SA man who later became a prominent member of the Resistance, was responsible for the documentation the vice squad enquiry had landed on his desk, and took it first to Wilhelm Keitel, then Blomberg's Chief of the Ministerial Office. Keitel was an old friend of Blomberg's – his daughter and the War Minister's son were later to marry – and backed off handling it, referring Helldorf to Göring.

There is a theory that Göring, who had his eye on the War Ministry in any case, may have masterminded the whole episode, manipulating the naive Blomberg like a puppet. Whatever the truth of the matter, he now had the War Minister completely at his mercy. Hitler probably knew nothing of the scandal until Göring placed it before him, uttering pious expressions of regret. Indeed, the case against Blomberg seems to have shocked the Führer at first; but that may have been more because of the sordidity of the potential scandal than anything else. As for Blomberg's colleagues, including Beck, it had been bad enough that he should have married so far beneath him; that it should turn out that he had married a whore was the last straw. He was ostracised and never admitted back into their company. It is touching to note that Blomberg stood by his wife throughout his ensuing disgrace and exile. He died shortly after the end of the war, never having re-entered active service.

When Hitler realised that he had to let Blomberg go his first reaction, despite Blomberg's reservations about his war plans, was panic. After all, Blomberg was a pliant soldier whose military expertise was useful. But the Officer Corps stood united against him: that his wife could call herself 'Frau Feldmarschallin' was quite intolerable. It fell to Fritsch to perform the unhappy task of putting this to the Führer.

Seeing that there was no way out, Hitler broke the news to Blomberg as gently as possible, assuring him that he would not be left completely out in the cold, and asking his advice on his successor. Ironically, Blomberg open-heartedly suggested Göring, the next most senior officer in the High Command, but Hitler rejected this. Göring was already on the road to ruin which would lead to his disgrace and, after his own abortive coup against Hitler, to the death sentence from the Führer – followed by his escape, and capture by American troops.

For the present, Hitler was prepared to turn a blind eye to the fact that his senior lieutenant was beginning to wear make-up, and the cocaine habit had not yet fully taken hold; but Göring was clearly more interested in personal self-aggrandisement than the wider ambitions of the Reich, and would have made at best an idle and at worst a scheming Number Two. The man Hitler chose was Wilhelm

Keitel – whom even Blomberg referred to as 'just an office manager'. A yes man, however, who happened to be a good administrator, was exactly what Hitler wanted. Keitel lived up to the role so well that he soon earned the nickname 'Lakeitel' – little lackey.

Concurrent with the toppling of Blomberg, plans were being laid against Fritsch. Fritsch was fifty-eight years old and had never married – not uncommon in Army officers of that day, but still leaving him exposed to accusations of homosexuality. Such stories were now concocted and again Göring was the man behind them, employing the services of Himmler's Gestapo and the head of the Security Service, Reinhard Heydrich, to set them up.[4]

A homosexual blackmailer called Otto Schmidt, who had been jailed a couple of years earlier, was dredged up to provide the 'evidence'. As we have seen, Hitler could switch on an aversion to homosexuals when he wanted to – though he scarcely bothered to conceal his hypocrisy. At exactly the same time as Fritsch was being brought down, on 5 February 1938, Walter Funk, whose homosexuality was well known, was appointed Reich Minister of Economics. Fritsch was a more positive character than Blomberg, and Hitler had no compunction in scheming to get rid of him. The evidence provided by Schmidt was that he had been propositioned by the Commander-in-Chief. Fritsch demanded a confrontation with his accuser in Hitler's presence, which occurred on 26 January 1938 – two days after the evidence concerning Erna Gruhn had landed on Hitler's desk. Schmidt coolly asserted that Fritsch was indeed the man.

At this point, Fritsch could have done a number of things. He could have consulted a lawyer, appealed to the Officer Corps that the Führer was taking the word of a convicted male prostitute and blackmailer against the Commander of the Army, or he could have resigned in a full and self-righteous glare of publicity. Instead, totally taken off guard by the outrageous and unprecedented accusation, which he was facing alone and without back-up, he lost his temper and left, on his dignity, but with his position considerably weakened. Hitler considered (for it was convenient to do so) that Fritsch was guilty by implication. Hence Fritsch's name did not come up during the consideration of Blomberg's successor.

Matters now moved very fast – as usual, Hitler left no time for any opposition to get a response organised. By early February the nature of the High Command was radically changed. The old War Ministry effectively became the Oberkommando Wehrmacht (OKW) – Overall High Command of the Armed Forces. He made Keitel head of it, but took over the job of Supreme Commander himself in a fully executive, not honorary, sense. Göring was promoted to Field Marshal – two years later he would be made Germany's first and last Reichsmarschall – and was able to add another specially designed uniform to his vast collection. Fritsch's job went to Walther von Brauchitsch, who was promoted Colonel-General.

Brauchitsch was to play a shadowy part in the battle between Hitler and the Resistance over the next three years. He seemed to want to join the forces ranging against the dictator, but he could never quite bring himself to. He was another weak man, but there was one practical contributory factor to his wavering. For five years he had lived separated from his wife, and in the meantime had started a passionate affair with a divorcée called Charlotte Schmid-Rüffer. There was no question of a divorce for Brauchitsch, because he did not have enough money to make an adequate settlement on his wife. To be fair to him, he had toyed with the idea of resignation, and Blomberg's case must have sharpened his sensibilities, but the offer through Keitel of Fritsch's old job was too much for Brauchitsch to resist. In addition when he opened his heart about his marital difficulties to Göring, the latter reassured him and pledged his support. Not long afterwards, his financial difficulties were miraculously resolved. His divorce was now affordable and he was able to marry his new love. Hitler had put another general into his pocket, and his cause was helped by the fact that Frau Schmid-Rüffer was, in the words of the German Ambassador to Rome, Ulrich von Hassell, who was already aligned with the Resistance, 'a two hundred per cent rabid National Socialist'. Brauchitsch took up his post on 3 February.

Fritsch did not come to trial until mid-March. By this time he had been effectively neutralised, and it did not matter much to the Nazis whether he was found guilty or not. The court of honour under – of all people – Göring's chairmanship acquitted him on the 18th of the month. A rearguard action had been fought. Hans Oster of the Abwehr had worked closely with his assistant Hans von Dohnanyi and with the co-operation of both Fritsch's lawyer and the examining judge of the military court, Karl Sack, to gather information proving the charges to be fabricated. Sack fought a lonely and consistent fight on behalf of true justice in the Reich courts as long as he could, and before his own downfall later did his best to prolong the trials of such men as Dohnanyi in the hope that the end of the war would overtake the Nazi prosecutions.

Sack's investigations led to the discovery of an elderly, retired Captain Achim von Frisch, who was homosexual, and had been a victim of Otto Schmidt's blackmail. When this evidence was brought to light the case against Fritsch collapsed.

That was not quite the end of the story. Fritsch was rehabilitated by Hitler, but not until June, and then he was shunted very far sideways, being given the command of Number 12 Artillery Regiment. The thin excuse for not restoring Fritsch to his old job was that Hitler could not expect Fritsch to have any confidence in him any more even though he had been exonerated; nor could he, as Führer, for the good of the nation, publicly admit such a major mistake. Fritsch responded to the shabby treatment he had been handed by challenging Himmler – whom he knew to have been behind the machinations against him – to a duel, but nothing came of it and he was persuaded to withdraw the challenge. After the outbreak of war, Fritsch, disgusted and disillusioned, sought death at the head of his troops in Poland and found it only days after hostilities had opened. As for Otto Schmidt, he ended up in Sachsenhausen concentration camp, but his old employers did not forget him. At the end of July 1942, Himmler concluded a report on him to Göring with the words, 'I request your agreement, dear Reichsmarschall, that I should submit Schmidt's case to the Führer for authorisation to execute him.' Göring scribbled in the margin of the memo: 'Yes. Ought to have been done *ages* ago.'

The fall of Blomberg and Fritsch weakened the Army's independence greatly. Hitler had replaced them with two spaniels. Arguably the moment for an effective Resistance had already passed, before it had even been formed. Why did the Officer Corps not stand up for its Commander-in-Chief, so crudely maligned? The reason is that Hitler had already diluted the Corps to such an extent that it could no longer adopt a unanimous stance. Since he had taken power the number of officers above the rank of Major-General had increased sevenfold. By 1943 there were over a thousand of them, as opposed to forty-four a decade earlier. Beck's subsequent call – later in 1938 – for a mass resignation of generals, the only possible way to stop Hitler without a coup, was a forlorn hope. Too many of the new appointments were

men like Walter von Reichenau, intelligent younger generals who had
thrown in their lot with the new regime. There were others whose
Party affiliations brought them promotion.

But there was another much simpler reason why Fritsch's fate
had been eclipsed. With the inspired timing of his prewar years,
Hitler had chosen 12 March 1938 to annex Austria.

This was a move which had long been on the agenda. In 1936, only
two years after his predecessor had been bloodily murdered by Nazis
in an abortive coup, the Austrian Chancellor, Kurt von Schuschnigg,
signed an agreement of friendly co-operation with Hitler. In one sense
this was temporising, for there were only seven million Austrians as
opposed to sixty-six million Germans. To strengthen his position,
Schuschnigg also created ties with Czechoslovakia, Yugoslavia and
Romania, but this move infuriated Hitler, who ordered a Nazi putsch
in January 1938. It came too soon, and misfired, but a month later
Hitler forced Schuschnigg to appoint the Austrian Nazi leader, Arthur
Seyss-Inquart, to his government as Minister of Public Security. The
Austrian Chancellor could see what was coming and tried to organise
a referendum for 13 March on the subject of Austrian independence.
However Hitler pre-empted this by getting the Nazis in Austria to stir
up trouble, upon which Seyss-Inquart asked the Germans to step in to
restore order. Hitler followed up this manoeuvre immediately with a
visit to Braunau, his birthplace, where he stood by his parents' graves.
The Austrians greeted the 'Anschluss' rapturously. Subsequently 75
per cent of the SS would be drawn from this country.

Hitler had scored another triumph. No one abroad objected –
there were even statements of approval in the British press, and
no one bothered about the reservations Czechoslovakia might have
had. At home, few, even among those opposed to Hitler, really took
exception to this unification of the German-speaking peoples. The
question of legality, and the fact that Schuschnigg was thrown into
Dachau concentration camp, were matters to be glossed over. But
Hitler was showing that he meant to do as he said. His position
was becoming as entrenched as his determination. Those close to the
centre of power saw that, unless action was taken soon, a disastrous
war could not be averted. And now, finally, the forces of Resistance
began to crystallise.

FIVE

Annus Fatalis

The leader of the civilian Resistance was Carl Goerdeler. He was born in 1884 in Schneidemühl in north-eastern Germany (the town is now in Poland and is called Pila – it lies just to the west of Bydgoczsz). The son of a dynasty of professional local government officials and civil servants, and a lifelong conservative, he followed in the family tradition and became deputy mayor of Königsberg (now Kaliningrad in Russia) and subsequently mayor of Leipzig. An economist, he served as Price Commissioner to the government in 1931, and was reappointed to this post by Hitler in 1934. He was, however, against self-sufficiency and massive rearmament. His biographer and friend Gerhard Ritter points out the crucial difference between him and Hitler:

> In his general political theory Goerdeler undeniably tended to au-
> thoritarianism; he mistrusted parliamentary government as under-
> stood by the western democracies, and in cultural matters he took
> a frankly conservative position, as was customary in the German
> Nationalist Party (of which he was a member). But the authority
> of the national government which he wished to strengthen was
> to depend not on brute force but on general confidence; it was
> to be strictly bound by law – though able, to be sure, to carry
> out unpopular measures required by the higher interests of the
> state.[1]

Thus Goerdeler was first a supporter of Hitler and later a fierce opponent.

He had become mayor of Leipzig in 1930. From the first his open, optimistic and sometimes almost overbearingly charismatic character boosted his political and national status. He was even in the running for Chancellor during the last days of Weimar, despite his support of unpopular 'squeeze' techniques to control the economy. Goerdeler was no friend of the Weimar Republic, whose extremely liberal constitution had made effective rule almost impossible. In the early days of Hitler's regime, the dictator was quite amenable to Goerdeler's political ideas, and Goerdeler played a leading role in the formulation of the new uniform code for local government which became law on 30 January 1935. In the early days Hitler promised him 'anything he might ask, and even placed his private aeroplane at his disposal'. It is interesting that Goerdeler accepted the post of Price Commissioner in November 1934 – well after the dictator had shown his true nature in no uncertain terms. But Goerdeler had sought advice from high Army circles, doubtless discussing the move with Kurt von Hammerstein, if not with Blomberg, before accepting the appointment, which lasted until his resignation the following April. Goerdeler had held the same post under Chancellor Brüning in 1932, and perhaps his decision to take it up again is best explained by what Gerhard Ritter has described as 'his unbounded energy, his insensitivity to the demonic powers of evil, and his optimistic belief in his own capacity to do good by talking sensibly to people'.

Goerdeler was never a fellow-traveller, and he left as soon as he saw that he could not use his position to influence the Führer for good. His subsequent criticism of the regime from outside (like Beck, Goerdeler was a compulsive and prolific writer) irritated Hitler. Goerdeler had also declined to join the Party, and while his position as mayor was reconfirmed for another twelve years when his first term of office expired in 1936, it was clear that tensions were such between him and the official line that he would be lucky to last another twelve months.

Matters came to a head late in 1936. By now he was not only out of national office, but, Göring having taken over control of the country's short-term economic affairs in a Four Year Plan, the knives were out for him.

During that year he travelled in Scandinavia, and in Sweden first made the acquaintance of the banker Jakob Wallenberg[2] whose friendship would stand him in such good stead later. In November he was in Helsinki, to give a lecture to the German-Finnish Chamber of Commerce. During his absence the Nazis struck.

Goerdeler had been a consistent opponent of the Nazis' anti-Semitic laws – there is a well-known story of his deliberately visiting his regular Jewish tobacconist on Boycott Day – and he had long withstood pressure from the local Leipzig Nazis to remove a statue of Felix Mendelssohn[3] from outside the Gewandhaus Concert Hall. On his return from Finland he found that his Nazi deputy had had the statue taken down. Goerdeler told this man – Haake – that, in view of his having gone against precise orders, either the statue would be replaced or he, Goerdeler, would resign.

Goerdeler was hugely popular in Leipzig, but that did not save him. His resignation duly went in and was accepted. The Nazis gained nothing by it, except perhaps proving once again that the German masses were eminently coercible. The mayor's duties ceased at the end of March 1937, but he did not lose out materially. He was able to retain his official pension, and he was immediately offered a job as an economic adviser – in reality an honorary post – by the elderly liberal industrialist and opponent of Hitler, Robert Bosch of Stuttgart.

Bosch was a vigorous white-bearded man. A Swabian democrat, he was a bitter personal enemy of Hitler on account of the Führer's politics, and he was always an active opponent of the regime. He helped Jews and theology students to escape persecution, and was allied with Bishop Theophil Wurm. He also supported Rudolf Pechel's opposition magazine *Deutsche Rundschau*. Bosch was protected from the Nazis by his standing, age (he was seventy-two when they first came to power), industrial clout and wealth. Goerdeler became financial adviser to the Bosch company as well as its representative to the Berlin authorities. It was at this time that he met Hans Bernd Gisevius in Berlin, the Resistance lawyer with whom he was to form a strong bond of comradeship. Bosch was immensely generous in financing the opposition, mainly from his private fortune, and even during the war he put his foreign connections at the service of the Resistance. He stood in contrast to Goerdeler, the Prussian conservative, but their alliance was another example of men of differing legitimate political views joining together against a common brutal enemy which threatened them both.

This splendid man also provided Goerdeler with the means to fund his own anti-Nazi activities, but he was not the only one to offer help. Friedrich Krupp,[4] one of the Ruhr industrial dynasty,

who by now had realised what a fatal error he had made in backing
Hitler, had offered Goerdeler a job if needed as early as 1935, but
now, since Hitler signalled distinct disapproval, he transmuted the
job offer into an ex gratia payment large enough to cover any travel
expenses Goerdeler might have, and indeed the former mayor was
soon to embark on an energetic series of journeys abroad warning
anyone who would listen of the dangers of Hitler's foreign policy.
There remained the problem of acquiring a passport, but help came
from the (at first sight) unlikely source of Göring. Göring was in fact
and as usual hedging his own bets, so there was never any question
of Goerdeler's collaborating with Göring against Hitler.

Goerdeler visited London in July 1937, following a journey to
Belgium. From London he went to Holland, and then to France,
Canada and the United States. He was in Paris in December. He
returned to London the following March to lecture, and was in France
later that spring. Then, as pressure mounted towards the end of 1938
– the most fateful year in the history of the Third Reich – he visited
Switzerland, Italy, Romania (whose oil supply Hitler coveted and
subsequently got), Yugoslavia and Bulgaria. He travelled to France
and Algeria, in spring 1939, and in the early summer visited Britain,
Libya, Egypt, Palestine, Syria, Turkey and Switzerland.

> From each country long reports on the impressions gained were
> sent to Krupp, Bosch, Göring and Schacht [Hjalmar Schacht was
> Minister of Economics until 1937 and president of the State Bank
> (Reichsbank) until 1939 – he had joined the Resistance by the out-
> break of war] and also to generals von Fritsch, Beck, Halder [Beck's
> successor as Chief of Staff in 1938] and Georg Thomas [Head of
> Army Economics Section and involved in the conspiracy] with whom
> he had long been in touch. At first the reports even went to the Reich
> Chancellery where Hitler's secretary, Captain Wiedemann, received
> them and promised to pass them on. Their purport was that peace
> depended mainly on the attitude of the German government. There
> were no signs of offensive action on the part of other countries;
> indeed the western democracies were ready for an economic and
> political understanding. There did however exist very definite limits
> of tolerance to German claims and plans of expansion. If these limits
> were overpassed, the danger to Germany could be fatal. His political
> impressions were buttressed by solid economic arguments.[5]

Unfortunately, by marching into Austria, Hitler undermined any
good Goerdeler might have done the cause of peace. None the

less Goerdeler's own political and territorial ambitions for Germany were not so terribly far from Hitler's. His bald statement of them to the Allies did not help the case of the Resistance either. One of the features of the conservative Resistance was its inability to grasp how little bargaining leeway Germany had until very late in the day; even in 1944 Stauffenberg was hoping that a peace could be agreed by which Germany retained Austria, the Sudetenland and German Poland, and Goerdeler would have concurred. One should also bear in mind the naivety of the Resistance members, especially in the early days. Oster was indiscreet. Goerdeler, unlike most of his fellows, would think nothing of visiting Beck (to the latter's horror) openly and in broad daylight at his home, when both were subject to security surveillance. Both Beck and Goerdeler committed their thoughts to paper extensively, and kept all their documents. Oster's aide Dohnanyi compiled a huge dossier on Nazi crimes, intended to be used in trials against them after the fall of the regime. Ulrich von Hassell kept a copious diary in which the names of the conspirators were only very thinly disguised. Oster's code name, for example, was *Hase*. In German, *Ostern* means Easter, and *Hase* a hare. The *Osterhase* is our Easter bunny!

Goerdeler was kept under observation by the Gestapo, but had enough powerful protectors to keep one step ahead of them until the very end. Thus, although representing conservative views, his role in the Resistance was not paradoxical. It was a different case with the more extreme right-wingers, such as Johannes Popitz. Popitz, by virtue of his position as Prussian Finance Minister, belonged to the higher echelons of the National Socialist State. He also held the Party Golden Badge – awarded to the first 100,000 members of the NSDAP. Like Beck's, his conversion to the anti-Nazi camp was a gradual one, and even when it had been completed he preferred to remain within the system in order to fight it, though he offered his resignation to Göring after the infamous national night of attacks against the Jews in November 1938 – the so-called *Kristallnacht*. He was an early helper of those Social Democrat colleagues who were now forced to become fugitives.

It was through Goerdeler and Hans Oster that Popitz found an entrée to the civilian Resistance, and he became a supporter of all the plans for a coup. Closely associated with him was Professor Jens Jessen, a right-wing economist who had also been attracted to the

Nazis at the outset. Jessen was a member of the Wednesday Club, as were Popitz, Ludwig Beck and Ulrich von Hassell, the Ambassador to Italy. The four men were involved in drafting early plans for the constitution of a new, albeit authoritarian, post-Nazi state.

By mid-1943, after the débâcle of Stalingrad, when only the most fanatical Nazis saw any hope of the war's still being won, Popitz, disillusioned at last by the failure of the Resistance to remove Hitler by direct means, decided on a plan of his own, operating from within. He was on good terms with Carl Langbehn, a lawyer who had been engaged in opposition work for Hassell and who was also close to Himmler. Through Langbehn, Popitz learnt just how much Himmler already knew about Resistance movements. Himmler had been putting out peace feelers of his own, unknown to Hitler, and had stayed his hand where the Resistance was concerned as part of his plan to remove Hitler if and when it became necessary and save his own skin by assuming power and negotiating a peace with the enemy. In view of this, Popitz had Langbehn arrange a meeting with Himmler for 26 August 1943. This took place, and although Himmler was reserved, future meetings on the delicate subject were not ruled out.

But Germany in the late summer of 1943 was a place where spies spied on spies, where everyone in any position of power had to watch his back, and where the stability of the government depended increasingly on the spread of personal insecurity. The secret scheme became known to the Security Service, from which even Himmler, its controller, was not immune. Langbehn was arrested and sent to the concentration camps. Himmler was able to distance himself from the plot, but Popitz, though left alone for the moment, knew that he was a marked man. Finally arrested in November 1944, he was executed at Plötzensee at the end of that month.

Popitz was working in relative isolation. Ernst von Weizsäcker, another leading Resistance figure who worked as a principal servant of the Nazi State, was, like Admiral Wilhelm Canaris of the Abwehr, responsible for a team of conspirators. After Hitler had appointed Joachim Ribbentrop as Foreign Minister in 1937, Weizsäcker was given the post of State Secretary to the Foreign Office. He was never a sympathiser with the regime, but like Popitz he believed that it was better to work against it from within and try to limit its evils than to tackle it from the outside. His most important contribution, similar to that of Canaris, was to provide a 'safe area' in which conspirators could operate, but the latter's work was of greater significance than his.

In the main the employees of the Foreign Office were drawn from the aristocracy and the professional middle classes. They came from an educated, liberal background, and the younger ones amongst them especially looked forward to a world in which internationalism, as opposed to nationalism, would be the keynote. They saw Hitler's policies as not only ultimately destructive to German interests, but grossly anachronistic – this quite apart from the moral and ethical questions raised. The Foreign Office was never a Nazi organisation, nor did the Party ever gain complete control over it. Ribbentrop set up his own bureau and largely ignored it, which was to the advantage of those working within it against the regime. The most significant members of this group, which was large, were the brothers Theo and Erich Kordt – Theo, the elder, being attached to the German Embassy in London, and Erich an adviser on Ribbentrop's staff in Berlin. Their cousin Suzanne Simonis acted as a courier between the two brothers, learning long, complicated messages by heart and repeating them verbatim, as to carry written material would have been far too risky. Also attached to the Foreign Office was the major Resistance figure, Adam von Trott zu Solz, and Hans-Bernd von Haeften, whose younger brother Werner later became Stauffenberg's ADC.

There were several others, and in the course of the war the official positions of the various members of the group changed, but these men formed the important core. They were at the centre of attempts both before and during the first years of the war to negotiate agreements with the Allies, principally in Britain and America. Negotiations were also carried on through different channels in Switzerland, Sweden and the Vatican. All could be said to have worked for the regime, but only in so far as they held positions within it which they then exploited as much as they could to the benefit of the Resistance. All were obliged to lead double lives, and all suffered from extremes of tension as a result.

Working closely with the Foreign Office was the Abwehr. Overall a very large organisation, it contained a relatively small but very effective cell of influential conspirators, who enjoyed the special protection of Wilhelm Canaris.

Canaris was a complex individual whose appointment as Chief of the Abwehr came at a time when his career might have been assumed to be over. He was a natural spy: he had a secretive nature and he either could not or would not show other people his true self. He was mistrustful of others, especially tall men (he was only five-foot-five), but he loved animals unreservedly. He was an accomplished rider, and his dog was probably his greatest friend.

His nickname was 'the little Greek'. Though his family had been in Germany for 300 years, and was of Lombard stock, it pleased him to claim descent from Konstantin Kanaris, the Greek freedom fighter and later prime minister, who may have shared Canaris's bloodline. His background was not military, but he joined the Imperial Navy aged eighteen in 1905. He served in submarines and later on the *Dresden*, which was scuttled after an encounter during the First World War with the superior British cruiser *Glasgow* off the Chilean coast. Avoiding internment, and speaking fluent Spanish (Canaris was a lifelong lover of Spain), he rode across South America and found his way back to Germany in time to take command of a submarine in spring 1918. Following the war, as a conservative officer and a Christian (his family was later to attend Niemöller's church in Dahlem), he was involved in anti-Communist activity, and he has been accused of complicity in the murders of the Communist leaders Karl Liebknecht and Rosa Luxemburg in the troubled days that followed the end of the First World War, when Berlin nearly witnessed a revolution.

He remained in the Navy after the war, and in 1922 became First Officer of the cruiser *Berlin*. On board, the senior officer gained the affection and respect of one of the cadets, an eighteen-year-old called Reinhard Heydrich. Heydrich was later to become Himmler's Number Two, and possibly the most dangerous man in the Reich. He was cashiered from the Navy in 1931 on account of dishonourably breaking off a promise of marriage – an experience which left him with an intense dislike of naval officers; but this antipathy was never extended to Canaris. Heydrich, whose death at the hands of Czech partisans in 1942 was to result in the revolting vengeance of the razing of the village of Lidice near Prague, was that rare mixture, a man of culture and intellect who was also a sadist and brutal killer. He was a past master at the ruthless in-fighting which typified the Security Service, and yet throughout his life his relationship with Canaris remained cordial. The Heydrichs and the Canarises were neighbours and socialised together, playing cards and holding soirées – for Heydrich was another gifted musician. It was this curious 'friendship' (for want of a better word) that protected the Abwehr for so long from Party pressure – the two men even agreed formally to leave each others' departments alone – though some poaching occurred on both sides. After Heydrich's death, his successor Ernst Kaltenbrunner proved to be a different kettle of fish, but by then the Resistance within the Abwehr was sailing ever closer to the wind. Himmler himself never worried Canaris – the Admiral thought the head of the SS a fool whom he could handle easily.

Canaris's monarchist and generally right-wing leanings often made him a butt for the radical press during the Weimar Republic. His relaxation and relief from such houndings was to travel to Spain, which he did often. He was an accomplished linguist, but he spoke Spanish with total fluency and could easily pass for a Spaniard. His love of the country was absolute. At home, he was an early supporter of Hitler's rearmament policies, and especially in favour of the rebuttal of the terms of the Treaty of Versailles, and the restoration of Germany's 1914 frontiers. However, his fastidious personality found Nazi officials distasteful, both in their manner and their persons.

His career was not distinguished, and 1934 found him in command of the coastal batteries and marine garrison at the bleak Baltic port of Swinemünde – directly north of Stettin (now in Poland). This looked like a dead-end job, the last posting before retirement. But meanwhile the head of the Abwehr, Naval Captain Conrad Patzig, was finding it difficult to get on with Himmler and had fallen out with Blomberg. It was Blomberg who ordered Admiral Erich Raeder to get rid of Patzig (since the Abwehr was a military department and Patzig under Raeder's ultimate command). This was duly done, but the Navy wanted to keep a man of theirs in the post, so Raeder proposed Canaris. He did not suggest Canaris out of any special warmth of feeling, for in fact he did not like the man. Canaris had a nervous, volatile temperament which worried the Admiral. He was also a sensitive man, and very alert to what was going on around him. These qualities, together with his natural secretiveness and his political acuteness, made him a dangerous underling. But he was the best man in the Navy for the job. He took up the appointment on 1 January 1935.

The Abwehr was divided into several departments, dealing with information gathering (using V-men – *Vertrauensleute* – what we

might call 'moles'), counter-espionage, the organisation of agents
provocateurs and sabotage in enemy countries, linked to a central
administrative office. The 'Overseas' department was responsible for
liaison with the OKW and the Foreign Office, and at the same time
it was entrusted with the surveillance of foreign embassy attachés in
Germany. The 'Overseas' department was to be subject to expansion
and change, as the National Socialists developed espionage and the
German secret service network to a degree of phenomenal complexity
(but not necessarily efficiency) because Hitler and Ribbentrop mistakenly believed that the British intelligence service was a paragon
of efficiency.

In the prewar years, Canaris served Hitler well, developing the
Abwehr from a 'little shop' into a large and sophisticated unit. He
would not, however, carry out any orders which he thought contra-
vened the Rules of War, and he fought cleverly and hard right up
until the time of his fall to prevent the annexation of the Abwehr
by the Party's State Security Service. He saw his unit as a brake
on Nazi extremism, but at the same time he felt that Hitler was
indeed 'Germany's fate', and that he would lead the country into
total destruction. That destruction was necessary, in Canaris's view,
for Germany to purge herself of the evil of Nazism.

Canaris was a workaholic who could not delegate. His subordi-
nate, General Erwin Lahousen, an Austrian officer who served in
the Abwehr and was a party to the conspiracy, said of him:

> Canaris was the most difficult superior I encountered in my thirty-
> year career as a soldier. Contradictory in his instructions, given to
> whims, and not always just, always mysterious, he had nevertheless
> developed intellectual and, above all, human qualities which raised
> him far above the military rubber stamps and marionettes that most
> of his colleagues and superiors were. He never struck me, Austrian
> that I am, as the typical German military man; rather he seemed a
> cosmopolitan in the uniform of a German admiral . . .[6]

He got on very well with Hans Oster, already in place and running the administrative department. The special relationship with
Heydrich (though Heydrich was tall and therefore fundamentally
mistrusted by Canaris) meant that:

> The Abwehr enjoyed more freedom from Gestapo control and
> direction than any other organisation in the Third Reich. For

instance, the Abwehr had its own passport office both for establishing passes for foreign travel and for visas. Moreover, the Abwehr personnel was, to some extent anyway, protected from 'screening' in the matter of investigation into 'Aryan' ancestry and descent. Among the officials of the Abwehr there were some good men – and among the so-called V-men . . . a good many who could not have complied with the requirements of the Nuremberg laws on racial purity.[7]

Like that of so many of his fellow conspirators, Canaris's political outlook seemed contradictory until seen in the light of his conservative background. It was his main concern to present Hitler with selected intelligence in an attempt to guide the Führer's political decisions, but he was not against all of them. Opposing the alliance with Mussolini, for example, he was irritated by Britain's weak line over the invasion of Abyssinia. On the other hand, he supported Franco to the extent of recruiting right-wing German 'volunteers' to fight on his side in the Spanish Civil War – a perfect training and testing ground for German men and weapons – and he helped organise the infamous airborne 'Condor' legion, which bombed Guernica.

And yet it was at about this time, 1936, that, almost certainly influenced by Oster, he began to view the Nazis with political as well as personal distaste. The main source of concern initially was the danger implicit in *Gleichschaltung* – Canaris could see that this signalled not just the beginning of a strong authoritarian regime which he might have welcomed, but of the destruction of personal and political freedom, which he did not. He retained his sense of humour, however, which more often than not expressed itself in sarcasm – a trait which did not increase his popularity. Within the Abwehr group of conspirators – and it must be stressed that it was a group, not the entire unit – he could be biting. 'Never', he once told a staff meeting with a straight face, 'neglect to give the "Heil Hitler" salute to any flock of sheep you might be passing. You never know: there may be some high-ranking official among them.' He shared with several officers of the old school, such as Beck, a horror of the decay in standards of simply decent behaviour. These were the early days of espionage and counter-espionage on their modern, cynical and highly technical level. Canaris's gentlemanly sense of what was ethical was horrified at Heydrich's manoeuvring. There was a distinct cooling of the social relationship for a time when Canaris learned that Heydrich had been supplying the OGPU (the Russian Secret Service) with false documents destroying the reputation of some of the Soviet Union's top generals in order to bring them down. This was part of Hitler's early plan to weaken the Red Army – a policy he continued throughout his 'alliance' with Stalin between 1939 and 1941.

Though Canaris toyed with the idea of resigning in 1937, he decided – like Weizsäcker – to continue in office and fight the regime from within. He was certainly privy to the plot hatched by Oster at about this time which would find its fruition in the coup scheduled against Hitler for the autumn of 1938. He had a large and complex network of foreign contacts to draw on, and he liaised with Beck over the Blomberg/Fritsch scandal, keeping him informed about Security Service tactics to bring the senior commanders down.

His closest aide in the so-called CC (Canaris Club) was Hans von Dohnanyi. He was born in 1902, the son of the composer Ernst von Dohnanyi. A brilliant lawyer who had been opposed to the National Socialist regime from the first, Dohnanyi was recruited to the Abwehr by Oster in late August 1939. Attached to Oster's Department Z, he enjoyed considerable power and freedom of movement. Department Z wasn't just concerned with Abwehr administration; it was responsible for personal data on personnel, finance and law. It also controlled the Abwehr's archive, the secret personnel index with 400,000 names, and the top secret index of *V-Leute*, to which access was strictly limited.

Dohnanyi was responsible for managing liaison abroad, in particular with the Bamberg Catholic diplomat Josef Müller's secret mission to the Vatican, and he played a leading role in 'Undertaking Seven' – a successful plan to help Jewish fugitives escape from Germany using Abwehr funds and by employing them as Abwehr agents. The plan derived its name from the original number of people helped, successfully sent to South America as Nazi spies with the blessing of the Security Service in 1942! It is a tribute to Canaris's ability to manipulate men like Himmler that the Abwehr was able to fulfil this plan.

Through his position in the Abwehr, Dohnanyi was able to facilitate travel abroad for his brother-in-law, Dietrich Bonhoeffer, when the latter became associated with the Resistance in the early forties. Bonhoeffer's older brother Klaus was also able to make a contribution from his senior position in the state airline, Lufthansa. As a trusted lieutenant of Hans Oster, Dohnanyi was closely involved in all coup planning up until the collapse of the Abwehr and his own arrest in

1943, but possibly his most important single contribution was the painstaking compilation of an archive of Nazi crimes. These papers, which were ultimately to bring such disaster upon the Resistance, came to be known as the Zossen Documents.

They took their name from the place they were stored – a safe in a secure office at Army Headquarters in the town of Zossen, a little way south of Berlin. Dohnanyi began to put the massive dossier together long before he joined the Abwehr, when he was working as the personal assistant to the Minister of Justice, and therefore in a position to see the paperwork attaching to all Nazi use and abuse of the law in the early days of its power, from getting rid of rivals and enemies in opposition to settling internal scores. As the archive grew – Dohnanyi was in the fortunate position of being responsible for its official filing – it came to include reports on the maltreatment of prisoners of war, notes by Goebbels on the handling of the Jewish 'problem', and film of the atrocities carried out in Poland after the conquest of that country. The Resistance took huge risks by storing documents dealing either with the conspiracy, with post-Nazi constitutional plans, or, as here, with the gathering of evidence for the prosecution of crimes against the proper constitution (that of the Weimar Republic, which was never formally revoked). Goerdeler, Beck and others seemed compelled to commit their thoughts and plans to paper, and if the Gestapo had developed more sophisticated methods of detection, the conspirators would not have survived for as long as they did. It is to the credit of those senior Army officers who were approached to join the conspiracy, and who declined, that they did not denounce their fellows to the Nazi authorities.

With his annexation of Austria unopposed and successfully achieved, Hitler began to turn his sights on Czechoslovakia. Aware of the dismay his proposals of November 1937 had caused, he was careful to ensure that senior generals whom he knew to be against any war plans were dispersed from Berlin and given postings at some distance from each other. A constant problem of the Resistance within the Army was to be that of postings: the conspirators might spend many painstaking months building up a key group in a given place, only to have it disrupted simply because the officers belonging to it were relocated elsewhere by the Army Personnel Office.

For the moment his popularity was such that Hitler may have been unaware, or felt that he could afford to ignore, the depth of feeling his treatment of Blomberg and, especially, of the popular von Fritsch had aroused in several of the older generals. Now for the first time soldiers outside the General Staff and the Abwehr – commanders of the Regular Army – began to see that Hitler was no statesman but a dangerous threat to world security, and one which could not be combated through the law. It was clear, too, that outside help could not necessarily be depended on, though the Resistance was to make appeals to Britain and France and, later, to the United States, from now until 1943.

Among the first such disabused men to declare himself was Erwin von Witzleben, whom Hitler was to make a Field Marshal in 1940. Witzleben was a career soldier from a military family. He was born in Breslau (now Wroclaw) in 1881 and had served both at the Front and on the General Staff during the First World War. In 1934 he took over the important post of Commander of Army District III, which included Berlin. Never a man to concern himself with politics, and lacking the intellectual capability of Beck or the complexity of Canaris or Oster, he had other crucial qualities. He was a practical man, whose common sense and knowledge of military affairs equipped him to cut straight through to the core of any problem which confronted him. He was the senior officer whom Oster had so appalled by bringing secret papers to a meeting openly in his car. It was he who, during the confusing and desperate afternoon and evening of 20 July 1944, was able to pull the disintegrating conspiracy together for one last effort. Once his decision to make a stand against Hitler had been made, he never wavered.

He brought with him into the conspiracy one of his divisional commanders, Walter von Brockdorff-Ahlefeld, whose troops were based in Potsdam, on the edge of Berlin. Potsdam was also the home of Number 9 Infantry Regiment, which had a higher percentage of officers opposed to Hitler than any other unit in the German Army. Thus it was that in 1938 the Resistance had at its disposal sufficient troops close to Berlin to crush the Nazi leadership before the SS could organise a counter-attack. Meanwhile, Oster's undercover activity and association with the former Gestapo lawyer, Hans Bernd Gisevius, had resulted in two more useful allies: Wolf von Helldorf, the Chief of Police of Berlin, and Artur Nebe, head of the Criminal Police Department. Through the offices of these disillusioned Party members it was later possible to trace the location of secret and newly established

SS barracks throughout the country, as the police had to be informed about all newly established brothels!

Hitler's excuse for moving against Czechoslovakia was the liberation of the Sudetenland, a broad strip of land along Czechoslovakia's frontier with Germany which was largely inhabited by ethnic Germans. The area was of vital strategic value to Czechoslovakia: its occupation by Germany would leave the Czechs virtually without defences. To add to the Czechs' problems, Poland, which had territorial pretensions on the Czechs' north-eastern border, was eager to take the area around the town of Teschen. Hitler had been careful to arrange a non-aggression pact with Poland. On the other hand, Czechoslovakia enjoyed the support of France and Russia.

Tension continued throughout the spring of 1938 as Hitler's move was awaited. At the end of April the French prime minister, Daladier, flew to London to seek Britain's support for Czechoslovakia. His British opposite number, Neville Chamberlain, was to disappoint him. Chamberlain's view was that Czechoslovakia was not worth risking a war over. Hitler knew that, however averse Chamberlain was to war, Britain would side with France if full-scale hostilities broke out. Meanwhile, Goebbels' Propaganda Ministry churned out emotional stories of Czech atrocities perpetrated on the Sudeten Germans.

Towards the end of May, the Czech president decided to bring matters to a head and ordered a partial mobilisation. Hitler saw this as a chance not to be missed and ordered a conference of his generals on 28 May. At it he said that the oppression of the Sudeten Germans had grown intolerable, that it was time they were granted autonomy, and that if they were not, he was determined to take it for them by force. In his estimation there would be no opposition. The Russians were in no position to help Czechoslovakia; the French would not attack without British support, and the British were not sufficiently armed to enter a war. Among those present were Brauchitsch and Beck, who sat 'granite-faced' as Göring effusively congratulated the Führer on his 'masterly plan'. In fact this plan had been under discussion for some time in secret as 'Operation Green', and two days after the meeting on 28 May Hitler issued a directive to the Commanders-in-Chief of the Army, the Navy and the Air Force: 'It is my unalterable decision to destroy Czechoslovakia by military action within the foreseeable future.' A deadline for preparations was set for 1 October.

By now any official line of defence was utterly compromised. Those present at the 28 May meeting were mainly men of straw: Brauchitsch, suborned by money (what had happened to the integrity of the senior German officer? Brauchitsch was no arriviste – his family down the years had provided Germany with a dozen decent generals); Keitel, the handsome lackey; Göring, the brave fighter ace of twenty years ago – now an overweight drug addict with a wardrobe and a make-up case to make the vainest woman envious. At least his new wife, the little provincial actress elevated by her marriage with the Reichsmarschall to leading lady of the Berlin Schauspielhaus, Emmi Sonnemann, worked hard at the State Theatre in what was then called Gendarmenmarkt in Berlin.[8] Part of her work was trying to do justice to major roles of which she was patently incapable. Another part, in collusion with the theatre's homosexual artistic director, Gustav Gründgens, was the protection of Jewish fellow artists. The theatre enjoyed Göring's special protection as part of his rivalry with Goebbels. Goebbels was the supreme arbiter as far as art was concerned; but Göring had the State Theatre and if it was going to be a bastion against 'Little Joe', then so much the better.

Hitler's decision to take Czechoslovakia by force concentrated the minds of those opposed to him. Beck had already sent a memorandum to Brauchitsch on 5 May in which he had clearly warned that such an action would inevitably lead to a pan-European war. That warning was ignored. After Hitler's directive of 30 May, Beck took up his pen again. At this stage, it must be remembered, men like Beck and Goerdeler still believed in the power of argument to sway Hitler – Goerdeler continued to do so for several years more. The question of actually killing the dictator had not yet occurred to them, though Oster at least already knew that that would be the only sure way to secure a coup.

Beck now wrote another memorandum to Brauchitsch in which he reiterated his warnings, politely and with close reasoning. He pointed out that there was a high likelihood that Czechoslovakia's allies would counter-attack, and that the resulting war would be disastrous for Germany, whose own rearmament programme was not yet complete. Though Beck's view was shared by many of the High Command, Brauchitsch refused to answer the questions he raised immediately, taking a few days' diplomatic leave instead.

As a result, Beck consulted Goerdeler and other senior colleagues associated with the conservative civilian opposition. Beck himself knew that sooner or later he would have to resign, but he wanted to sound others out on this matter as well – a mass resignation in protest at his plans might still just be enough to deflect Hitler from his plan. But Beck was a reluctant revolutionary, too modest to believe that his own isolated action would do any good, and he was in a difficult position. His duty was clear, but his loyalty was still torn. During June and July, he had a number of long talks with Oster, during which the Abwehr General (Oster had been reinstated and promoted since joining the Abwehr) sought to persuade him to lead a more drastic action. This was very far from the traditional role of a Chief of the General Staff, and still Beck hesitated. Yet his words of warning through official channels continued to fall on deaf ears. Hitler would reply to Beck with counter-arguments, alluding to his reliable military intuition. Beck would answer these politely, point by point. But he got nowhere. In response to a memorandum of 3 June, Hitler remarked in exasperation: 'I'm not asking my generals to understand my orders, but to obey them!'

Finally, on 16 July, knowing that his opinion was shared by the vast majority of the General Staff and the High Command, Beck wrote a memorandum to Brauchitsch, in which he did not mince his words. Repeating his warning that France and Britain would certainly declare war if Germany marched on Czechoslovakia, he concluded:

> On the basis of the data given above, I now feel duty bound . . . to ask insistently that the Supreme Commander of the Wehrmacht [Hitler] should be compelled to abandon the preparations he has ordered for war, and to postpone his intention of solving the Czech problem by force until the military situation is basically changed. For the present I consider it hopeless, and this view is shared by all my Quartermasters-General and departmental chiefs of the General Staff who would have to deal with the preparation and execution of a war against Czechoslovakia.[9]

Beck also formally proposed to Brauchitsch that a representative group of leading generals should now approach Hitler and, if unsuccessful in getting him to change his mind, resign. The delegation, Beck suggested, should not only raise the already outlined objections to the Czech campaign, but take the opportunity to protest against the totalitarian conduct of the regime and demand an end to the rule of terror, political arrest and imprisonment, the curbing of free speech, and official corruption. There should be a return to the rule of law, and to the fundamental Prussian principles of cleanness and simplicity.

This was the moment when, if they had held firm, the generals could have toppled the regime. This was still a time when they believed that Hitler could be separated from the Party – in that way, their Oath of Loyalty would not be compromised and Germany could retain its popular head of state: the Army would have acted in the best interests of its ultimate leader. Had Beck been followed at this juncture, a bloodless coup might have been the outcome. The SS was still building up its strength. But the plan did not really have a strong chance. Not only was Brauchitsch the last man to cross Hitler at this point; but Beck himself had not understood that Hitler and the Party were one and the same. Hitler was not a good man misled by his minions, however much Beck might have wanted to believe that. Men like Oster, who for a long time had understood precisely which way the land lay, could only wring their hands in frustration and wait for another opportunity.

Brauchitsch had to respond to Beck's memorandum. One can imagine his state of mind. He was himself an experienced enough soldier to see that Beck was right; but he had a job which put him at the height of his career, he owed his private happiness to Hitler, his new wife was an ardent supporter of the Führer, Brauchitsch himself lacked moral fibre, and he was personally scared of his leader. He finally called a meeting of all senior generals and divisional commanders at the Armed Forces Central Administrative Building in Bendlerstrasse in Berlin for 4 August. By that time a commission under the British Lord Runciman had been set up to look into peaceful ways of settling the Sudeten problem – a move by the Allies which made Beck look something of a Jeremiah. However the senior generals stood behind him still – notably Witzleben, but also Kurt von Hammerstein and two other generals who would play key roles in the Resistance: Karl-Heinrich von Stülpnagel and Erich Hoepner. There were only two dissenting voices, those of Generals Reichenau and Busch – but they had already nailed their colours to Hitler's mast.

Unfortunately, while agreeing with Beck's point of view, the generals reached no consensus on action. Brauchitsch did not encourage them to, and offered them no firm leadership. Instead of making the speech Beck and Oster had prepared for him, he merely read out the memorandum of 16 July and made no appeal for a démarche.

The generals had lost the initiative, and now – either through Reichenau or Brauchitsch himself – Hitler learnt of their meeting. At about the same time the Abwehr learnt that Britain had no intention of letting the Sudetenland become a *casus belli*: Chamberlain was already showing himself to be a man prepared to avoid war whatever the moral or ethical cost of peace. On 10 August Hitler called a meeting at the Berghof, his country residence at Berchtesgaden in Austria (where Himmler took over the former home of the von Trapp family). There the chiefs of the Armed Forces were treated to a three-hour harangue in the course of which Hitler worked himself into a violent rage, brushing aside objections that German defences in the West were nowhere near strong enough to withstand a French assault, and reasserting his determination to crush Czechoslovakia.

A week later, Brauchitsch summoned Beck and told him that Hitler had issued a general order forbidding interference by the Army in political questions at any level, and demanding 'unconditional obedience' from all generals including the Chief of the General Staff. This was the last straw for Beck, who nevertheless made one last appeal to Brauchitsch to join him in resigning. Brauchitsch refused, taking refuge behind the principle which so many senior officers were to use to evade responsibility: 'I am a soldier. It is my duty to obey.'

Beck felt that he owed his country a greater duty than blindly to follow a leader bent on its destruction. Despite the reluctance of Britain and France to confront Hitler, he was sure that the Führer would not rest until he had committed Germany to a war of territorial conquest. He had done his utmost to avert this while in office, and now he had no option but to resign.

He did so forthwith and, after two days' hesitation, Hitler accepted his resignation on 21 August. He handed over to his deputy, Franz Halder, on 27 August. General Hossbach remembers the impression Beck made on him as he said farewell: 'He was the last real Chief of the General Staff of Germany, directing the gaze of his beautiful eyes into the distance . . .'

Beck remained in the Army, taking over the command of 1st Army in Wiesbaden, but Hitler would not feel safe with such an intelligent and influential opponent in any position of power. Beck was obliged to retire at the end of October, ending a career of forty years' distinguished service. He was never to wear uniform again, and thenceforward dressed in dark, sober suits. His health was not good, and he looked older than he was, his face marked by disappointment and stress. In 1943 he underwent a successful operation for cancer at the hands of Professor Ferdinand Sauerbruch, his old friend of the Wednesday Club, and was thus able to continue at the head of the Resistance until the final crisis of 20 July 1944. After retiring, he took up residence in Goethestrasse, in the quiet south Berlin suburb of Lichterfelde. He attended meetings of the Wednesday Club, and worked in his garden, where he took special pleasure in growing fruit and vegetables.

Beck was still too much an old-fashioned officer to make publicity capital out of his resignation as Chief of Staff, but he may also have been disappointed that none of his brother officers followed him. He had expected his resignation to result in a cry of protest, demands for an explanation, even that it might trigger a popular condemnation of Hitler. But there was barely a ripple. Beck might have withdrawn completely, but he had already confided in his brother his determination to continue his fight against Hitler whatever happened to his career, and now that he was without other employment he was able to give the Resistance not only his full time, but, in his person, a point of focus and a respected leader. His unusually broad outlook and his intellectual strength enabled him to bridge the gap between military and political opponents of the regime, and his close relationship and collaboration with Carl Goerdeler led to some of the most important conservative political theory to come out of Resistance thinking. The most urgent task for the present, however, was not how the country would be managed after the fall of Nazism – temporary rule by the Army would have to be accepted – but to get rid of Hitler before he could plunge Germany into war.

Beck and Goerdeler now formed the core of a developing Resistance network which had representatives in the Army, the Church, the Abwehr, the Foreign Office, the conservative opposition and the Berlin police force. Links were kept loose and constantly changed, though the Abwehr and the Foreign Office worked closely together. Despite the relative inefficiency of the Gestapo in the early days, the conspirators had to be on constant guard against informers, and those of them who were well known to the authorities had to exercise extreme discretion when meeting – though it is sometimes hard to imagine why they were not arrested far earlier than they were. By the time Beck resigned, plans for a coup were already well advanced, under the auspices of Hans Oster – a practical man with no personal political ambition, but possessed by a profound moral drive. Witzleben and Brockdorff-Ahlefeld were prepared to stand their men by, and General Erich Hoepner, in command of 1st Light Division in Thuringia, was ready to move against the large SS garrison in Munich, if its men should be ordered to march north to the aid of the Führer in Berlin. In Berlin itself, police neutrality during the coup was guaranteed by Helldorf. Though regarded with some suspicion by other members of the conspiracy on account of his long connection with the Party, and his tough and volatile temperament, Helldorf had been influenced by his own deputy, Fritz-Dietlof Graf von der Schulenburg, and would prove to be a consistent opponent of the regime. Schulenburg, an aristocrat who had joined the Party for idealistic reasons, having believed in its socialist message, had long been disillusioned by Hitler.

The plan was to isolate the Reich Chancellery and then for a small unit of hand-picked officers to enter the building and seize Hitler. Oster did not underestimate the difficulty of this final assault. Hitler was protected by a bodyguard of about forty men at all times, and these belonged to the fanatical SS unit 'Leibstandarte Adolf Hitler'. The Resistance was divided in its opinion of what to do with Hitler, once he had been arrested. The difficulty was compounded because public reaction was an unknown quantity. The older conspirators, especially Beck and Canaris, were concerned that Hitler be taken alive and publicly tried for his crimes, to avoid the risk of making a martyr of him. Goerdeler also supported the idea of bringing Hitler to trial – and would cling to this principle as the years passed, long after his colleagues had accepted the necessity of assassination. Hans von Dohnanyi was already preparing a case for the prosecution, assisted by Karl Sack of the Judge-Advocate-General's Department. Meanwhile, Dr Karl Bonhoeffer, father of Klaus and Dietrich, was engaged in secretly preparing a report on Hitler's mental condition to be used as a basis for declaring him insane.

This was the official line of the Resistance, but Oster had private reservations, and not for the last time he took a lonely decision that cut through all the discussion. As long as Hitler was alive, he argued, there would be a risk of forces loyal to him mobilising to rescue him. He was a popular figure and it would be better to demonstrate to the nation what crimes he had in fact committed – but this should take place only after he was dead. Accordingly he gave secret instructions to the leader of the team detailed to arrest Hitler – a tough former Freikorps fighter called Friedrich Heinz – to arrange a mêlée in the Reich Chancellery during which Hitler would be 'accidentally' killed.

To prevent anarchy and reduce the risk of civil war in the event of one of the other Nazi leaders providing a rallying-point, it was crucial that the Army take control of the country following the coup. This could be achieved legally, but it would require Brauchitsch's complete collaboration, and Brauchitsch could not be trusted. The conspirators decided to involve him only at the last possible moment. Beck's successor as Chief of Staff, Franz Halder, though not a whole-hearted supporter of the Resistance, at least seemed sympathetic, and Beck had a high opinion of him.

Preparations took until mid-September. Meanwhile, the conspirators kept an anxious eye on the negotiations which were continuing over Czechoslovakia. It was essential for the justification of the coup that it would take place immediately after Hitler had given the final order for Operation Green – the invasion of Czechoslovakia – to take place, but before hostilities broke out. It was Halder's job to signal this hiatus to the conspirators, at which time Witzleben would use his troops to isolate Berlin. It was equally crucial that neither Britain nor France should reach any peaceful compromise with Hitler. Indeed, it was essential, if the coup was to be presented to the German public as the only means of avoiding war (and war was not a popular idea), that the Allies should confront Hitler with the unequivocal threat of it if he persisted in pushing his territorial designs on Czechoslovakia.

Carl Goerdeler had already visited Britain to urge the government there to take a firm line with Hitler. He had not succeeded in convincing the British authorities, but he had unsettled them. A series of emissaries from the Resistance – their travel funded and organised by the Abwehr and the Foreign Office – followed his lead during the summer of 1938.[10] Goerdeler's approaches were not met with success. In Britain he had enjoyed the confidence of Sir Robert Vansittart, who until recently had been Permanent Under-Secretary at the Foreign Office; but Vansittart's star was waning. He was a staunch opponent of appeasement, and thus earned the disfavour of Chamberlain and his Foreign Secretary, Anthony Eden. 'Van' was kicked upstairs to an advisory post at the end of 1937. Chamberlain wrote to his sister with unconscious irony:

> After all the months that S.B. [Stanley Baldwin – his predecessor in office] wasted in futile attempts to push Van out of the FO [Foreign Office] it is amusing to record that I have done it in 3 days . . . I hope to announce it after the House [of Commons] has safely dispersed . . . Van will be removed from active direction of FO policy and I suspect that in Rome and Berlin rejoicings will be loud and deep.

Goerdeler did not help the case of the Resistance by making demands on behalf of the putative German government which was supposed to replace Hitler that were not dissimilar in their territorial aspects from Hitler's own. Viewed from outside, Hitler was the legitimate leader of his country and he had certainly done nothing to justify committing one's country to a war with him. By asking for, among other things, the cession of the Sudetenland, Goerdeler only muddied the water further. In most of its dealings abroad, the German Resistance suffered from parochialism: its own, and that of its interlocutors.

In mid-August 1938 Hans Oster organised a visit to London for Ewald von Kleist-Schmenzin. His credentials were impeccable and his contacts were good. The mission had come about as the result of a chance meeting between Kleist and a twenty-five-year-old British journalist called Ian Colvin, who had been in Berlin for eighteen months as the *News Chronicle*'s junior correspondent. Colvin's father was Ian Duncan Colvin, the leader writer on the *Morning Post*, and a friend of Robert Vansittart and Winston Churchill. While in Berlin, the young journalist had been introduced to the Casino Club in Bendlerstrasse, not far from Armed Forces Headquarters. The Casino was a bastion of the Establishment, not unlike the Reform Club in London or the Downtown Association in New York. He knew that here if anywhere he would learn what men of influence who were opposed to the regime were thinking.[11]

Colvin was introduced to Kleist by Hubertus von Weyrauch, the club's secretary and a close personal friend. The journalist was impressed by the slightly built grey-haired man whose signet ring bore a heraldic running fox. After a cautious lunch during which the two men sounded each other out, Kleist confided in Colvin his own fears for the future of Europe. 'Czechoslovakia is the next step,' he told Colvin. 'The Wehrmacht insists that this is a real military venture and must be organised by the Army. Hitler says that the Party can deal with Czechoslovakia and that the Army only has to obey instructions. One thing I know for certain – if England says "No", be it only through diplomatic channels, the adventure must be put off. Hitler admits this and fears like the plague that England will warn him. For he would have to give way and that would be a grave blow to his prestige in Germany. When the pendulum is checked, it swings the other way. That is what would happen here.'

The upshot of this meeting and those that followed was mutual respect and the idea that Kleist should go to England to make his views known there. He flew out on a Junkers 52 bound for Croydon from Tempelhof on 18 August, with introductions to Vansittart, Churchill and Lord Lloyd. As a man who was already recognised by the Nazi State as its enemy, he was taking a grave risk; but Oster's department at the Abwehr had organised his passport, and he was seen off by his cousin, General (later Field Marshal) Erwin von Kleist. Although he made a better case than Goerdeler, Kleist was no more successful. The British cast a wary eye on such emissaries. Policy was strictly concerned with avoiding war, and reports from the Ambassador in Berlin, Sir Nevile Henderson, of Hitler's achievements were full of praise. Ironically Henderson, one of the most disastrously misplaced diplomats ever, owed his appointment to Vansittart, who gave it to him as a reward after a long stint in South America. Henderson was more of a fool than a knave, but his naive approval of the regime seriously discoloured British thinking.

It is perfectly fair to accuse the British of blinkered and even pusillanimous thinking at this stage of the run-up to war. Chamberlain spent crucial periods in August 1938 and 1939 in Scotland grouse-shooting, and his Foreign Secretary (between the two periods in which the office was held by Eden), Lord Halifax, was niggardly in the discharge of his duty. Worse, on a personal level, Halifax had been at Eton with Vansittart, and was envious of the latter, who had been a member of Pop and Captain of the Oppidans. Eden was anti-Semitic and sympathetic to Hitler. He suppressed reports from Germany to the prime minister, and regarded the representations of the Resistance with an undue degree of suspicion. Chamberlain, a former mayor of Birmingham, was sadly out of his depth as prime minister at such a time. His own remarks 'if only we could get on terms with the Germans' or 'I confess some feeling of uneasiness and I don't feel sure we ought not to do something' may be compared with Hitler's 'I have given the command and I will shoot anyone who utters a word of criticism' as a measure of how ill-matched the pair were.

Kleist was entrusted by Beck to give the British the specific message that failure to stand up to Hitler over Czechoslovakia would result in war. This was not even followed up properly. That there is no excuse is borne out by the fact that British agents in place in Germany from the mid-thirties (including one who held the highest rank in British Intelligence after the war) were consistently sending information home confirming Hitler's warlike intentions. Some still privately express their anger at Chamberlain today.

On the other hand one must remember that Britain was still at the tail-end of its world superiority, and to a certain extent its leaders were living in the past. Even Churchill expressed admiration for Hitler as late as 1937, and no one would take the representations of the Resistance regarding Hitler's ambitions seriously. At the same time Chamberlain was nervous of taking a belligerent stance because his traditional Allies showed no sign of supporting him if push came to shove. In May 1937 the USA passed the Neutrality Act, divesting itself of the traditional rights of a neutral to trade with a belligerent (Sweden made a killing out of its iron-ore trade with Germany during the war). This was a heavy blow to Britain and France, because it made the purchase of American military equipment in peacetime of questionable value, since supplies could not then be assured in war. At the same time, Commonwealth prime ministers stated that they could not support a European war. Mackenzie King refused to have Canada made the long-stop arsenal for British rearmament, Robert Menzies indicated that tensions in the Far East would make it impossible for Australia to participate in a European war (though doubtless Gallipoli was still fresh in his memory), and in South Africa, General Hertzog said that a central European land war could not be the concern of his country. Above all, there was the spectre of the First World War. Barely twenty years had passed since that monumental, pointless slaughter, and the political and emotional scars it had left were still fresh. Ultimately no one can wholly blame Chamberlain for the worse carnage to come.[12]

Having said all that, one must also remember in fairness that Eden did pay close attention to an early report by his friend Nigel Law on Nazi oppression in 1936, that later on he seems genuinely to have been waiting for the German Resistance to 'put its money where its mouth was' before proffering help, and that even Sir Nevile Henderson, described by Colvin as having 'the most calamitous personality of all time', relented from his admiration of Hitler and the Nuremberg rallies for long enough in August 1938 to mention in a dispatch (Number 647) that 'I believe that if we saw any utility in war, now would be the time to make it, rather than later'.

But, whatever signals Chamberlain received, and despite the efforts of a series of Resistance emissaries and the Resistance man at the German Embassy in London, Theo Kordt, his decision was peace at all costs. The late summer and autumn of 1938 present a depressing picture of the British prime minister travelling across to Germany almost, as it were, at Hitler's beck and call, and, even less sympathetically, prepared to sell Czechoslovakia down the river and be an accessory to Hitler's illegal rape of that country if only he could buy the dictator off by such means. Despite the mobilisation of the British Fleet at the end of September at the behest of Sir Alfred Duff Cooper (who subsequently resigned as First Lord of the Admiralty in disgust at Chamberlain's appeasement policy), and despite an ultimatum issued to Germany (though couched in the most circumspect of terms) on 10 September, Chamberlain continued to spike his own guns by placating Hitler. With what contempt must the dictator have entertained the overtures of this man. His own nickname for the British prime minister was 'The Arsehole'. But Chamberlain continued to see himself as the man who might pull Europe back from the very brink. He knew that Hitler was mad; he knew what a disaster a fresh world war would mean. He knew that the mobilisation of the Fleet had made Hitler hesitate. He was blind only to his own limitations.

Chamberlain concocted his own secret plan, known as Plan Z, in which he featured as 'Mr X'. By its terms he would sort out the Sudeten crisis with Hitler personally. In pursuit of it, and flying in the face of urgent appeals from the German anti-Hitler faction in their Foreign Office, from no less an authority than Ernst von Weizsäcker via the eminent Swiss High Commissioner for Danzig, Carl Burckhardt, Neville Chamberlain went to Berchtesgaden to see Hitler on 15 September. This was a blow in the face for the Resistance, poised as they were to bring the dictator down. At the meeting, Chamberlain, who had brought no interpreter of his own, was not even allowed a record of his conversation with the Führer because Ribbentrop, who had been excluded from it and was in a fury as a result, refused permission for him to be given one. Chamberlain swallowed this humiliation and trusted his memory when he gave his report to the Cabinet in London on the following day. He advocated letting Hitler have his way over the Sudetenland, adding that he believed this would satisfy the Führer's territorial ambitions. Less than a week later, having finished consultations with the British parliament and with the French, the prime minister was back in Germany ready to grant the peaceful cession of the Sudetenland, only to find that the dictator had raised the stakes. Hitler now insisted on a military occupation and the evacuation of Czech dwellers in the Sudetenland. This should begin immediately and be completed by 28 September. Otherwise, he said, he would declare war on Czechoslovakia on 1 October.

This demand was unacceptable to the French who said so immediately and mobilised fourteen divisions. Hitler continued to brazen it out. The unit primed to storm the Chancellery and arrest him stood on red alert. On 27 September Hitler ordered a march past of armoured divisions in Berlin. To his fury it met with an apathetic reaction from the populace. 'With people like this, I cannot go to war,' he said, sullenly. But he stood by his bluff. He knew that Chamberlain was a broken reed; at that moment the British prime minister was his best ally. The mobilisation of the British Fleet made him hesitate, but the action was undercut by yet another conciliatory note from Chamberlain suggesting that Hitler could 'get all essentials without war and without delay'.

Matters were at breaking point. So sure were the conspirators that Hitler would brazen it out and go to war that even Brauchitsch had been persuaded to join them and give the necessary counter-orders the moment Hitler authorised the go-ahead for Operation Green. But meanwhile, and at the eleventh hour, Chamberlain had instructed the Ambassador in Rome, Lord Perth, to suggest to Mussolini that he might intercede with Hitler to avoid a final confrontation. Mussolini was ill-equipped and uneager to join his ally in a war of the dimensions likely to unfold, and picked up the cue with alacrity. Hitler was no less happy to seek an honourable settlement without bloodshed: the fourteen French divisions and the British Fleet had shaken him. The French were as keen as the British to avoid a fight, and a conference was hastily convened in Munich. At it, Hitler was not only able to retain the prestige he had very nearly lost, but he also scored another singular diplomatic triumph: the Sudetenland was his. Not a shot had been fired, the Czechs had been betrayed, and now the rest of their country, to which the German dictator referred contemptuously as 'the rump', was at his mercy, together with its renowned arms industry.

But apparently peace had been preserved. The Resistance looked on helplessly. Its chances of a coup had been shattered just hours before fulfilment, for even if Hitler had backed down, the resultant loss of standing might have been enough to destroy him. Now he was more triumphant than ever, and he would celebrate his victory, and demonstrate his contempt for everyone else, by a bloody stroke against the Jews which would wipe out any last illusions anyone might have entertained about his intentions or his morality.

Part Two

1938–1944

Late one night in the war, a Berliner was making his way home during the blackout. Suddenly he heard a sharp voice behind him hiss: 'Hands up or I shoot.' He could see the barrel of a pistol glinting. Then the voice said: 'OK – hand over your wallet and make it snappy.' The Berliner breathed a huge sigh of relief. 'Man, you gave me a shock,' he said. 'For a moment there I thought you were the police.'

SIX

The End of Germany

On 10 October 1938, the Sudetenland became part of Greater Germany, and Czechoslovakia lost its mountain defences. Most of the Jews living in the area fled to the unoccupied provinces of Moravia and Bohemia. In Germany, Hitler turned his attention to those Jews who had been born in what had been Polish provinces of the former Russian Empire. These people, he decreed, would have to be expelled. Eighteen thousand of them were thrust towards the Polish frontier on the night of 27 October in a massive SS 'action'. Before the reluctant Poles would accept them, they had to remain in misery in the no-man's-land between the two countries, and many died.

The son of one of these Jewish families was a student in Paris at the time. When, on 6 November, he heard the news of what had happened, he went to the German Embassy in a rage, and shot and mortally wounded the German official who received him, the young Third Secretary, Ernst vom Rath.

Vom Rath was very far from being a Nazi, but that did not stop Hitler's making a martyr out of him. There followed, on the night of 9 November, a nationwide attack on Jews, their property and their synagogues. George Ogilvie-Forbes, a British diplomat in Berlin who was also part of the anti-appeasement camp, reported to London that the German people seemed to have mortgaged their right to be part of the international community. The British consul at Frankfurt wrote:

It seems to me that mass sexual perversity may offer an explanation for this otherwise inexplicable attack. I am persuaded that, if the government of Germany depended on the suffrage of the people, those in power and responsible for these outrages would be swept away by a storm of indignation, if not put up against a wall and shot.[1]

But how vigorous the mass of the population was by now, was another question. Two years earlier Nigel Law had reported to Anthony Eden from Berlin:

> To return to the individual and the uncertainty which surrounded him. Night and day he feels himself spied upon. [He] anxiously looks behind the door before answering your question and then decides, after all, that it is wiser not to reply . . . People no longer read the papers: they are bored with the repetition of speeches and the accounts of parades. They contain no other news and, as someone said to me: 'We have no information on which to base ideas of the future and it is wise and more pleasant not to think. The problems of each day are enough . . .' To sum up, I found a depressed people without hope for the future and obsessed by fears . . .[2]

Kristallnacht as the Nazis called it – 'the night of broken glass' – stripped those Jews who had remained in Germany of any illusions about what would happen to them if the Nazis continued in power. Over 190 synagogues were smashed or burnt down, graveyards were desecrated. The action derived its name from the number of shop windows smashed. When it was all over, the Jews were accused of having provoked the attack and presented with a bill for the damage. While the German people cannot be excused from guilt for this atrocity, from the point of view of the story of the Resistance it has to be said that many hundreds of Jews found shelter and protection at the hands of German neighbours – Quakers and Jehovah's Witnesses were especially courageous – and that *Kristallnacht* marked a turning point away from Nazism for many Germans who had wavered hitherto. The action was fomented and principally carried out by SS and SA groups, and one Brigade-leader wrote complainingly to Himmler that local anti-Semitic forces were 'induced during the first few hours to start pogroms against the Jews, though it proved very difficult to persuade them'. In terms of the central Resistance group, Hjalmar Schacht made a public protest, saying that there was no place in the Reichsbank for anyone connected with such thuggery; and von

Helldorf, who had been absent from Berlin at the time of the riots there, berated his police for their passivity. 'To the dismay of all the Nazis,' reports Gisevius, 'he announced that if he had been present he would have ordered the police to shoot the rioters and looters. It was a remarkably courageous statement for a chief of police and high officer of the SA to make. Precisely because of Helldorf's position it was particularly dangerous for him to condemn the . . . Party line.'[3]

It is interesting that even this late it was still possible for prominent men to voice their opinions without disappearing into the concentration camps. Gisevius argues that if more such people had been less craven public opinion could still have been turned against the Nazis. He adds that 'to the credit of the people it must be said that the overwhelming majority had no part in this hideous affair'. Naturally it will never be possible to establish the truth or otherwise of that statement, but it is reasonable to assume that most Germans did nothing for or against *Kristallnacht*. In the kind of society Germany had become, it was better to keep your head down if you wanted to survive. The German people were beginning to see the kind of man they had elected, and greeted with such enthusiasm, only six years earlier. But they were being swept along too fast to think of a revolution, and all opposition politicians were either dead, in prison or in exile. There were no popular rallying-points, and insidiously, like a cancer, the Gestapo was spreading its tentacles into every walk of life. The most horrifying truth about Nazi Germany is that a country can, at such a time, throw up more than enough people to support a vicious and oppressive regime quite voluntarily. 'Say no,' wrote Wolfgang Borchert, the greatest German anti-war poet of the Second World War. 'Don't play ball with them.' But it was far easier to say yes, or to say nothing. Borchert was called up in 1940 and served two prison sentences as a result of a series of brushes with authority. While in prison he was badly mistreated. His health was broken, and he died in Basle in 1947, aged twenty-six.

For those in the Resistance – by which I mean men (and, due to the structure of society at the time, to a far lesser extent women) in official positions of authority and power – there remained the problem of basic loyalty. A man like Hans Oster was a rarity: he saw his duty as a Christian and as a citizen of the world, and once he had perceived it and was sure of its moral rectitude, he had no difficulty in pursuing the aims it set him. Though a more political creature, and more of a

German nationalist, Carl Goerdeler had much in common with him. Beck, once on the road, would stick to it doggedly, having arrived at his course by a mixture of rationalism and *force majeure*. Canaris, Gisevius, Helldorf and Schulenburg all found a way to square their Resistance to the regime with their consciences, their background and their upbringing – and these factors made it harder for some than for others. Some members of the Resistance could not help, by virtue of the posts they held, but work for the Reich while they simultaneously opposed it. Some were never clear cut about where they stood. Great generals like Guderian and Manstein never supported the Resistance but equally never betrayed it.

In addition to the loneliness and isolation membership of the Resistance brought in its train – quite apart from the sheer danger – the traditional background of the conspirators made them acutely aware of the question of loyalty. The Resistance in France or Yugoslavia had clear goals and no doubt about the heroism and patriotism of its actions. In Germany, though there was a legal distinction between treason against the country (*Landesverrat*) and against the government (*Hochverrat*), Hitler had so identified himself with the country that despite his crimes those in authority under him who disagreed with him strongly enough to want him removed still found themselves in a moral and political quandary which we may find difficult to understand. They were also without a single central government in exile, or, as was the case in Italy, a monarchy, to which they could transfer loyalty. They had nothing to fall back on, and these were mostly men who supported the idea of an authoritarian government; men who saw in Hitler's rule much to approve of.

> The men of the Opposition were unanimous in attributing Germany's decline to lack of leader-material and absence of desire for leadership. Beck's study of Ludendorff was basically concerned with this problem, and Goerdeler's favourite historical theme was the failure of political leadership in the Reich since the departure of Bismarck. Schulenburg joined the NSDAP [Nazi Party] because he believed 'party politics' to be the opposite of true political leadership, which he saw personified in Otto Strasser . . . [Goerdeler] decried democracy as 'rule by the masses', and went on to say that England [sic] was not a true democracy since her electoral system enabled a minority to appoint a government.[4]

At the same time as considering the human inconsistency which pervaded attitudes to the Resistance, one must remember the historical context. The political outlook of the conspirators was outmoded: they had been disillusioned by the failure of democracy in the Weimar Republic, and their central concept was an authoritarian oligarchy for Germany, or at best a pyramid-style meritocracy. Had the Resistance succeeded in toppling Hitler, it is very unlikely that any of their theoretical schemes for government would have come to fruition. Traditional admiration of Britain's constitutional monarchy still existed, but was tempered by memories of Kaiser Wilhelm II and Weimar. The American system seems to have been an unknown quantity, despite the association with the USA of such men as Dietrich Bonhoeffer and, more significantly, the part-American diplomat and aristocrat Adam von Trott zu Solz. The men of the Resistance were great theorisers, and they were children not only of their own time but of their parents' time. Among the aristocrats in their ranks, and there were not a few, even the left-wing Fritz-Dietlof von der Schulenburg and Claus von Stauffenberg desired a continuation of the old aristocracy as political leaders. Von der Schulenburg even looked the part, with his monocle and duelling scars. It is significant that the German politicians after 1945 came from the middle and working classes (on both sides of the East-West divide). Nazis and the old-fashioned German leadership that opposed them went down together.

In one sense it was very ironical that the main burden of Resistance fell on the Army, and not insignificant that most of the conspirators were drawn from the ranks of the intellectual General Staff. The Army's tradition was always one of aloofness, and this continued during the early Nazi years in harmony with Prussian military history and aristocratic concepts of caste. We have seen that neither the Navy nor the Air Force were in the running, and in passing it may be added that the bulk of their officers were middle-class. The crack (and brand new as a military concept) paratroopers were attached to the Air Force and were supportive of the regime. As Hans Rothfels, one of the earliest and best commentators on the Resistance, comments: 'Before 1914 [the Army's aloofness] meant avoidance of interfering in public affairs, which in those days appeared "improper".' After 1919, it meant that the German Army formed a kind of state within a state and reserved its own policy. Under conditions created by the

Nazi regime, however, the 'hands off' attitude 'meant in practice the toleration of crime and murder by those who possessed the necessary force to prevent them . . . remaining aloof contradicted another highly honourable and aristocratic tradition, that of noblesse oblige and of a duty to protect the weak.'

In view of all this, it seems that officers who attended divine service in full uniform (and in large numbers) were making no more than a token and rather idle gesture against the regime, which they regarded as something beneath them. But one should not forget what a young and unstable country Germany was – and is. As a true unified democracy, it has only existed twice, from 1919 to 1932, and since 1990. The Germans have always been saddled with two national vices – love of uniforms and love of order, but they have a far worse – though related – one: insecurity.

To understand the notions of the generals it is necessary to look ahead a little into the Second World War. Even a glance indicates that no profound sense of honour motivated them. Several defected from the Resistance (with which they had dallied) in the wake of Hitler's early successes – Austria, Czechoslovakia, Poland, France. It may be that some of them believed Goebbels' propaganda, that in Hitler Germany had found the 'greatest military commander of all time', and it may be that some responded to the new sense of pride that Hitler had instilled in the nation. But on what foundation was that pride built? Surely not on a political police network that came to mean prison or a hideous concentration camp barrack for anyone who raised the mildest objection to the regime? Surely not on a determined policy of genocide regarding the Jews, and of land theft in the occupied territories, and the slaughter of the intelligentsia and clergy in Russia and Poland? And yet, it seems, that so it was, and few excuses can be found. Three matters must be taken into account: a deep-rooted fear of 'Bolshevism' – Germany almost became a Soviet State in 1919 – traditional anti-Semitism, and traditional contempt for Poland. It should be stressed again that Hitler did not have one original thought, and his ambitions and prejudices mirrored, in an uninhibited way, those of his time. That Army commanders could turn a blind eye to the activities of the SS behind the lines in Russia and Poland can be explained, though not excused, by these attitudes.

'Chamberlain has saved Hitler,' Gisevius complained bitterly as hopes of bringing down the regime shattered. There were more cautious regroupings of senior officers by the OKW, but the Resistance continued its appeals to Britain – with continuing lack of success. Brauchitsch withdrew hastily from any association with the Resistance. Halder, the Chief of Staff, dithered.

Halder is a man over whom people have argued. He has been presented as a model administrator, but a man torn between conscience and duty. Less charitably, he has been seen as someone who never quite had the courage of his convictions, but who at the same time could not bear to let go of them. He seems, on balance, to have been a man whose heart was in the right place, but who was too spineless to follow its promptings. Unfortunately, like so many of his colleagues, he bent with the wind: many a general who would have supported a coup had it succeeded, would do nothing to help instigate one. Halder, at least in the early days, could be counted as a participant in the Resistance.

With his cropped grey hair and stubbly moustache, his pince-nez and his pedantic expression, he resembled a slightly nervous little schoolmaster, and to several of his brother officers who had crossed the divide and stood squarely against Hitler, he was indeed 'the very stuff of a petit bourgeois'; but he was in a supremely difficult position, and not quite man enough to cope with it. His own postwar recollection of his situation sounds honest at least, and does not smack of self-justification or hand-washing:

> Resignation – the way Beck went – or treacherous murder. In the making of a German officer there are deep and earnest inhibitions against the idea of shooting down an unarmed man . . . The German Army did not grow up in the Balkans where regicide is always recurring in history. We are not professional revolutionists. Against this speaks the predominantly conservative attitude in which we grew up. I ask my critics, who are still very numerous, what should I have done, i.e. what should I have prevented? Start a hopeless coup for which the time was not ripe, or become a treacherous murderer as a German staff officer, as a top representative of the German General Staff, who would act not only for his own person but as representative of the German tradition? I say honestly, for that I was not fitted, that I have learnt. The idea that was at stake was clear to me. To burden it in the first stage with a political murder, of that as a German officer I was not capable.[5]

Halder believed that the people were behind Hitler and that an

Army coup could not succeed unless it had the assured support
of a majority of middle-ranking officers. This, contended Halder,
the coup would not have. At the same time, he discussed (with
Gisevius, among others) the idea of a bomb attack on Hitler's train
made to look like an accident. Gisevius is cutting about how this
rather underhand assassination idea sat with Halder's pretensions to
a high moral stance. Halder's reasons for not doing anything looked
like excuses for cowardly inaction. And yet Halder, in what seems
to have been genuine agitation, talked about having a pistol in his
pocket ready for the express purpose of shooting Hitler down – it
was just that, when it came to it, he could not bring himself to do
it.

Where Halder indisputably failed was by not coming down on
one side of the fence or the other. For such a key man to dither
was a great hindrance to the Resistance.

Meanwhile, Hitler was not remotely appeased by the Munich
Agreement. Within a month secret operations were afoot to take
over what remained of Czechoslovakia. Despite being let down so
badly by Britain once, the conspirators, when they learned of Hitler's
intention, again began to plan against the dictator. Britain and France
had, after all, said at Munich 'thus far and no farther' – and Britain
had speeded up its rearmament programme. But Hitler, ever vigilant,
caused anyone suspected of disloyalty to be removed from the centre
of activity. Witzleben was transferred from his Berlin command to
Frankfurt in November 1938.

The Führer had outfaced the Allies once again and his stature
was at its height. Although there was no enthusiasm for war in
Germany, the popular feeling shared by the generals was that
Hitler stood a good chance of taking the rest of Czechoslovakia
without risking hostilities, and so it proved. There could be no
unity against him, therefore any coup risked plunging the country
into civil war. Even Witzleben recognised this, and top generals
like Alexander von Falkenhausen, who later joined the conspiracy
when he was Commander-in-Chief of Belgium and Northern France,
declined – though not unsympathetically – an approach to join the
Resistance made at about this time by Adam von Trott zu Solz, an
old acquaintance from the days when they had both been working
in China, Trott as a diplomat, Falkenhausen as military adviser to
Chiang Kai-shek.

Taking advantage of a threat of annexation which Hungary was hanging over Slovakia, Hitler so engineered matters politically that on 14 March 1939 the regional government in Pressburg (Bratislava) declared Slovakia's autonomy, and placed the new country under German protection. At the same time, the elderly and ill new president of Czechoslovakia (following Beneš' resignation), Emil Hácha, was summoned to Berlin. There, he was forced to wait several hours at the Adlon Hotel before being summoned down Wilhelmstrasse to the Reich Chancellery in the small hours, where he was subjected to a long, bullying tirade from Hitler, the gist of which was: hand over what you've got left or we'll smash it to pieces. Hácha knew by now that no one would come to his aid if he fought. He succumbed.

On 16 March Hitler proclaimed the creation of the Protectorate of Bohemia and Moravia from the great castle of Prague, which was also the seat of government. France and Britain did little more than grumble disapproval, though a fortnight later Britain, realising where would be next on Hitler's list and awakening at last to the real danger he posed, signed an agreement promising unconditional support to Poland in the event of an enemy invasion, and signed similar agreements with Greece, Romania and Turkey. France followed suit.

This action had been taken with the indirect help of the German Resistance. Through the agency of Gisevius, who by now had a consular post in Zurich, Goerdeler had made representations to British contacts in Switzerland. At the same time, briefed by Kleist-Schmenzin, the young Ian Colvin approached his formidable contacts in the British Foreign Office. At last the British lion showed some signs of stirring, and not before time. At the beginning of April, Hitler issued his first orders for 'Operation White' – the invasion of Poland.

This was what Beck and Oster had imagined would happen. By now it was clear that Hitler thought he could smash through any obstacle set in his path to get what he wanted; equally, the dictator did not believe that, given their record over Czechoslovakia, the Allies would really do anything for Poland. And if they did decide on action, he had one more diplomatic iron in the fire with the help of which he proposed to crush even them.

On 23 May he summoned his commanders-in-chief to another meeting. He told them that he planned to attack Poland as soon as possible and that, in order to pre-empt a counter-attack from the west, the key military positions in Belgium and Holland would have to be taken over immediately. The fact that those countries were neutral 'must be ignored', declared Hitler. 'The idea that we can get off cheaply is dangerous; there is no such possibility. We must burn our boats; it is no longer a question of justice or injustice, but of life or death for 80 million people.' And now, realising that the generals would panic at the thought of a two-front war when Germany was not only still not ready, but had not the resources to supply the arms industry with raw materials in the event, he played his trump card: it was possible, he hinted, that Russia might not oppose the invasion of Poland.

Once again Poland was to fulfil its self-perceived destiny of being 'Christ between two thieves'. The great flat plain of farmland which constituted the country would be swallowed up and shared again between its two powerful neighbours, as it had been between Imperial Russia, Prussia and the Austro-Hungarian Empire for the whole of the nineteenth century.

When Weizsäcker and his fellow conspirators in the Foreign Office learnt this news, they hastened to transmit it to colleagues in the Abwehr. Immediately, preparations were made to communicate Germany's diplomatic overtures to Russia to the Allies. The British were themselves engaged in negotiating a treaty with Stalin. A series of visits to Britain by a number of different German conspirators with strong British contacts was the result – among them were Goerdeler, the Kordt brothers and the young Adam von Trott zu Solz – but the British were increasingly inclined to view any German with suspicion, and even Chamberlain knew by now that peace could not be maintained for much longer. It is sad to reflect that the one opportunity for peace was still the collapse of the Nazi regime, and the only chance of that was for the British to give credence to, and act on, the information given them by the conspirators. But the conspirators did not represent an alternative party, nor did they seem, to British eyes, to be much more than a loose collection of conservative and liberal individuals: and might they not be German agents? And these emissaries wanted to keep the land Hitler had gained for his adopted country. Also, there was no physical sign of a movement against Hitler which could be encouraged. Now, as so often, Fate was playing along with the Führer.

At home, there had been not a word of dissent by the generals at Hitler's proposal to launch an unprovoked attack on Poland. Operational plans were in his hands by mid-June. But whereas several generals were still tempted by the idea of a quick war of occupation followed by a quick peace in Poland – in other words, a localised war – there was a handful of others not so sure. Among the most influential was Georg Thomas, the Army's economic administrator. Thomas was another example of the kind of military man who opposed the regime and yet aided it in the efficient fulfilment of his duty. He did, however, with the encouragement of Oster and Canaris, draft a long memorandum to Hitler's lackey, Keitel, in which he stated that there was no way in his view that a localised war could be realised: that the balance of power would thereby have been tipped so far that the Allies would have to react in the interests of international security; and that in such a case the war Germany would be drawn into would be one which she could not physically sustain – in the medium term she would inevitably be starved of munitions and food. Coupled with this, Germany had started the recent arms race, and was ahead in terms of quantity – just; but in terms of sophistication it was the Allies who were ahead, developing weaponry (particularly in the field of warplanes) which was already more advanced than Germany's.

At the beginning of his career, Hitler had been willing to listen to rational arguments and at times even act on them. Now, even Keitel dismissed Thomas's ideas. The danger of war did not exist.

> France was too degenerate, Britain too decadent, America too uninterested to fight for Poland; and when Thomas begged leave to disagree on the grounds of better information, he was sharply reproved for becoming infected with defeatist pacifism. The Führer's greatness and superior intelligence, said Keitel, would solve the whole problem to the advantage of Germany.[6]

In the meantime, despite the best efforts of the Resistance to jolt the British out of their complacency over the possibility of a pact being signed between Hitler and Stalin before they could agree on one, Joachim Ribbentrop scored the greatest victory of his diplomatic career. On 23 August he concluded a German–Soviet Pact of Non-Aggression with Molotov in Moscow. The British, outmanoeuvred again, at least had the strength to create even closer ties of obligation with Poland as an immediate result. In fact, the British had made no secret of their intention to do this, something which had infuriated Hitler, who had snarled to Canaris a few months earlier when this likelihood had been revealed to him, 'I'll cook them a stew they'll choke on!' On 22 August, after Ribbentrop had set off for Moscow, Hitler convened a meeting of his top brass at Berchtesgaden, where he gave vent to a four-hour speech – with an interval for an opulent dinner at which caviare was served. The speech was confidential – copies were forbidden, as it amounted to a call to arms; but Canaris was present and able to take it all down verbatim.[7] Canaris was thus forewarned of Hitler's intentions and appalled by them. He later handed his copy of the transcript to Oster for the file Dohnanyi was still building up against the regime, but it has been lost. In it Hitler spoke in no uncertain terms about his projected policy of mass extermination. Was it convenient for most of them to believe that he did not mean to be taken literally?

Hitler was positively crowing. The wavering generals had swung round behind him again, and again his genius appeared to be vindicated. The wild gamble had paid off and it looked, not least to him, as if he could not lose. The Russian alliance had been snatched from the feeble grasp of the British and the French: without it, how could they hope to protect Poland militarily? 'Our enemies', boasted the Führer, 'are men below average, not men of action, not masters. They are little worms. I saw them at Munich . . . My only fear is that at the last moment some Schweinehund will make a proposal for mediation [over Poland].'

Still the Resistance hung on, though this was one of their darkest hours. The generals, who had barely responded to the events of *Kristallnacht*, made no objection now when Hitler told them that he planned to unleash SS death squads behind the lines of a conquered Poland. With their double-standard morality and sense of honour they seemed to be able to lull themselves into thinking that so long as their own hands were clean, it did not matter what the government saw fit to do with the people they had placed at its mercy. Schacht told Brauchitsch and Halder that a declaration of war without reference to the Reichstag was an illegal and unconstitutional act, but any hope the Resistance might have had of the commanders of the Army arresting Hitler as a result were torpedoed by their reply, which was that Schacht himself would be arrested if he tried to set foot in OKH HQ. Beck's own last-minute appeals too fell on deaf ears. The date of the invasion of Poland was set for 26 August.

And then, at the very last minute, in one of those baffling volte-faces that were, curiously, his preservation, Hitler cancelled the order to advance.

Hitler was worried by Britain and France after all. No offer of mediation had come, and the two countries appeared to be standing firm. The Führer's ambitions had always been eastward, not westward; but he could not leave his barely constructed West Wall at the mercy of an Allied attack while he drove into Poland. His intelligence network had given a very strong picture (which was exaggerated) of France's military preparation. What was more, Italy announced that it could not carry out its supportive role owing to a lack of *matériel*. Mussolini had never wanted to chance his arm for Hitler's benefit in any case, and now once again he was looking for a way out of the Pact of Steel he had signed with Germany in late May.

These influences had caused the generals to waver once more. Hitler addressed the Reichstag in muted tones. On 26 August he even summoned Sir Nevile Henderson, the British Ambassador who had formed such a favourable impression of Nazi Germany, and proposed a non-aggression pact with Britain, though this was an irrelevancy in view of Britain's agreements with Poland. For a moment the Resistance held its breath, and then gave way to jubilation. They had still hoped at the last minute to persuade Brauchitsch and Halder to support Schacht with a detachment of troops to arrest Hitler the moment he declared war on Poland. So close did they come that it was only when Schacht, Gisevius and General Thomas arrived by car at Canaris's office to collect him in order to go to Brauchitsch and Halder that they learned, from a delighted Oster, that Hitler had called the invasion off three-quarters of an hour earlier. He had announced it at 2.50p.m. on 25 August; it was now 7p.m.

'The Führer is finished,' said Oster. 'Peace has been saved for the next twenty years,' said Canaris. But once again, violently and without warning, Hitler was to change his mind. Perhaps he knew that to save himself he had to go on; perhaps something in his make-up impelled him towards war, no matter what.

On 28 August he told Brauchitsch that he would fight a war on two fronts after all if he had to, and proceeded hastily to map out a plan whereby an act of Polish 'aggression' could be engineered to give him the excuse to attack – and a new date was set for 1 September. In the two intervening days he also managed to present to the British Ambassador a conciliatory sixteen-point plan by which the Polish 'problem' might be resolved; but refused (via Ribbentrop) to let Henderson have a copy of them. They were merely read out to him in German. Henderson did not take the proffered translation from Hitler's translator, Paul Schmidt (who was also on the side of the conspiracy), which would have helped, as Henderson's German, though good, was not up to diplomatic finesse. The conspirators Ulrich von Hassell and State Secretary Ernst von Weizsäcker had copies of the sixteen points, but before they could relay them to Henderson (in any case not the most secure of men even at such a crucial moment as this), they were expressly forbidden to have any more diplomatic contact with the British by Ribbentrop. However, Weizsäcker managed to telegraph the contents to Theo Kordt, still on the staff of the German Embassy in London, who, under conditions of strict secrecy, was able to show them to Sir Robert Vansittart. But, even as he did so, his wife rang from Germany to say that they had just been publicly announced over the wireless, with the comment that Poland had failed to send a representative to sign agreement to these reasonable proposals – Hitler had made sure to set an impossible deadline for such a signing, but this was not revealed. He had duped the British into thinking he meant to keep secret something he had every intention of making public – his stratagem had been simple and totally effective.

It was past the eleventh hour now, but if Brauchitsch and Halder could have changed their minds even this late the situation might have been saved. It was a vain hope. Hitler gave the final order for Operation White, and this time he did not revoke it. Canaris wept. '*Finis Germaniae*,' he said to Gisevius, quoting the words of the Chief of the Imperial Civil Cabinet when, in 1917, he had learnt of the decision to wage unrestricted submarine warfare on neutral shipping: 'This means the end of Germany.' There was no more question of a coup – in reality, there had not been since 25 August – events had unrolled too quickly and too crazily. Also, Hitler had felt confident enough to lay down a clear challenge to those of his senior officers who might be planning anything: 'I have just one thing to say to anyone who's thinking of stabbing me in the back: watch out!'

But still, on its eve, only a few Germans had any conception of the war that was about to be unleashed, and what it would bring to their country. The school holidays were still on, the cities were empty, and the coastal resorts packed. In Berlin, Wilhelm Furtwängler was conducting Bruckner's 7th Symphony at the Philharmonia; and *Die Fledermaus* was playing at the Metropol. The following morning at 3.15a.m. German divisions moved into Poland.

The campaign was ruthless, brilliantly executed and completely successful. In less than a month Poland was at Germany's feet. The Poles had fought bravely, but how can you attack armoured divisions with cavalry, or shoot down Messerschmitts with rifles? And by the terms of the treaty with the USSR, Soviet forces had moved in to occupy the eastern areas allocated to them by late September. The Poles had had no help from Britain or France. There had been no attack on Germany from the west. The sixty-seven-year-old General Maurice Gamelin, wary of the locked front of the First World War, had decided on a strategy of dug-in defence, from which even Poland's fall would not move him. He was replaced in 1940 by the even older General Maxime Weygand, whose thinly spread line of defence ensured that the Germans' deep penetration attack was utterly successful, just as it had been in Poland. Ironically, Hitler's star tank general, Erich Hoepner, would soon become one of his most determined opponents.

But the fall of France was still in the future, and at the end of the Polish campaign Germany drew breath. To go on now would be to sacrifice any last grain of a chance of avoiding world war. During this period of phoney war, another chance of a coup seemed momentarily to offer itself. Even enthusiastic Nazis thought that Germany could not cope with a long campaign on several fronts for many months, and few could have been blind to the potential threat of the inexhaustible resources of Russia and America, should Germany's ambitions become too much for them to tolerate.

The first person to grasp the new possibility of bringing Hitler down was Kurt von Hammerstein. Two of his sons, both young officers, were also involved in the Resistance from an early date, and he had retained his commitment to it. With the war, he had been recalled from retirement and placed in command of Army Section A, based in Cologne. Unimpressed by any of Hitler's early successes, he shared Ludwig Beck's conviction that 'this war was lost before the first shot was fired', and his disgust at Hitler was subsequently reinforced by reports of the atrocities committed in Poland. He was appalled that the generals in the east said nothing in protest. He said to his acquaintance, the anti-Nazi journalist, Rudolf Pechel: 'I am an old soldier, but these people have turned me into an anti-militarist.'

His plan, developed in liaison with the Resistance centres in Berlin, was to persuade Hitler to visit the West Front, and arrest him. By now the infrastructure of the Resistance was quite firm in Berlin. Regular contact between conspirators in the Foreign Office, the Abwehr and the Regular Army, as well as the police, had been developed using junior officers, and officers whose official duties made them go-betweens, as couriers. Nevertheless, the number of people involved was kept as small as possible as a security precaution, and wherever feasible conspirators operating at ground level did not know each other's identity. Two important additions to the Army's group of conspirators were General Karl-Heinrich von Stülpnagel, Halder's deputy, who had been involved with the proposed coup of 1938, and General Eduard Wagner, the Quartermaster-General-in-Chief.

Hammerstein's go-between was Lieutenant Fabian von Schlabrendorff, who in the very first days of the war had been able to maintain contact with the last remaining British diplomats in Berlin, among them Sir George Ogilvie-Forbes, the Chargé d'Affaires. On 3 September, after the British ultimatum to Germany had expired at 11a.m., Schlabrendorff was given the job of seeking out Sir George and telling him what Hammerstein planned.

> The British Embassy in Berlin was already closed. But I succeeded, between 1 and 2 in the afternoon, in making contact with Sir George Ogilvie-Forbes at the Hotel Adlon in Unter den Linden and in giving him my news. While I was still speaking to Sir George in the foyer of the hotel several SS Officers came in and immediately went up to a waiter [waiters were notorious Gestapo informers], who pointed in our direction. For a moment I was worried that the SS gentlemen would take an interest in me, since I was taking refreshment with a senior British diplomat immediately after war had been declared between Britain and Germany, but luckily they took no notice of me. After a short conversation with Sir George, they left. He had not lost his composure for an instant, and returned to our table to tell me that the SS had merely wanted to settle a few details relating to the departure of the remaining British diplomats and embassy staff.[8]

Hammerstein made every effort to persuade Hitler to visit Cologne, insisting that a visit by the Führer to the west while his forces were campaigning in the east would bolster morale and show the French how seriously he was taking their threat; but Hitler, obedient to his sensitive instinct of self-preservation, stayed away. Not long after, with the end of the Polish campaign, Hammerstein was put on the retired list once more. Still by no means an old man, he would shortly fall victim to the cancer that would kill him in 1943, his sixty-fifth year. But although out of the Army, and from now on burdened with failing health, he remained a source of advice and moral support for the more active conspirators.

While it was true that the generals of the Polish campaign had returned flushed with triumph – the technique of Blitzkrieg had paid off – some of them were also disgusted at what they had seen. Hitler was not slow to send in murder squads of SS behind the front line, and on 12 September Ribbentrop had delivered to Keitel the Führer's order for the slaughter of the Jews, the clergy, the aristocracy and the intelligentsia: the Jews because it was part of Hitler's plan to wipe them from the face of the earth, the others because all potential leadership in Poland had to be liquidated.

The conquest of Poland was completed by 27 September. There was some hope among the generals now of a peace treaty to prevent the escalation of the war, but Hitler was already in pursuit of plans to open up the offensive on the West Front. Curiously though, almost before the High Command had time to react, the Führer addressed the Reichstag in a speech which definitely suggested peace feelers directed at the Allies. The terms were impossible: Britain and France should recognise Germany's territorial gains up to and including Poland. Britain should cause Germany's colonies, confiscated under the Treaty of Versailles, to be returned; but Germany would drop its claim to Alsace-Lorraine. Both Daladier and Chamberlain rejected the proposal, which may only have been made to gain time, but before they had even reacted, Hitler had swung round once more to the idea of an invasion of the west – 'Operation Yellow' – to be carried out as soon as possible, and in the same manner as the Polish campaign.

In this atmosphere Halder, under the influence of Ludwig Beck, began to warm towards the idea of a coup once more. One of his closest associates was Major (later Lieutenant-Colonel) Helmuth Groscurth, who was a liaison officer between the Regular Army and the Abwehr, and who also had close contact with Weizsäcker's Army liaison officer,

Hasso von Etzdorf. Halder knew that Groscurth was involved in the Resistance – it was to Groscurth that he had confided his desire to shoot Hitler personally. Groscurth wrote in his personal diary for 1 November 1939: 'With tears in his eyes H[alder] said he had been going to see Emil [one of the Resistance's nicknames for Hitler] with a pistol in his pocket for weeks in order to shoot him down.' But, as we have seen, Halder could never bring himself to the point. Now, despite his evident desire to see this latest coup attempt work, and the resurrection and adaptation by Oster of the 1938 plans to help him – for the Chief of the General Staff was a powerful figure and the Resistance could not but assist Halder if he showed himself willing, however unreliable he had proved in the past – he fudged the attempt. It was almost a replay of 1938 – everything depended on Hitler's declaring war on the west this time – but the doubts remained the same. How far would the population and the bulk of the Army react to a coup? What would happen if it misfired?

On 22 October Halder learned that Hitler proposed to launch his attack on 12 November. Senior Army commanders immediately objected that they could not possibly be ready in time to meet that date. The conspirators, who also knew Hitler's plans, were quick to foment military discontent. Oster in particular discussed the matter with Stülpnagel, the Deputy Chief of Staff already involved in the Resistance, at Army HQ in Zossen.

But it was as if Hitler knew what was going on. On 27 October he invited Brauchitsch and Halder to lunch, along with a dozen other officers, and awarded them all the Knight's Cross – one of the highest military decorations. After the ceremony the Commander-in-Chief and the Chief of the General Staff attempted to dissuade Hitler from his attack date, but without success. The following day Brauchitsch was already in defeat, but Halder tried again. Hitler would not listen. Halder, who knew Stülpnagel was involved in the conspiracy, sent him to the West to inspect the front line. Stülpnagel told Halder to put Brauchitsch under lock and key and appeal to the senior generals (all of whom were opposed to a western offensive at this time) to range themselves behind him. The true purpose of Stülpnagel's visit to the West Front was to sound out the Commanders of Army Groups A and B, Gerd von Rundstedt and Fedor von Bock. Neither of these old guard officers would commit himself to a coup, but Wilhelm von Leeb, the commander of Group C, who had already spoken out against the French campaign, agreed to be associated with it. Moreover Witzleben commanded the 1st Army, within von Leeb's Group.

But that was not enough for Halder. He did approach the head of the Reserve Army, Friedrich Fromm, who would play such an ignoble role in the 20 July plot, but Fromm would not commit himself. The Reserve Army would be needed as it had internal military control of Germany. Nevertheless, there was still a chance of success, but it was risky – too risky for Halder.

Meanwhile Beck strained every nerve to convince him and Brauchitsch of the disastrous consequences of war. As was his manner, he presented them with memoranda in which he pointed out once again the suicidal nature of a world war, backing up his arguments with statistical data drawn from General Thomas. He also pointed out that on 27 October the USA had lifted the embargo on arms which had been the result of the earlier American declaration of neutrality. By 31 October, Halder sent a message to Oster via Groscurth, in which he asked Goerdeler and Beck – as potential heads of state in waiting – to hold themselves in readiness. It is likely that Goerdeler, in his optimistic way, would have set about drawing up one of the many lists of potential cabinet ministers he wrote, along with the vast amount of theoretical political writing his energetic but frustrated mind threw up. Halder also told Groscurth personally that fatal accidents could be arranged for the Nazi top table, including Hitler, but he was not specific and there was still an ominous note of 'if only' in his tone.

Nevertheless, the Resistance set itself once more on an alert footing. Schacht, who had been obliged to resign from his post as head of the State Bank in January, but was still a Minister Without Portfolio, was also told to prepare himself.

Hitler's security arrangements were still relatively lax at this stage, but Oster was taking no chances. When Erich Kordt, the suburban-looking career diplomat who gave the impression that the most exciting part of his day was a beer and sausage lunch, boiled over with frustration and offered himself, following a meeting at Beck's Goethestrasse house, as a potential assassin, Oster accepted. It would never hurt to have a second string to the bow, and Halder had proved too often in the past to have feet of clay. Oster also took counsel with Dohnanyi, Gisevius and Thomas. Perhaps a last memorandum to the Chief of the General Staff might stiffen his sinews. Clearly Groscurth was still sceptical about Halder.

But Halder had seen Hitler three times between 25 and 31 October and each time tried to dissuade him from his attack date. At the military councils of 25 and 31 October, Wilhelm von Leeb reported that all senior officers were against the attack, that Brauchitsch had supported them, but that Hitler would listen to no one. He dug in. Here one sees Hitler's own deep-seated mistrust of the generals at work, coupled with the contempt and fear of the little man come to power with regard to those born to it. Hitler had seen how spineless the generals could be; he knew too that he was successful. He must have been drunk with success. But he had fought, we must assume, courageously in the First World War as a corporal, and from that experience he also thought he knew better than the generals about the psychology of soldiers, and how to command them.

Brauchitsch and Halder spent 2 and 3 November inspecting the West Wall. Everything confirmed what they already knew: Germany was not ready for war. Back in Berlin on 4 November, Thomas presented Halder with yet more pessimistic statistical data about supplies of munitions and food. There was also the obvious problem of a winter campaign: rain and snow created mud and frozen terrain, which affected men and machinery alike, as well as making it hard going for the horses on which the German Army still depended to a large extent for transport.

Halder returned apparently still determined to go ahead with a coup, but he did not have Brauchitsch's wholehearted support, and even committed conspirators like Witzleben feared that too many junior officers were 'drunk with Hitler' to follow their leaders against him. After the war Brauchitsch said, 'The whole thing [would have been] plain high treason . . . Why should I have taken such action? It would have been against the German people. Let us be honest . . . the German people were all for Hitler.' No military logic could get the generals out of their cleft stick, and logic could not move the masses as Hitler could. A civil war would mean at worst the end of Germany and an opening up of the country to the dreaded forces of Bolshevism; at best it would mean the end of the Army, to which by tradition and training most of the generals owed their fiercest loyalty.

But Oster, who with Dohnanyi had the most modern outlook of all the conspirators, stuck to his plan of action. Halder's intention was still to arrest Hitler, but Oster knew, as he had done a year ago, that the only way to finish the Nazis was to chop off their head. When Kordt had come to see him in his office at the Abwehr on Tirpitzufer on All Saints' Day, the day after the meeting at Beck's house, and had offered his services: 'I'm prepared to throw the bomb, to rescue the generals from their scruples,' Oster accepted immediately. Kordt, as a senior Foreign Office man in Ribbentrop's entourage, was among the few who had easy access to Hitler (Beck, for example, met Hitler only once, in 1937, and Canaris only five or six times in the course of an eight-year career). 'Give me eleven days,' Oster told him. Eleven days to organise the explosives. He contacted Erwin Lahousen, the Austrian officer who was Groscurth's successor as head of Abwehr Department II – the section which dealt with sabotage among other things. Lahousen, already involved in the Resistance – as were all of Oster's immediate senior colleagues – could justify the drawing of explosives and fuses from stores, and also arrange for Erich Kordt to undergo a quick course at the secret Abwehr training camp on the shores of Lake Quenz near Brandenburg. Kordt would be presented to the staff there as a trainee V-man. There was no question but that explosives should be used, and Oster could not afford to think of the innocent lives which might be lost along with Hitler and his crew. Kordt could never get to see Hitler alone, but only in the context of a planning meeting. So, even if Kordt had been a crack marksman, the likelihood of being able to draw a pistol, aim and fire one fatal shot in a crowded room was very remote.

Brauchitsch was summoned to the Reich Chancellery's Congress Hall at noon on 5 November to make his report to Hitler on the West Front. Halder, despite his position as Chief of the General Staff, would be in attendance, but would have to sit out the actual meeting in an ante-room. Brauchitsch was very nervous beforehand. Once again the schedule was insanely tight. A decision on whether or not to go ahead with the 12 November attack date would have to be made by 1p.m. because the Army would need a week to gear up. Much now hung on which way Brauchitsch would swing. If he stood firm, Halder's coup still had the ghost of a chance. If not . . . well, the few who knew about Kordt and Oster could at least cling to a last hope. But 11 November – the day scheduled for Kordt's attempt – was barely twenty-four hours before the attack date for Operation Yellow.

The meeting lasted twenty minutes. Perhaps on account of his nervousness, Brauchitsch was sharper than he had intended to be from the outset, and both he and Hitler became furious. The Commander-in-Chief presented his statistics, and added, exaggerating slightly, that the morale of the men could not be compared with that of 1914. He also pointed out that during the recent Polish campaign discipline and *esprit de corps* had been about as low among the troops as it had been in late 1917 and 1918. He could not have said anything worse, for the collapse of the Army in 1918 and its betrayal (as Hitler perceived it) by its leaders had unleashed the revolution of winter 1918–19. This had been the most traumatic moment of Hitler's life, and the experience which had turned him into a politician. He now became incandescent with rage and demanded proof of this allegation. Did Brauchitsch perhaps think that the Army was on the verge of breaking up, as it had in 1918? If there had been acts of indiscipline, how many of the culprits had been hanged?

Above all, before storming off to leave the normally reserved and dignified Brauchitsch white-faced and trembling with anger and humiliation, Hitler spat out that he was well aware of the 'spirit of Zossen' that existed among the generals of the Regular Army, and that any cowards would be crushed.

On the way back to Zossen, the shaken Brauchitsch gave an appalled Halder all the details of the interview. They had scarcely arrived back than they heard that Hitler had given the order for Operation Yellow to begin as scheduled, without further consultation. This was another slap in the face – Hitler was not even trying to hide his contempt – but the two men panicked. Halder immediately gave orders that all papers relating to his coup should be destroyed before the Gestapo arrived. Neither Halder nor Brauchitsch had forgotten what had happened on 30 June 1934, nor the fate of Generals Schleicher and Bredow on that day.

Personal fear of Hitler had robbed Halder of any sense of what he was standing for. His coup was designed precisely to bring to an end such effective bullying tactics as those Hitler had just employed. Halder's only excuse is that it took a very strong personality indeed to stand up to the dictator. Those who knew him still speak of the overwhelming power of Hitler's presence – something no photograph or film can convey. One should never forget that he was very far from the ridiculous figure he has become to us through overexposure and pastiche. He was the most formidable enemy humanity has ever known. The German Resistance could not have been up against anything worse.

Groscurth and Dohnanyi subsequently saved many of the papers scheduled for destruction, but Halder spent the rest of the day in a panic. Brauchitsch later calmed himself down, but effectively washed his hands of the business. He was still in favour of the coup, he said, and he still felt that the western offensive should be stopped – the original point of the coup anyway. Hitler had ordered it to proceed and thus provided the conspirators with their justification. They would have the backing of the western commanders. The Gestapo had not, after all, shown up in Zossen – in fact they were in total ignorance of Halder's plans, as was Hitler. Halder began to swing again. Now he dispatched Groscurth to Canaris in Berlin with a report of what had happened and a request to remove Hitler by assassination as soon as possible.

Canaris took the news badly, and would not agree to the idea of an out-of-hand assassination. Oster had been wise not to involve him in the plan with Kordt. A coup which could be justified by the two moral leaders of the Resistance, Beck and Goerdeler, was what was needed to legitimise a replacement administration in Germany in the eyes of the world and to the German public. To Oster, already involved in other secret plans to avert the war, the news of Canaris's rejection of Halder's request came as no surprise. Never downcast by setbacks for long, he must have comforted himself with the thought of his other iron in the fire. But he knew how much more satisfactory and how much more assured of success a proper coup led by a man in Halder's position would have been.

Meanwhile, Canaris had suffered another blow. On 6 November he was summoned to Hitler's office and ordered to prepare Abwehr agents to be dressed in Dutch and Belgian uniforms to be dropped into those neutral countries and stand guard at the bridges, to prevent them from being blown up. The Polish campaign had been triggered by Gestapo agents in Polish uniforms staging an 'attack' on the radio station at Gleiwitz. These 'gangster methods' upset Canaris profoundly.[9]

One last hope was Witzleben, but he was far away at 1st Army Headquarters in Bad Kreuznach, beyond Frankfurt, and Oster would have to get official permission from Canaris to use a car to drive there: petrol was already rationed. Canaris was so out of sorts that he refused

to give it, so Oster was forced to telephone Witzleben to get him
to ring Canaris and request a meeting about military security with
Oster. Finally, on the following day, Oster set out to see Witzleben
with Gisevius.

Unfortunately Witzleben remained pessimistic about the chances
of a coup's success. He still firmly believed that Brauchitsch and
Halder were men of straw and that the rank and file officers were
firmly behind Hitler. Thus, despite one or two more efforts to save
it, the second great chance to dismount the Nazis and stop the Second
World War was missed, largely on account of one fit of temper from
the Führer.

In the event, the attack date of 12 November was shortly afterwards put back on account of bad weather – this would not be the
last postponement of Operation Yellow. On the other hand Hitler
firmly turned his back on peace initiatives from the King of Belgium
and the Queen of the Netherlands, which had been engineered secretly
by Oster but also by two 'Nazi' generals, Reichenau and Warlimont,
acting independently and out of purely military considerations.

There remained the possibility of Kordt's attempt, but in the
meantime Hitler had travelled down to Munich to celebrate – as he
always did – the 8 November anniversary of his own failed 1923 coup.
It was there that something happened which would rock the Party as
much as it did the Resistance. One simple man working alone tried
to kill him and came within a hair's breadth of success.

Georg Elser was born in the Schwäbische Alb area south of
Stuttgart in 1903. He came from a modest background and was
apprenticed to a cabinet maker, to learn a craft at which he became
exceptionally skilled. For five years, between 1925 and 1930, he
worked as a joiner at a clock factory in Konstanz, and during that
time he joined the Red Front Fighters' League. From 1936 to 1939
he worked in an armature factory in Heidenheim, and from April 1939
he took a job in a quarry from which he was able to steal fuses and
explosives. In July he designed his bomb, and the following month
he left Heidenheim for Munich, where he took a room, living on
his savings from now on. Between September and the beginning of
November he worked patiently, concealed in the Bürgerbräukeller
in Munich, for thirty-five nights, hollowing out and preparing the
column in which he would conceal his bomb. He placed it on 1
November 1939, primed it on the 2nd, and on the 5th he set the

time fuse he had designed to explode on 8 November at 9.20p.m., when Hitler would be making his annual address to the Old Guard who had taken part in the 1923 coup attempt.

Elser was a small, quiet, shabby man who gave the impression of being shy. He had no interests beyond his carpentry and his love of music, which was a passion with him. He was not especially politically inclined – the fierce-sounding Red Front League was a socialist organisation which he had joined at the suggestion of a colleague at the clock factory simply because he had left-wing sympathies. He played in its band. However, he had hated the Nazi ideology of *Gleichschaltung* – making everyone conform – from the first, and had never been carried away by National Socialist enthusiasm. Above all, he was a loner who kept his thoughts to himself, not confiding much to his family, to his only close friend, Eugen Rau, or even to his girlfriend of many years' standing, Elsa Heller.

He decided to kill Hitler some time in 1938, when it was clear that the dictator wanted war. Elser knew what another war would mean, and he instinctively saw that in the current political climate the only way to stop it would be to kill Hitler. Once having reached this decision, he set about accomplishing his end methodically and without hesitation. The Bürgerbräukeller, a large restaurant-cum-brasserie which had been one of the centres of the 1923 coup attempt, was where the Führer always held his annual get-together, and the ceremony was one of the few fixed points in Hitler's calendar. Most of the bearers of the 'Blood Order' would be there, wearing their red and silver medal on the right breast, with its eagle and oak wreath, its view of the Feldherrnhalle in Munich, with swastika and sunbeams, and the words: 'You were victorious.'

Elser attended the gathering in November 1938, with a view to getting the lie of the land. When he returned to Heidenheim he set about his preparations in earnest, his work in the armature factory providing tools and some of the materials for his bomb, and his experience in the clock factory also coming in handy. He even built a model bomb to test his mechanism.

Back in Munich almost a year later, he knew where he would plant the bomb – in a column which backed the podium where Hitler would stand to make his speech. On the nights that he worked in the Bürgerbräukeller he would go there for a meal and then hide until the place emptied and closed, mingling with the first customers the following morning. He was not a man to attract attention and, as he was working entirely alone, his security was complete. He would chisel away at the brick column for hours, slowly and deliberately, working on his knees, which became bruised and swollen.

Once his bomb was installed and the timer mechanism set, he paid a quick visit to his sister in Stuttgart to leave his few belongings with her. Then he went back to Munich to check that everything was still in order. He barely ever read anything, not even newspapers. If he had, he would have seen some disquieting news in the *Völkischer Beobachter* of 6 November: for the first time in fifteen years, Hitler had it in mind not to attend the Old Guards' reunion. The reason was that, after his row with Brauchitsch, the Führer had decided momentarily to visit the Front for himself. But, as was usual with him, he changed his mind again. However, fate was still with the dictator. Instead of speaking from 8.30p.m. until 10.00p.m. as scheduled, when he would have caught his private aeroplane back to Berlin, he was obliged by adverse weather conditions to use his train. In order to get back to Berlin in time to get on with his work schedule, Hitler had to leave Munich earlier. Thus it was that he addressed the meeting from 8.10p.m. until only 9.07p.m., giving a very childish speech in which he laid the blame for the coming war squarely on Britain's shoulders. Then he left abruptly, not even waiting, as was his habit, to chat with his old comrades.

The bomb went off at 9.20p.m. exactly as planned. It brought the roof down, killing eight and wounding another sixty-three. It would certainly have killed Hitler. But by then Elser had already been arrested.

He was stopped by officials at the Konstanz frontier crossing to Switzerland at 8.45p.m. He was wearing an illegal Red Front badge on the reverse of his lapel, and he had incriminating material in his pockets, including springs and cogwheels from an alarm clock. Immediately Germany's top detective, SS Brigade-leader Artur Nebe, head of the Criminal Investigation Department, but already involved in the Resistance, was called in. He interrogated Elser in detail, found the man taciturn and a shade ingenuous, but did not believe that he was lying when he said that he had worked on his own initiative. This neither Hitler nor Himmler would accept. Himmler especially was eager for Elser to be linked with the British Secret Service, or with the Black Front, the breakaway National Socialist group in exile, led by Gregor Strasser's brother, Otto. Because of this, Elser was sent to the Gestapo Headquarters in Prinz-Albrecht-Strasse, Berlin, where he was given what was known as 'intensive interrogation', but they got no more out of him than Nebe had. Finally he was sent to the concentration camp at Sachsenhausen, where he spent the next five years. At the end of 1944, he was transferred to the 'VIP' barrack at Dachau, where he joined other victims of the regime, among whom were the former Austrian Chancellor, Kurt Schuschnigg, and his wife and daughter, Hjalmar Schacht, Martin Niemöller, and Franz Halder, for it was here that the hesitant Chief of the General Staff finally ended up.

Elser was well treated throughout his imprisonment. It was Hitler's intention to stage an anti-British show trial of him at the end of the war, at which he would be proved to be an agent of the enemy. In the meantime, Elser was allowed a workbench and tools in his cell, and he made chairs and bookcases for his guards in return for cigarettes. He became a heavy smoker during the years in prison, and smoking and playing the zither were his last remaining pleasures. He was never shaken in his belief that he had done the right thing, nor for a moment did he think that the Nazis would not kill him. And they did, when it was certain that the war was lost. The order came from Berlin on 5 April 1945 to stage the man's death, making it look as if he'd been killed in one of the frequent Allied air raids. An opportunity presented itself to the camp administration to do so on 9 April.

After the explosion in the Bürgerbräukeller there was pandemonium. The Nazis suspected an elaborate international plot. The central Resistance wondered if some anti-Nazi group within their ranks had managed to get so close while they had shilly-shallied in Berlin. It was even considered that the whole event had been staged by Hitler himself in order to increase his prestige. Only after the war was Nebe's original finding confirmed, that Elser had done it alone. His was the first of only two bomb attempts at which the bomb exploded – the second would be Stauffenberg's on 20 July 1944. Stauffenberg's was the result of years of Army attempts and planning; Elser's anonymity was his best ally.

Elser is a neglected hero. Had he succeeded, he would probably never have taken credit publicly for the deed. His failure, ironically, aided the Nazis – there was a general wave of sympathy for Hitler, and the dictator's security was immediately tightened – which meant in turn that Kordt's plan was scuppered.

There was an additional way in which the Nazis turned the event to their advantage. At the end of September 1939, two British secret agents in Holland made contact with a German exile who told them of a planned anti-Nazi coup, to be carried out by members of the Army. They collected further details regarding the demands of this Resistance group, and these were confirmed by reports from London of meetings with Goerdeler and other members of the central Resistance. The two British agents were then authorised to make contact with the Germans, and did so over a series of meetings between late October and early November, all of which took place at Backhus, near Venlo.

But the Germans were in fact members of the Security Service, and the chief 'Resistance' officer was Walter Schellenberg, the twenty-nine-year-old head of Gestapo International Counter-Intelligence. On 9 November the British agents were taken to a point close to the German frontier and there arrested. This event, known as the 'Venlo Incident', could not have happened at a better time for the Nazis, who insisted publicly that the activity of the British spies was linked to a conspiracy which also involved Elser. At the same time the British, seeing themselves outmanoeuvred yet again – and by German agents posing as conspirators – turned an even colder and more suspicious eye on the genuine German Resistance. One man who would suffer particularly unfairly from the personal obloquy of his former Oxford 'friends' was Adam von Trott zu Solz – as will be seen. But it was a severer blow that his credibility suffered. Thus, unfortunately, more harm than good came to the Resistance out of Elser's failure; but the result, had he been successful, cannot be estimated. There would certainly have been chaos in Germany; but it is unlikely that any of the surviving Nazi leaders would have committed the country to war. Hitler was the head and the heart of Nazism. However dangerous as a group, the others were just fellow-travellers.

As for the British, their Secret Service learnt a lesson. At the time – under the authority of officers who became very senior in MI5 and MI6 after the war but who were then cutting their teeth in espionage and information gathering – the Secret Service (to use a blanket term for the various departments) was a group of imaginative amateurs. Academics and intellectuals were recruited on a semiprofessional basis, and while some discharged their duties with great responsibility and got little thanks, others behaved like overgrown schoolboys. To an extent the two Englishmen involved in the Venlo Incident mirrored this. Sigismund Payne Best had lived in Holland since 1916 (when he had also served in Intelligence). He had married a Dutchwoman and ran a business there. His associate, R. H. Stevens, was an ex-Indian Army man sent out to join Best by the head of the service, Stuart Menzies, though Menzies' predecessor, the outspoken Admiral Sir Hugh 'Quex' Sinclair, had described him as 'an absolute fool'.

The German Secret Service departments were capable of disasters equal to the Venlo Incident – from a plan to put bombs into crates of oranges shipped from Spain to the British Navy, to Operation Pastorius, a plan to land ten young Nazis fluent in American English on the shores of the USA so that they could sabotage the American warplane industry. Canaris took the lead in this 'show' very reluctantly, and, as he privately predicted, it was a disaster. One of the ten dropped out before departure owing to an attack of VD; of the nine who went, all were arrested as they landed, and seven were executed shortly afterwards. The two survivors were imprisoned but pardoned after the war and may have betrayed the operation. But both sides now began to learn the efficiency and ruthlessness that fathered modern espionage and counter-espionage work, creating another minefield through which the Resistance had to tread.

SEVEN

In the Shadows

The invasion of France was postponed but not cancelled. What was more, initiative was passing from Brauchitsch and Halder to the generals who stood close to Hitler: Keitel and his deputy, Jodl. In other words, the Army High Command was losing ground to the Overall High Command – the office which had been Hitler's creation. It was becoming clear that Hitler's next move, based on past experience, would be simply to take over Brauchitsch's job himself. It would be 1941 before he finally did so, but from now on Hitler was effectively in direct control.

Hans Oster had foreseen for a long time that the phoney war would come to an end. Even before the projected coup of 1939, he had made a lonely decision about how he might at least contain the Blitzkrieg in the West.

Not only in France, but also in Holland and Belgium, military leaders had been looking cautiously at Hitler's mounting ambitions. There was no channel of sea to protect them, and though Holland's neutrality had been respected in the First World War, Belgium and France had bitter memories of German occupation. It was from Holland that an unexpected and welcome ally came to Oster, when Major (later Colonel) Gijsbertus Sas was reappointed Military Attaché in Berlin by the Dutch Commander-in-Chief, General Reynders, in view of his political perspicacity and special understanding of German affairs.

Sas had been Military Attaché for the first time in 1936, when Oster was Sas's host at the Olympic Games. Both shared a passion for riding, and the strong friendship which grew up between them and their families was based on their mutual enjoyment of the equestrian events. Oster's daughter, however, remembers that at the beginning he cautiously warned his children not to breathe a word against the Nazis in Sas's hearing. Indeed, in 1936, the Sas family were enthusiastic about the appearance of the New Germany. But as the friendship deepened and Sas came to see behind the veneer of Nazism, so Oster's confidence in him grew. After his recall to Holland, Sas and Oster remained in close contact.

The Dutchman took up his reappointment in April 1939. Oster was delighted, and Sas was soon a regular visitor at the Osters' spacious flat in Bayerische Strasse. It was in the course of a conversation they had there quite early on that the topic of Hitler's war plans first came up. At first all Oster was prepared to do was not deny Sas's presumption that Hitler indeed had intentions in the West. General Reynders read his Military Attaché's reports on the situation throughout the summer and found them sober and responsible. But then, at the end of September, their tone became much more urgent.

On 28 September Sas reported that the West could expect an offensive in about six weeks' time, and that Holland had better not count on the protection of its neutrality. He had reached this conclusion by himself, but when Reynders communicated back his scepticism, the Military Attaché went to see Oster again, who received him in the study of his flat. Once Sas had taken him into his confidence and told him about his 28 September report, and the thousand rumours and sources which had brought him to his conclusion, Oster did not hesitate for long before answering. 'I think you are right. I am not, however, privy to the plans of the General Staff Operations Section; but I will try to find out what the exact current situation is.'

One of the problems of the story of the Resistance is that few of the conspirators left copious written material behind them. Much that was written was destroyed by the Gestapo in the purges following the failure of the 20 July 1944 Plot. Key men like Oster and Stauffenberg committed little to paper, certainly not of their private thoughts. So at first sight it is hard to say whether or not Oster came to the momentous decision to offer secret military information to a potentially enemy state spontaneously, or whether it was a measure he had already considered adopting if an opportunity to do so ever presented itself. He had certainly talked freely theoretically with Sas for several months about the situation in Germany, but specific information was quite another matter.

There is no doubt that he took the decision and operated the liaison with Sas alone, though he took Beck into his confidence and gained his agreement. The whole operation did not come to light until after the war, and until recently the debate about whether his action was justified still raged fiercely. Only in 1991 was a plaque to his memory affixed to his old Berlin home. The old question of the difference between treason against the government and treason against the country was raised, not without reason: had Oster crossed the border between the two, and entered forbidden territory? His daughter (not the only relative of a conspirator to do so) has made the point that even many decades after the war it was not always a good thing to bear the same surname as a prominent conspirator.

Oster knew that if he gave precise information to Sas about German invasion plans, he would be putting the lives of tens of thousands of German soldiers at risk. The fact is that he would have taken this into his calculations, accepting responsibility for a lesser evil in order to avoid a greater one. He was not an unreflective man, but he was able to make a decision and then stick to it. His daughter remembers:

> My father had no anxiety. He just wasn't frightened of things. He wasn't incautious, he just saw his way and went ahead and did it. He was energetic and decisive. If you were a victim of anxiety during the Third Reich, you'd be good for absolutely nothing – look at Halder. My father's views never changed, whatever Hitler's fortunes were.

As a professional soldier, Oster would have weighed the pros and cons carefully. His thinking would have been coloured too by his deep regret at the failure of the 1938 coup attempt – the one which came closest to success, and by which any war at all would have been avoided. Now, a year later, he regarded the vacillations of the generals with increasing scepticism. He was as convinced as Beck and Canaris that a European war, let alone one that involved America, would mean the end of Germany and the deaths of millions of people. He had as little doubt as Beck (a view scoffed at by Hitler) that America, with its vast resources, would not stand by and let Britain be destroyed. For better or worse, Britain was the cradle of America, and language, history and much of the culture were things the two countries held in common.

Finally, and just as importantly, Oster was convinced of the essential criminality of the Nazi regime. Among the staff of the Abwehr, in their cramped little offices ranged along the narrow corridors of the Tirpitzufer building, few wore uniforms. Oster was barely to be seen in one since the Nazis had taken power – he felt that it had been sullied; nor did he accept his promotion to Major-General willingly at Hitler's hands. He knew about the euthanasia programmes, he knew what Hitler planned against the Jews, and he was outraged that Germany should consider for a moment flouting the neutrality of Belgium and Holland.

Sas told Oster that any information he received would be transmitted to his Belgian opposite number, Colonel Goethals. Oster accepted this and said to the Dutchman, in his usual undemonstrative way: 'It is my plan and my duty to rid Germany and the world of this plague.'

There followed a series of secret meetings with Sas. Getting into his car at the end of the first one, Oster said to his friend, Corvette-Captain Fritz Liedig, whom he had taken into his confidence, and who was waiting for him at the wheel, 'There's no going back for me now.' He sat in the car in silence as they drove through the dark October streets of Berlin, then added: 'It's much easier to take a pistol and shoot someone down, it's much easier to storm a machine-gun emplacement, than to do what I have decided to do. And if I should die, I beg you to remain my friend after my death – a friend who knew the circumstances under which I took this decision, and what drove me to do things which perhaps others will never understand, or at least would never have done themselves.'

That night, 8 October 1939, Oster had told Sas that while nothing was yet planned against Holland, the approach to France would certainly be made by force across Belgium. He had crossed his lonely Rubicon.

The reaction of the Dutch authorities to the news transmitted to them by Sas in confidence was at first sceptical, but fourteen days later, Oster communicated additional information that the invasion plan now included Holland, and that the attack date was likely to be mid-November, depending on weather conditions.

Now the Belgians put themselves on guard. They mobilised, but quietly, to Oster's great relief. There was certainly no doubt that they took the warning seriously. In Holland the case was different. Sas was told by the head of the Dutch Secret Service that he had their full confidence; but in The Hague he learnt from a friend, the Adjutant to the Minister of War, that the opposite was true. His friend also showed him a report by the Secret Service which stated that Sas was not a credible source, and which, further, argued that his warnings were 'ridiculous'. This was at the beginning of November. He returned to Berlin on the 7th, to find a message from Oster: 'Come immediately. Every second counts.'

At their meeting, Oster was able to tell Sas every detail of what had happened between Hitler and Brauchitsch, and that the order had been given to attack on 12 November. But barely had this date been communicated to Holland, than it was deferred, first to the 15th and then almost immediately to the 19th. Then to the 22nd, then to 3 December. This was typical of Hitler's unpredictable and impatient style, and as usual it served as protection for him. Oster never lost credibility in Sas's eyes, but it was no wonder that the Dutch authorities looked at Sas askance.

The story of the next few months is so long and complicated that it becomes a mire of simultaneously occurring and contradictory events. The essentials are that the planned invasion of France was put off so frequently that Resistance warnings ceased to be taken at all seriously. On 10 January 1940, two German airmen had to force-land at Mechelen, Belgium. They were carrying invasion documents, but despite this breach of security, or perhaps because of it, Hitler decided to aim for an offensive on the 17th. Bad weather intervened again, however, and finally, on 16 January, the Führer decided to put the whole thing off until the spring.

Meanwhile, in Rome, the Bamberg lawyer, Dr Josef Müller, continued his efforts on behalf of the Resistance to persuade the Pope (Eugenio Pacelli had ascended the Papal throne in 1939 as Pius XII) to act as a peace broker between the Allies and a government of liberation in Germany. The negotiations were tortuous but the Pope was not unsympathetic to the role, which encouraged the conspirators greatly. However, the British Minister, Sir Francis D'Arcy Osborne, was doubtful of the Resistance: who were they, actually, and what political groupings did they represent? Furthermore, through Müller the Resistance had made this approach primarily to Britain, which in turn pointed out that it could do nothing without France. Secret meetings also took place with British representatives in Switzerland, but achieved nothing in the end. Nor did the efforts of a colourful but definitely dubious self-styled diplomat called James Lonsdale Bryans. Bryans was an old Etonian sponger who had a slender contact with Lord Halifax (then Foreign Secretary of Britain), and with Detalmo Pirzio-Biroli, whom Bryans met in Rome and who was engaged to the German Ambassador Ulrich von Hassell's daughter, Fey. Bryans clearly saw an opportunity for self-aggrandisement in acting as go-between for Hassell and Halifax, and it is a measure of the Resistance's anxiety to follow up any channel to the Allies that Hassell took the risk of meeting such a doubtful emissary. Bryans, to his credit, persevered until March 1940, but his representations on behalf of the Resistance fell on increasingly deaf British ears and finally Sir Alexander Cadogan, Vansittart's glacial successor at the Foreign Office, showed him the door.

Oster's friend, Corvette-Captain Liedig, came up with a plan late in 1939 based on the ever-present fear of Bolshevism. After the fall of Poland, in which that country had been split between Germany and the USSR more to the former's benefit than had been suggested by the Treaty of 23 August, Stalin had made no difficulties but requested Germany's connivance at his including Lithuania in his 'sphere of influence'. The Soviets had attacked Finland in November, and there was, argued Liedig, every chance that they would sweep down on western Europe from the north. Hitler, the self-appointed bulwark against Bolshevism, now seemed to be opening the gates of Europe to Russia. If Germany toppled him now, and placed her forces at the disposal of Europe against the USSR, then the new German government could claim a generous peace settlement as a reward. Britain and Germany could even fight side by side against the common menace. Romantic as this sounded, in the end it proved at least partially true, though not until after the collapse of the Third Reich.

But again everything hinged on a decisive move from Brauchitsch and Halder, which did not materialise. Nor was there any help from the commanders in the West, though Wilhelm von Leeb remained willing to support Resistance plans. Beck, Goerdeler and their group, including the Abwehr conspirators, had revived their hope in a combined rising of the western Army at the very end of 1939, following vociferous protests from Colonel-General Johannes von Blaskowitz, the sixty-two-year-old Commander-in-Chief in the East.

Blaskowitz was complaining about the atrocities committed by the SS and the so-called *Einsatzgruppen* – task forces – behind the lines in Poland. In the days before the 'Final Solution' (formulated in January 1942), the massive deportations to those concentration camps which were developed specifically as death camps had not yet begun. But the slaughter had. There were four *Einsatzgruppen*, each numbering between 500 and 1000 men. Their official function was 'the removal of all elements hostile to the Reich and to Germany behind the fighting line'. Among them, over their period of operation in Poland and later in Russia between autumn 1939 and about summer 1942, they were responsible for the deaths of two million people. On 29 August 1941, one such group killed 1469 Jewish children in Moletai and Utena in Lithuania. Their method of operation was very simple:

> A squad would arrive at a town or village and round up the people they sought, sometimes assisted by the local police. They would then take them to the outskirts, or to a nearby wood or open land. The victims would then be forced to dig a pit, which would become their grave after they had been shot.[1]

These atrocities sometimes took place under the very noses of the Regular Army, and not all senior officers did as Field Marshal Ernst Busch, who merely instructed his ADC to 'draw the curtains'. For some, witnessing such horror was enough to make them withdraw their support for Nazism. And yet, in this ghastly world, one of the principal members of the police Resistance, Artur Nebe, was none the less obliged to take command of such a group for a period in order to maintain his Nazi credibility. He led Task Force B from June to November 1941 in Russia. Statistics for the four main groups between June 1941 and April 1942 are available:

Task Force A: 250,000 deaths
Task Force B: 70,000 deaths
Task Force C: 150,000 deaths
Task Force D: 90,000 deaths.

Nebe himself always contended that he kept his killings down to a minimum and that, if anyone else had been in command, the rate would have been very much higher. The number he himself claimed to have been responsible for was 45,467. His colleague Otto Ohlendorf, commanding Task Force D between June 1941 and June 1942, suggested ingenuously at his own postwar trial that Nebe had exaggerated to Himmler even the relatively low figures that he gave, in order to draw credit upon himself. Nebe also claimed later to have tried to avoid the posting altogether, and get himself transferred to the International Police Commission, but that Beck and Oster persuaded him not to move away from his important position inside the RSHA (State Security Head Office, comprising the Security Service and the Gestapo) to which the police were attached. This may be true: we have seen what personal moral compromises Beck and Oster were prepared to make in pursuit of an ultimate good. But Nebe remains a shadowy figure whose usefulness to the State may even have equalled his service to the Resistance. He was the leading investigator in both the Fritsch and the Elser cases, and his first Gestapo assignment (as early as 1933) was to try to arrange the liquidation of Gregor Strasser. Few papers have been either left behind or yet discovered about him, and the one eyewitness account of him, a biography, *Where's Nebe?*, is by his close personal friend and associate, Hans Bernd Gisevius, who is not known for absolute accuracy or impartiality, who was for a time in the Gestapo himself and doubtless had to make compromises, and whose portrait of Claus von Stauffenberg is a masterpiece of character assassination.[2] German historians I talked to remain unsure about Nebe but are inclined not to give him the benefit of the doubt. On the other hand, after his arrest following the 20 July 1944 attempt, he endured two months of torture without giving anyone away before they executed him.

Blaskowitz's protests against the atrocities in Poland were smothered by Keitel, but Groscurth had obtained a secret, detailed report from the general, which he used when on an official tour of inspection to the western commanders in mid-December 1939. Though they were outraged by what they heard, it was still not enough to sway them into action. Meanwhile, as the western offensive continued to be delayed, so the German Army grew stronger. The arms factories did not cease to produce the weapons of war, though among the population standards of living began to decrease and Führer worship had distinctly lost its edge.

The early part of 1940 saw the Resistance in the doldrums. Despite all their efforts, their emissaries abroad had made little progress and at home the generals were as intractable as ever. A typically German fatalism was engendered in some, a sense that Hitler was the country's lot and had to be borne until destiny saw fit to remove him. At least there was comfort in the fact that, historically, no such reign of terror had lasted very long. Seven years had gone by since Germany had been plunged into dictatorship, and now a war of similar length seemed inevitable.

But such a prospect was intolerable to most. A visit by the American Under-Secretary of State, Sumner Welles, was scheduled for the first week in March. This gave the Resistance a glimmer of hope. Perhaps even now American diplomatic intervention would bring a solution for peace.

It would be nice to believe that Sumner Welles's visit was due at least in part to the efforts in America of the young Adam von Trott zu Solz, who had by now worked for several months tirelessly in the interests of the Resistance, but it is unlikely.[3]

He was the son of an old Hessian family so ancient that they had given their name – Trott – to the wood which grew near their castle of Solz. Adam was born in 1909 at nearby Imshausen, which he loved, and which was his home all of his short life. He came from a solid line of public servants, and had one American grandmother. He was very tall (six foot four), and his rapidly receding hairline made him look older than he was, but he was a handsome man and he had a smile which Christabel Bielenberg, wife of his best friend Peter, thought he should not be allowed to use on any unattached woman without accepting the consequences.

Trott grew up speaking all but fluent English and looked set to embark on a career in the family tradition of public service, but after taking his final university examinations in Germany he elected instead to go to Oxford, where he had spent a term in the late twenties and where he now returned as a Rhodes Scholar, going up to Balliol College in autumn 1931. Balliol was then still a power-house for British intellectuals, and Adam made many friends who were later to become either famous or influential. They became contacts in his work for the Resistance and some, like David Astor, who went on to be editor of the British Sunday newspaper the *Observer*, did not fail him. Three who did were the academics Maurice Bowra and A. L. Rowse, both of whom stabbed him in the back after hostilities had broken out, and the future politician Richard Crossman.

Trott was still at Oxford when Hitler seized power, news which affected him deeply, as David Astor remembered:

> Trott's first reaction, as I recall, was gloom, tempered by challenge. I remember a walk in the country when I told him that if he defied the Nazis they wouldn't answer him with arguments. I tripped him up and pushed him to the ground to suggest what they would do . . .[4]

Trott returned to Germany at last in August 1933, breaking off his Rhodes Scholarship two thirds of the way through, and after brief spells in Hamburg and Berlin settled back in Hessen, where he took up a career in public law. It quickly became clear to him that the process of law as he understood it was on the brink of fundamental disruption by the Nazis, and all his worst fears about them were confirmed. However his misgivings were balanced by his natural (and deep) patriotism, and he could accept the good qualities of Nazi social policy, especially as it affected the rural life which surrounded him:

> Children were taught how to wash themselves and how to brush their teeth; parents were taught that milk was more wholesome for babies than beer; the peasants as a whole, who had been living on a diet of starch . . . were taught to grow vegetables which up to then had been enjoyed only in towns.[5]

Although he did not join the Party, and remained true to his anti-Nazi stance, Trott bridled slightly at the anti-German posture taken by some of his British friends. This friction led to misunderstanding and in some cases alienation which would not help him in his missions to Britain on behalf of the Resistance, but which were perhaps insignificant against the backdrop of growing tension of the time. Meanwhile he continued with his work in the law, and prepared a selected critical edition of the works of Heinrich von Kleist, a famous German author who died in 1811. The edition got into some trouble with the authorities, as Trott had sought to use the angle of the selection and some of his commentary as covert criticism of the regime. Nevertheless the book was published, but not before Trott had moved to Berlin where he met, and was greatly influenced by, Ewald von Kleist-Schmenzin, a descendant of Heinrich von Kleist.

He worked in the office of the lawyer Paul Leverkühn, who later became head of the Abwehr in Istanbul. Among others in Berlin, he met Hans von Dohnanyi, Klaus Bonhoeffer and Louis P. Lochner, the American head of the Associated Press Bureau in the capital.

Work, however, was not going well, and it is likely that Trott felt himself to be in limbo. He may also have felt stifled in Germany, and despite his new contacts and his antipathy to the regime, he had not yet fully committed himself to the Resistance. He had always been attracted by travel, and he still had one year of his Rhodes Scholarship to go. He decided to use it while he still had the opportunity, and elected to go to China, travelling via the USA and Canada, in 1937–38, taking a teaching post at Yenching University in Peking. It is possible that he may have considered staying abroad, though his future behaviour bears out that he was as fatally drawn to Germany and to fighting the enemy from within as Dietrich Bonhoeffer. In any event he returned late in 1938, having at least had the benefit of distance from which to view the problem of Hitler's Germany, and to consider how he might serve his country without serving the present State.

Through a cousin, Hubertus von Weyrauch (who had introduced Ian Colvin to Ewald von Kleist-Schmenzin), Adam von Trott zu Solz got to know Walter Hewel, an intimate of Hitler's who now served as the dictator's liaison officer with the Foreign Office. Hewel was pro-British and against war, and agreed to send Trott to Britain both to sound out his excellent British contacts and to prepare a confidential report for the Führer on the morale and general mood in England. At the same time, Trott strengthened his personal links with the German Foreign Office.

He made three trips to England in the spring and early summer of 1939, staying mainly at the Astors' homes at Cliveden in Hampshire and St James's Square, London. However, he was playing a dangerous double game, and not only from the German point of view. His visits, though made on his own initiative, had been organised with Hewel's help, and looked at least semi-official. It was no wonder that his former friends looked on him askance, and his troubles were compounded by his inability to express the difference between his ambitions for his country and his association with the Third Reich. Nevertheless, on his return he was able to draw up a report (which was translated into Nazispeak for Hitler's benefit by Trott with the help of Dohnanyi and his friend Peter Bielenberg) aimed at pretending to be positive while discomfiting the Führer. It presents Britain as determined to fight, confident of American solidarity, and totally opposed to the forcible annexation of neighbouring lands and the violation of neutrality.

The report had no effect on Hitler, but by the autumn Trott was engaged in a similar mission to America, under the auspices of attending a conference of the Institute of Pacific Relations at Virginia Beach. Here again he was well endowed with contacts. He knew the British Ambassador, Lord Lothian, from his Oxford days, and he had the backing and collaboration of the eminent German journalist Paul Scheffer and the former German Chancellor, Heinrich Brüning, both now in exile. At first things went well. Scheffer wrote a memorandum, to be presented under Trott's name, which took the form of a request to the Allies to outline clearly and publicly their war aims. Germany should not be made to feel unduly threatened, or the atmosphere for a successful coup could not be created; but if the country were made to feel that, after the collapse of Nazism, it would be accepted and made welcome as an equal in the commonwealth of nations, and not stigmatised as the eternal ne'er do well, then the Resistance would be able to go to work with confidence.

This document was presented to George Messersmith, the Assistant Secretary of State in the State Department. At first Messersmith was enthusiastic, and he certainly recommended Sumner Welles to read the memorandum. But then the old doubts began to appear: if Trott were permitted to leave and return to Germany freely, how far could he be trusted? FBI agents were set to tail him. Then Felix Frankfurter got hold of a copy of the memorandum. Frankfurter had also known Trott since Oxford, and had been warned by Maurice Bowra that he was not a man to be trusted. Frankfurter, a member of the Supreme Court and a Zionist, was not further endeared to Trott by the 'sound but tactless advice' he received from him that Jews should keep a low profile in anti-Nazi propaganda.[6] By the time Trott left for Germany in January 1940, he had not quite mortgaged all trust – Messersmith told Alexander Kirk at the US Embassy in Berlin to keep channels to him open – but none of his missions can be regarded as successful, and Trott was aware of this himself. After America joined the war in 1941, he was regarded as a Nazi double agent by the US authorities. In Germany, he was looked upon with equal suspicion, and was not able to take a job in the Foreign Office until June 1940, despite all

Weizsäcker's efforts to get him on board. Once there, however, he was able to continue his Resistance activities unabated.

At the beginning of March 1940, Hitler presented a new proposition to the Armed Forces. This time he was to take complete control himself, however, and manage the operation through Overall High Command, ignoring Army High Command.

For some time he had been brooding about Stalin's attack on Finland. It was very possible that the Allies might take aiding the Finns as a pretext for entering Norway. Once there, they could attack Germany from the north, and from there they could also hamper the supply route of Swedish iron-ore to Germany. On the other hand, if the Germans took it, the fjords could be used as naval bases. Denmark would provide air bases for the Luftwaffe, and provide a bridge to Norway, at the same time securing the Baltic.

Hitler announced the date for so-called Exercise Weser on 27 March 1940. On 1 April Liedig was briefing Oster on the state of play. Oster, hugely frustrated, said to him: 'I simply don't understand the British. How can they be so blind? Surely they can see that a show of force would send Hitler packing . . .' The following day he went to Sas and told him that the invasion of Denmark and Norway would take place immediately after the first week of April – between the 8th and 10th. Sas told not only The Hague, but also informed Goethals, and went to see the Norwegian legation counsellor and the Danish Naval Attaché. The Dane informed Copenhagen, but Stang, the Norwegian, dismissed Sas's information as nonsense. In fact, Stang was a supporter of Quisling, the Norwegian Nazi leader. But in the end it was Britain and France which distracted the attention of the Scandinavian states. On 5 April the Allies accused Norway and Sweden of materially aiding Germany, and warned them against taking a pro-German stance. On 8 April, British minelayers were at work along the Norwegian coast. The German Fleet and troop transports were already at sea. Oster, with a touch of Goerdeler's optimism, bent over the map and said, tapping it, 'The British Navy will engage us about here. They'll defeat us, that'll be the end of Emil [Hitler], and we'll be able to negotiate a peace.'

But the minelayers had finished their work, and the British Fleet arrived too late. Cruiser Squadron 1 was still loading on 7 April at the Firth of Forth as a German squadron passed out of the northern end of the Kattegat. On 9 April the Germans made their landings according to plan. Denmark fell in a day. Norway collapsed in a month.

With this totally successful act of aggression the Resistance saw their chances of negotiating with the Allies slip even further away. At the same time, Hitler's triumph suppressed all the more forcefully any hope of a successful coup. It was impossible to predict the reaction of the masses, and his string of easy victories with minimal loss of life was head-turning. Hitler had gained more territory for Germany with less difficulty than Bismarck himself. Obstacles seemed to melt away at his touch. Only one slender possibility of a favourable outcome remained – that war with France could be averted. But this expectation was beginning to look more like wishful thinking.

Plans for the invasion of France had been on the table for some time. The Blitzkrieg technique had proved successful, and there was no sign that the French had adapted their defences to it. Reconnaissance flights had also shown that the French were not as strong as had been supposed. Now it was well into spring, and Hitler's patience was at an end. After a row with Göring about waiting for the right weather conditions for fighters and bombers, the Führer set the time and date for invasion, in deep secrecy, for 5.35a.m. on 10 May.

Contrary to forecasts, 9 May was a beautiful day all over Europe. Oster sat it out grimly. All the Resistance could hope for now was a last-minute cancellation, the code word for which was 'Augsburg' which could be given only by Hitler from his special train. The dictator had set out from Berlin in the late afternoon, ostensibly to visit units in Denmark and Norway. But at Hamburg the train had changed direction and headed south to Hanover, due east of which lay Holland. The change of direction could mean only one thing.

If the 'Augsburg' signal had not been given by 9p.m., Operation Yellow could not be called off. Oster and Sas met at the former's flat at 7p.m. Both men's nerves were taut. At 8.30p.m. they could stand the waiting no longer and took a taxi to Tirpitzufer. Sas waited downstairs while Oster ran upstairs to the Abwehr offices. Twenty minutes later, he returned, his face set.

'My dear friend, it's all up with us at last. There's been no counter order. The bastard's gone off to the West Front; it's all over. Let's hope we meet again after the war.' He added bitterly: 'Blow up the bridges over the Maas for me.'[7]

EIGHT

Holding On

As soon as he had the news, Sas communicated it to his own authorities and to Colonel Goethals. At midnight he received a lightly coded message from The Hague to enquire if there really were to be no change in the arrangements for 'the operation on your wife'. Sas told them it would take place in under six hours. But the Dutch did not take the warning seriously, and even the Belgians did not mobilise until 3a.m. The German forces swept over them, driving the British Expeditionary Force, severely depleted, back across the Channel, and decimating the French units which had fought alongside it. General Hoth raced along the north coast of France, while Generals Guderian and Kleist (the latter a cousin of Ewald von Kleist-Schmenzin) headed south and east, smashing through the Ardennes. Paris fell on 14 June, the French capitulated on 22, and hostilities ceased on 25. Hitler ordered that church bells be rung throughout the Reich for a week in celebration. He also created twelve new field marshals – ironically, among them were Leeb and Witzleben – nineteen colonel-generals, and seven generals. Göring now became the first and only 'Reichsmarschall' of the Greater German Empire.

The Resistance now entered a long period of abeyance. The phoney war was over, and the new conditions that ensued made it much more difficult to meet, to plan and to carry out any attempt at a coup. Quite apart from anything else, many conspirators were simply kept too busy with their regular duties to contribute; others were posted far away, or to the Front; others decided that now they had to make Germany their priority, and fight for their country rather than against its leaders. Gisevius expresses the dilemma well:

> The opposition had to consider its stand in the new situation. A
> man might have fought bitterly against Hitler's insane war policy,
> but now the war was there. How was he to react towards it? As an
> oppositionist? As a patriot? As a European? Or as none of these, but
> quite simply as a soldier whose business it was to obey orders?
>   Let us not forget that totalitarianism and opposition are mutually
> exclusive political ideas. In a democracy it is possible to practise
> opposition, but dictatorship permits no antagonists . . . Opposition
> is a struggle against an existing regime; it is an attempt to bring
> about a shift in course or a change in personnel, without directly
> overthrowing a system . . . The people of a nation [subjected to
> evil dictatorship] must take upon their conscience the tremendous
> burden of devoting all their imagination and zeal to the purely
> destructive activities of underground work . . .

As far as peace negotiations were concerned, it soon became clear
that any hope of temporising with Britain was gone too (that is,
for the Nazis, though the Resistance continued – vainly – to try to
talk terms at least). Early in May 1940 the belligerent and ambitious
Winston Churchill, leader of a rebel faction within the Conservative
Party, staged a coup of his own and forced the waning Chamberlain
out of office. Chamberlain died, worn out, soon afterwards.

As he had shown in his treatment of striking workers early in
his career, Churchill was an aggressive man whose chief approach
to problems was to fight them head on. Hitler was a problem. Now
that Churchill was Prime Minister, he would fight him. That was the
way to get rid of him. Though crude and intemperate, Churchill was
the perfect match for Hitler, and perhaps the only man who could
have united the will of the British at this isolated moment in their
history. Hitler certainly feared him.

Despite the loss of momentum, the spirit of the Resistance was
kept alive through a number of groups and individuals. Several people made, or at least thought very seriously about, an assassination
attempt on Hitler.[1] In 1938, the Swiss theology student Maurice
Bavaud had tried three times to get a shot off at Hitler, making him
the one man other than Stauffenberg to make more than one attempt.
He was caught, and executed in 1941. In 1939 the British Military
Attaché, Colonel F. Noël Mason-Macfarlane ('Mason-Mac', as he is
affectionately remembered by his friends) quite seriously suggested

to the British government that he should take a shot at Hitler from the
window of his flat at 1 Sophienstrasse, because it conveniently overlooked the Führer's platform opposite the Technical High School,
from which Hitler frequently made speeches.

There were two other remarkable lone attempts to undermine
Hitler by less direct means. Albrecht Haushofer was the academic
son of a famous professor at Berlin University. Professor Karl
Haushofer enjoyed a close friendship with Rudolf Hess, Hitler's
ill-fated deputy, and the family thus had a certain degree of protection, which was important because Frau Professor Haushofer was
part Jewish. Albrecht was on the staff of the Foreign Office. His
father was the founder in Germany of the science of geopolitics,
and Albrecht, a great traveller himself, had a very close knowledge
of Britain. He was therefore in a better position than most to see
that a world war threatened. He tried to use his own influence with
Hess to block the promotion of the warmongering Ribbentrop and,
though he failed in this, Hess approached him in September 1940
with a view to making peace overtures to Britain. Hess suggested
that a meeting on neutral ground – possibly in Lisbon – might be
set up between himself and Haushofer's acquaintance, the Duke of
Hamilton. The proposal entailed much discussion, but finally a letter
was dispatched to the Duke, who did not, however, reply. In the
course of time Operation Sealion – the planned invasion of Britain
– was dropped and German attention once more turned towards an
eastern campaign, but in the spring of 1941 another possibility arose
for Haushofer to communicate with the British, this time via a Swiss
contact. Hess was not against the idea, but it came to nothing. The
crux of this episode was that Hess, a man of very limited intelligence,
developed an *idée fixe* about the Duke of Hamilton. On 10 May 1941
he set off on his famous flight to Britain, with the idea of contacting
the Duke, and through him seeking an audience with King George
VI.

Haushofer had nothing to do with this mad scheme, but his
association with Hess was known and now, with Hess's protection
gone, the Gestapo arrested him and went through his papers. He was
released, but his reputation was severely damaged both at home and
abroad, where he had painstakingly sought to send out peace feelers.
The regime never trusted him again, and like so many others he was
re-arrested following 20 July 1944. In prison he wrote a sequence of

sonnets which are well-known in Germany, one of which celebrates the fortuitous death during an air raid of the infamous Nazi hanging judge, Roland Freisler:

> But yesterday he sent four to their deaths,
> And today he lies dead in the ruins himself.
> He'll send no more to meet the rope or axe;
> A pile of rubble's all his office now.
>
> . . .
>
> Justice by chance? A thousand bombs descend
> On this great city, killing high and low –
> Was one bomb used by Destiny as its judge?
>
> . . .

Haushofer was killed on the same April night, and in the same group, as his friend Guttenberg.

A lonelier course was taken by the young mining engineer Kurt Gerstein. His story is a unique one in the history of the Resistance, and does not fit in easily, but it is a tragic illustration of moral paradox.[2]

Kurt Gerstein was found hanging in his cell at the Cherche-Midi prison in Paris on 25 July 1945, a fortnight before his fortieth birthday. His whole life had been an inversion. His profound Christianity had driven him to join the SS to expose it from within; but his technical expertise had condemned him to a job at the very centre of its rotten heart.

He came from a conservative, traditional family in Münster, where the values of obedience and stoicism had been bred into him from childhood. Obedience was not something to which he was inclined naturally, but he grew up conventionally, though his attachment to the Evangelical Church was noticeably passionate. At the end of 1933, despite having already joined the SA, Gerstein sent two telegrams protesting against the disruption by the Nazis of German evangelical youth work, in which he was deeply involved. The recipients of these, Nazi Youth Leader Baldur von Schirach and State Bishop Ludwig Müller, did not react, but the early protest was a courageous one. Further moves against the Church compounded Gerstein's outrage, and as Nazi skulduggery all round him became unbearably evident, so there grew within him a need to bear witness to the crimes of the regime which would not be denied.

In Hagen in 1935, the local Roman Catholics demonstrated at a performance of the anti-Christian play *Wittekind* by Edmund Kiss. The riot was quashed by the police. The following day, Gerstein booked a front-row ticket and from it conducted his own solo demonstration. In the fight which followed he lost several teeth. Although the introduction of the Nuremberg laws against Jews does not appear to have affected him (he came from a conventionally, but not violently, anti-Semitic background), he did help one Jewish convert friend to continue his theological studies. His reaction to further depredations by the Nazis on the Church was always extreme. His stance for what he saw as purity, and against Nazi obscenity, was fanatical, and yet friends remember a man who had a good sense of humour and a great capacity for irony.

He was first arrested in 1936 for organising the First Congress of the Miners' Association of the Saar, and though the Confessing Church, with which he was closely associated, interceded for him and prevented his imprisonment, he was dismissed from the Party. His dominant father forced him to apologise and recant. All his older brothers and his father were by now Party members. Not belonging was a severe hindrance to a career. He obeyed, but nevertheless continued his fight, through pamphlets and publications which he financed from the private income he derived from the family firm in Düsseldorf. Significantly, one series of pamphlets was called 'Of Honour and Purity', in which he was clearly trying to square his conscience and beliefs with Nazi ideology, but he was re-arrested in summer 1938 and accused of monarchist plotting. By now he was married and had started a family.

He was sent to a concentration camp for six months, but was then released owing to lack of evidence. Although his father continued to support him, Gerstein became depressed and pessimistic. He had used up his private supply of money on his pamphleteering, and had not been in work for a year. An attempt to take up medical studies foundered, as did another to read theology. Finally, with the help of a powerful industrialist, Hugo Stinnes Jnr, he got a job in a potassium mine in Thuringia in the summer of 1939.

His spirits lifted slightly, but the comfort was not to last. His sister-in-law, Bertha Ebeling, of whom he was very fond, became one of the early victims of the Nazi euthanasia programme at one of the centres in Hadamar and Grafeneck. These centres, supervised by the former CID chief of Stuttgart, Christian Wirth, who was to go on to run one of the death camps in Poland, were to be the first to use gas chambers disguised as shower rooms. Bishop Galen's sermons against the programme followed soon after.

This event triggered Gerstein's plan to join the SS and become a 'spy for God', though the idea seems to have been with him since the end of 1939. He joined in March 1941 and because of his engineering background and his smattering of medicine they allocated him to the Medico-Technical Service of the Waffen-SS Group D (Hygiene), which was working on water disinfection systems for front-line troops and prisoners of war. Stationed at Arnhem, he contacted an old Dutch friend and immediately confided his plans to him. By now he was committing a number of crimes against the State – he listened to the BBC, for example, and read banned books. He was also convinced of the need for Germany to lose the war. Nevertheless he received a glowing report at the end of his SS training period, and when it was discovered by the Party that he was an expelled member, the SS refused to let him go because of his invaluable technical knowledge.

That was at the end of 1941. Early the following year his friend Helmut Franz described Gerstein as 'a bundle of nerves made up of hate, fear and despair'. It will be remembered that in January 1942 the plan for the Final Solution was drawn up. In June Gerstein, by now head of Technical Disinfection Services of the Waffen-SS, became involved in the work of the extermination camps. His role was to improve their efficiency.

He was considered an expert in cyanide disinfectants. One of his first experiences of the camps was at the side of Christian Wirth, at Belzec. There he was able to witness the procedure of gassing people with carbon monoxide. The Jews were stripped and crammed into a shed, into which exhaust fumes were fed by pipes. It then took the technical team at the camp two hours and forty-nine minutes (it was timed exactly) to get the big diesel started; a further thirty-two minutes were needed for all the people in the shed to die. Wirth, a champion of carbon monoxide over the far more efficient Zyklon-B, the new crystallised cyanide gas originally developed for disinfection purposes, was embarrassed and upset.

As a cyanide expert, Gerstein could pronounce shipments of Zyklon-B (which quickly replaced carbon monoxide as the killing method) useless because it degenerated in transit, and no one questioned his word; but he could not do this with every shipment and he could only delay and disrupt, not prevent, the slaughter. There were four camps in Poland specifically dedicated to slaughtering Jews, not including the massive death factory of Auschwitz-Birkenau and other concentration camps with smaller gas chamber complexes. He was caught in a terrible trap, but he did not commit suicide, or apply to be sent to the East Front, or seek refuge in alcohol, as some SS men did. He stuck to his mission.

Returning by train from Warsaw to Berlin at the end of his first tour of duty to the camps, he fell in with Baron von Otter, the thirty-five-year-old secretary to the Swedish Legation, and told him the whole story of what he had seen, begging him to report it to the Swedish Government and to the Allies. Von Otter was sceptical: Gerstein had no proof, no photographs, and he was wearing the uniform of an SS Obersturmführer (lieutenant). For a referee, Gerstein gave him the name of Otto Dibelius, a leading cleric in Berlin who was closely associated with the Confessing Church. Von Otter duly made a report to his government, but it was suppressed because the Swedes did not want to damage their trade relations with Germany.

Gerstein did not stop at von Otter. He was convinced that once the German people knew what was going on, and especially where the clothes handed out to the poor as part of Hitler's annual Winter Aid campaigns came from, they would spontaneously rise against their Nazi masters, but it was to no avail. He could not even get a rumour started. Nor did an approach to Diego Cesare Orsenigo, the pro-Nazi Papal Nuncio, meet with any more success. Nevertheless he continued, doggedly, obsessed with what he had seen. Confidence in a British reaction to the news relayed via von Otter faded: Gerstein had hoped the RAF might drop leaflets over Germany. By the end of 1942 the Allies certainly knew from other sources of the existence of the camps and their purpose, but did nothing.

Gerstein, who with his clean-cut features looked the model SS man, even acted the part. His camouflage was almost too good. To observers at Auschwitz he appeared 'brutal', and 'a very typical SS officer'. Under the surface, he was falling apart. The stress of the double game, common to all the conspirators, was telling on him, but he had to bear it alone, and bear it he did, still telling anyone he thought he could trust, and who might be able to relay the information abroad, about what he was seeing every day in the camps. His consistent failure never deterred him; this was a mission he was locked into. From 1943 to 1944, the height of its operational period, he was in charge of deliveries of Zyklon-B to Auschwitz from the German pest control company which manufactured it.[3] He continued his efforts at sabotage, but in the end his position made it impossible for him not to aid the system. As a lieutenant, he could not even dent the massive machinery of death, as the horrific statistics of the camps show.

By the winter of 1944–45 he was desperately ill – but by then the work of the camps had been done. The gas chambers of Auschwitz were dismantled that winter and the camp evacuated in January.

March 1945 found Gerstein with his family in Tübingen, a pretty university town south of Stuttgart. He managed to surrender to the French a month later, who treated him well until he came under suspicion of complicity in the Final Solution and was transferred to Cherche-Midi, where he was kept in conditions of harshness and squalor for which the French prison system at its worst was notorious.

After his death he was condemned by the Tübingen Denazification Court in 1950, not so much for his complicity as for his inability to have effected a better Resistance. He was not rehabilitated until 1965.

While Gerstein was fighting his lonely and doubtful battle, much of the time of other larger groups of the Resistance during the war was spent in discussion, and of planning for the future when the war (as most Resistance leaders realised) would be lost and the time came to rebuild Germany. Such planning served a dual purpose: Germans are great theorisers, and this was the time when many intellectuals started to develop their constitutional plans for the new state which would emerge. The planning was also therapeutic, a means of escape from the awfulness of having to accept that Hitler, despite every effort, had succeeded in every one of his aims, and was now more firmly in the saddle than ever. He had not, after all, lost popular support and, for those who disagreed with him, the growing number of concentration camps waited. At the same time the efficiency and scope of the various police forces in the service of the state grew.

One way in which the Resistance could still operate practically was through its unceasing contacts abroad. The group within the Foreign Office was still able to travel to neutral countries; Gisevius was in place in Zurich, where Canaris had organised a position in the consulate for him. The other group in a position either to facilitate foreign travel or act as couriers was that inside Lufthansa. Dr Otto John was a lawyer who worked as a legal adviser to the company, and he was in close association with the head lawyer, Klaus Bonhoeffer, brother of Dietrich.

Klaus Bonhoeffer was quite unlike his brothers and sisters. He was physically much darker, more south European in his looks. His godson Klaus, the son of Hans von Dohnanyi, remembers him as a 'jovial man, who loved the Mediterranean, and was full of life'. His passion was travelling, and he visited all the countries of Europe; but his favourite place was France. Its language and its culture were spiritually his own.

He was against Hitler from the very beginning, pointing out that such tyrannies as his should be nipped in the bud, but the setbacks of the Resistance did not shake him. Above all he was in a unique position as a middleman between his brother-in-law Dohnanyi in the Abwehr, his brother Dietrich in the Confessing Church, and the Lufthansa group.

To close the family circle, Otto John's brother Hans worked for Dr Rüdiger Schleicher, a senior civil servant in the Ministry of Aviation, and head of the Institute for Aeronautical Law at Berlin University. Schleicher was another of the Bonhoeffers' brothers-in-law. Otto John had worked with the group around Canaris and Oster in the Abwehr since before the war, and went on two missions to Madrid in the course of 1943 to establish contact with the Americans. One of these concerned another colleague at Lufthansa, Prince Louis Ferdinand.

Prince Louis Ferdinand was the second son of Crown Prince Wilhelm, and a grandson of Kaiser Wilhelm II, who died in 1941 at Doorn, near Arnhem in Holland, where he had spent most of his years in exile following his flight from Germany in 1918. There were various monarchist Resistance groups, including one in the south which proposed to put one of the Bavarian Wittelsbach kings back on the throne, but the most serious contenders for the role of constitutional monarch in a resurrected, post-Nazi Germany came from the old and dominant Royal Family of the Hohenzollerns. Early on, a group within the Resistance made up of Oster, his associate Friedrich Heinz, the deputy police chief Fritz-Dietlof von der Schulenburg, and, for a time at least, Goerdeler, had considered the idea of replacing the National Socialist regime with a constitutional monarchy along British lines. However it is likely that they would have adopted the more democratic system of proportional representation, despite the difficulties this had created for the Weimar Republic, rather than the 'first past the post' system used in Britain, whereby a Party can form a government without the mandate of the majority of the people.

At first their choice fell on Prince Wilhelm, the older son of Crown Prince Wilhelm. He seemed to have every noble quality, but he was also – which was an advantage – unadventurous, and lacked personal ambition. Equally, he was modern in his outlook, and a supporter of democracy. Unfortunately, Prince Wilhelm lost hope of a restoration of the monarchy after war had broken out. He was killed on active service in France on 26 May 1940, and his heroic death made such an impression on the public that 50,000 people attended his funeral in Potsdam. Such popularity raised the hopes of the Resistance, but at the same time it so terrified Hitler that he forbade any member of any of the old reigning houses to serve in the Armed Forces from then on.

Beck was the most respected leading member of the Resistance, and his name had been written down as the potential President of a new democratic republic in which Goerdeler would be Chancellor; but neither man had popular appeal. After the death of Prince Wilhelm, the thoughts of the Resistance turned to his younger brother.

Louis Ferdinand, like Wilhelm, had excellent credentials: he had been brought into the Resistance at the age of thirty in 1937 by Otto John, in whose department at Lufthansa he worked, and whose protégé he was. He had contact with Dohnanyi and the Bonhoeffers, but also with Kurt von Hammerstein, Goerdeler, the Catholic Resistance conspirators Josef Wirmer, a lawyer; Jakob Kaiser, of the Catholic Trade Union Movement; and Justus Delbrück, the brother of Karl Bonhoeffer's wife Emmi and another Resistance worker in the Abwehr. Louis Ferdinand was also a progressive liberal, and had strong connections in the USA where he had worked for Ford in Detroit for five years. Personal opinions of him are hard to pin down. Goerdeler's biographer Gerhard Ritter speaks coolly of 'a man to whom life seems in the main a kind of sport', but others are much more generous. Sir John Wheeler-Bennett, one of the earliest chroniclers of the Resistance, who had the opportunity to interview many of the surviving participants soon after the war, positively glows in his praise.

He certainly had qualities to bind the various disparate elements
of the Resistance together, from progressive liberals and left-wingers
to young aristocrats, conservative senior officers and older politicians. But, alas, this was to prove another blind alley. When Louis
Ferdinand asked his father's permission to be put forward as potential
head of state, and his father refused it, the young man acquiesced to
his wish. It was 1943 by then. All was clearly lost. There was nothing
more for it but a long slog to the end, and many Germans, not least
in the ranks of the Resistance, were becoming fatalistic.

Among the Catholic conservatives in the Abwehr who supported
Louis Ferdinand was Karl Ludwig Freiherr von und zu Guttenberg.
Guttenberg's contribution to the Resistance was the production of
a literary magazine, *White Pages*, which survived from 1934 until
1943.

The purpose of *White Pages* was to keep the human spirit of the
Resistance going, to remind people that there was another Germany
– the Germany of Goethe and Schiller, of Hegel and Schopenhauer,
of Bach and Beethoven. Contributors were all critical of the regime,
but in their articles, especially those which dealt with elements of
German history, they were able to give vent to their criticism without
fear of trouble from the Gestapo. This was not a unique idea – several
academics had escaped into their work in this way, producing papers
so erudite that they went right over the Nazi censors' heads. There was
an anti-Nazi group of philosophers in Frankfurt which was left alone
throughout the war for this reason. Not that all Nazis were stupid,
but at the street level of policing they left much to desire. There is
one story of a Gestapo raid on an academic's house: during it, one of
the policemen noticed a book on archaeology lying on a table. Picking
up only the 'arch' part of the word, he bellowed: 'Ah! So you're an
anarchist too!' Nazi rule was yob rule.

White Pages appeared as a monthly subscription magazine (the list
of its subscribers was destroyed by the Gestapo after 20 July 1944),
and during its life Guttenberg not only ensured that no reference to
National Socialism ever appeared in it, but that it pushed anti-Nazi
opinion to the limit without openly expressing it. This it did in what
appear to be delicate, but were in fact very brave, ways. For example,
in the 'Letters to the Editor' section, published letters were not signed
off with the prescribed 'Heil Hitler', but with 'Yours faithfully' or
'Yours sincerely'. Such things were more than enough to lead to

difficulties with the printer, but Guttenberg could charm the birds from the trees.

Contributors included Ulrich von Hassell and Klaus Bonhoeffer. For a young officer like Axel von dem Bussche, who was later to make his own bomb attempt on Hitler, the magazine was a turning point. He was introduced to it by Fritz-Dietlof von der Schulenburg. Beck and Goerdeler were on the consultative board of the magazine, whose meetings served as cover for conspiratorial discussions. Guttenberg himself never contributed a line, though he was an intelligent young aristocrat with a great interest in journalism. His real strength was the spoken word, and his flair was for creating contacts, many of which grew from the seeds of university friendships. In his own close circle were Nikolaus von Halem and Herbert Mumm von Schwarzenstein, who were to be involved with Beppo Römer in their own misguided attempt on Hitler's life.

With the outbreak of the Second World War, *White Pages* became a quarterly, to conform (as did all other magazines) with paper rationing. This restriction however was a help, since the editorial staff were being reduced by conscription anyway. Guttenberg himself was recruited into the Abwehr by Canaris in 1940, and from there continued to use his network of contacts in the service of the Resistance. He was especially close to the group around Goerdeler and Beck. But he continued to run *White Pages*, which closed in January 1943 only because of the acute paper shortage in Germany. When it did so, the wave of letters he received was a tribute to his achievement. All the magazine's readers felt themselves bereft, and much lonelier in the Nazi world without it. It was a loneliness Guttenberg himself was soon to feel. Oster temporarily posted him to Agram (Zagreb) for his own safety. From the spring of 1943 onwards he led the life of an exile. He was arrested in the great purge following 20 July 1944, and was murdered with many friends by the SS as the bombs fell on Berlin at the end of April 1945.

Among the groups of intellectuals who tried to keep the spirit of free expression alive, and who would have subscribed to *White Pages*, one of the most prominent was the Solf Circle. It took its name from Hanna (Johanna) Solf, the widow of a former ambassador to Japan. His memory was held in such high regard by the Japanese that they interceded with Hitler to spare his widow's life after the 'teatime discussion group' she belonged to had been infiltrated and betrayed to the Gestapo in September 1943. The group met regularly for tea at the Berlin homes of either Frau Solf or her friend, Elisabeth von Thadden. Its purpose was to find out humanitarian ways of countering the regime. Elisabeth von Thadden was a Christian educational reformer who, when her girls' school near Heidelberg was closed down by the Nazis in 1941, joined the Red Cross. In the course of her work with it she learnt that the Gestapo were destroying letters sent home by German prisoners of war, on Hitler's orders, on the grounds that they might undermine morale. In fact the Nazi top brass wanted to keep alive the myth created by themselves that the Russians took no prisoners.

Other members of the group included Nikolaus von Halem, Herbert Mumm von Schwarzenstein and the former diplomat in America, Karl Otto Kiep. Kiep was a very important man in the Resistance. Now holding the rank of major in the Reserve, he headed the Foreign Policy Desk in the Overall Command of the Armed Forces (OKW), and was a link between Overall Command and Weizsäcker's group in the Foreign Office. The Solf Circle, though relatively harmless in itself to the Nazis, had members whose contacts elsewhere were of the first importance to the Resistance.

The Gestapo informer responsible for exposing it was Dr Paul Reckzeh of the Charité Hospital. He had got an introduction to Frau von Thadden through a mutual acquaintance of known anti-Nazi views who lived in Switzerland. She in turn invited him to accompany her to a meeting of the Solf Circle on 10 September 1943, at which he heard enough to encourage him to have phone taps put on each of those present. He also offered to deliver a letter for Frau von Thadden to Professor Friedrich Siegmund-Schultze, a German who had emigrated to Switzerland soon after the Nazis came to power. He was connected to the World Council of Churches there, an organisation which the Gestapo correctly believed to have contacts with the Resistance.

Very soon after this, a prominent member of another Resistance group, the Kreisau Circle, von Moltke, was tipped off about the phone tapping order and passed the warning on. Once the Gestapo realised that this had happened, they moved in and made their arrests.

Nearly all the participants were executed during the purge that followed 20 July 1944, though by then already in prison. As will be seen, the repercussions of the breaking of the Solf Circle had even wider implications for the Resistance.

The Kreisau Circle was a much more important part of the Resistance than the Solf Circle. It was so called by the Nazi Security Service during their investigation of it after 20 July 1944. The name comes from the estate of Helmuth James Graf von Moltke, one of the group's leaders. It is now Krzyzowa in Poland.[4]

The name the Gestapo gave it is misleading, for it gives the impression of an organised, coherent group, with definite aims. This is not true. The circle, which met formally at Kreisau only three times, was a large, loosely knit group of people who came mainly from the young landowning aristocracy, the Foreign Office, the Civil Service, the old Social Democratic Party and the Church. Its membership shifted and changed, and for a long time its leaders were averse to taking action of any kind against Hitler, preferring instead to let him run his course – a matter which they considered inevitable – while in the meantime they discussed what sort of Germany they would rebuild after his equally inevitable fall. Its most useful practical function was as a forum where members of different Resistance centres who also belonged to it could exchange ideas and information. It may also be described as the cradle of the government of the New Germany that might have been if the 20 July 1944 Plot had succeeded.[5]

There were perhaps twenty core members of the circle, and they were all relatively young men. Half were under thirty-six and only two were over fifty. The young landowning aristocrats had left-wing ideals and sympathies – within reason – and created a welcome haven for leading Social Democrats who had elected to stay in Germany, and survived several years in camps like Dachau. Men like the journalist-turned-politician Carlo Mierendorff, and, after his death, Julius Leber, were the political leaders of the group, and their ideas struck lively sparks off older members of the Resistance like Goerdeler. Church contacts included Bishops Preysing and Wurm.

At the heart of the group sat two young aristocrats, Helmuth James von Moltke and Peter Yorck von Wartenburg, both descendants of famous early nineteenth-century Prussian generals. They have been described respectively as the head and the heart of the circle, and certainly it was with the arrest of Moltke early in 1944, following his attempt to warn the Solf Circle that it had been infiltrated, that the Kreisauers fell apart.

Moltke was a thirty-two-year-old lawyer when the war broke out, and he joined the International Law sector of the Abwehr. Throughout the war years he wrote from Berlin to his wife Freya almost daily, and the correspondence, saved by a miracle from the Gestapo, now forms one of the most delightful and interesting records of that time.[6] He was a very tall man, even taller than von Trott, at six foot seven. He enjoyed cooking, and he shared cultural interests with the friends he made in Berlin before the Nazis came to power: Bertolt Brecht, Carl Zuckmayer, the architect Adolf Loos, Arnold Schönberg and Rudolf Serkin. His mother, Dorothy Rose Innes, was the daughter of the South African Minister of Justice. Moltke spent some time there before the war, spoke English fluently, and dabbled in journalism, contributing articles to such papers as the *Chicago Daily News*, for which he was assistant Berlin correspondent for a time before 1933.

He was opposed to Nazism from the start, and spent long parts of 1934 and 1935 looking for jobs abroad. Later he was to use his English contacts in yet another vain attempt to persuade the British to collaborate with the Resistance. He never once wore a uniform, and, with Canaris, he fought hard against the mishandling of Russian prisoners of war and against the use of the *Einsatzgruppen* behind the front line in the East. Through his office he did his best to help Jews in occupied territories. He met the more right-wing Peter von Wartenburg in 1940. Three years his senior, Wartenburg, who was a cousin of Stauffenberg, had originally had a certain sympathy for the Nazis, but quickly became disaffected, and as early as 1937 became the centre of a series of discussions held by a circle of friends which became known to the Gestapo as the 'Counts' Group'. Also a lawyer, Wartenburg worked for the Overall High Command in the Economics Division, Eastern Theatre of War.

The first meetings of the group – often no more than two or three people at a time attending – were held in Moltke's tiny Berlin flat. Among the earliest members were Adam von Trott zu Solz, whom Moltke had met in London in 1937, and Adolf Reichwein. Reichwein was a philosopher, teacher, educationalist and traveller of prodigious intellect who was later to associate himself closely with Julius Leber, the man whom Stauffenberg wished to see become Chancellor. Reichwein was in Berlin working at the Folklore Museum, a post he had been allowed to take up after the Nazis had obliged him (as a socialist) to resign from his teaching job in Halle. Once in Berlin, he was able to build up his own network of socialist Resistance contacts, and it was through him that the left-wing journalists Carlo Mierendorff and Theodor Haubach joined the Kreisau Circle. The other important left-winger in the group was the trade unionist Wilhelm Leuschner, who by reason of his seniority (he was born in 1890) was given the nickname 'Uncle'.

Leuschner had already been in the camps, arrested after the German Trade Union Congress was shut down in 1933. The chairman collapsed under the harsh treatment dealt out to him and Leuschner, his deputy, was nominated to take over by his fellows on the executive committee while they were all still in custody and did not know what the future held. He was ordered to accompany Robert Ley, the head of the Nazi German Labour Front which replaced the trade unions, to Geneva, to place Ley's credentials before the International Labour Organisation. He agreed to do this on condition that his colleagues be released, which they were, but once there, he refused to say anything at any meeting. Offstage, as it were, Leuschner told his foreign colleagues exactly what the situation was at home, and Ley got a frosty reception. Leuschner was arrested the moment he recrossed the German frontier. He was released in 1934 before the next meeting of the ILO, as the Nazis wished to avoid adverse publicity relating to him.

Back in Berlin, he was able to take over a small factory in a working-class district which manufactured beer barrel taps.

> This business gave him a good pretext for travelling all over Germany, visiting in particular the inns which local unionists had used as meeting places. He further got an exclusive licence for using a special non-corrosive type of non-ferrous metal. Screws made of this rapidly became important for types of naval and air armaments, enabling him to invoke the help of the Armed Forces if anyone threatened to interfere with his production.[7]

Leuschner's 'cover' was similar to that used by Leber, who had also been through the camps before the war and now lived in Berlin running a small coal haulage business. Both men were arrested in the purge following 20 July 1944 and later executed, but their contribution to the ideas factory of the Kreisau Circle was inestimable, and they are two of the most important men lost to postwar German politics.

Their names appeared constantly on potential Cabinet lists drawn up by the Resistance.

Karl Ludwig von Guttenberg was a member of the Circle, and he provided a very important link with two Munich Jesuits, Augustin Rösch and Alfred Delp. Delp's role was to sound out for Moltke the possibilities in the Catholic community of support for a new, post-Nazi Germany.

Another great friend of Guttenberg, Ulrich Wilhelm Schwerin von Schwanenfeld, had great-grandparents in common with Schulenburg. Like him, he had joined the Party, but never from conviction. His aim from the outset had been to oppose the regime. He knew Haushofer, and in 1920 at the age of eighteen he had been given riding lessons by Oster. It was through Oster that Schwerin obtained a staff posting with the Brandenburg Division in Berlin in 1943 – a division earmarked for use in any subsequent coup.

Representing the evangelical side of the Church was Eugen Gerstenmaier. Dr Gerstenmaier was perhaps a less spiritual man than Father Delp, though by extreme adroitness in his defence at the trial after his arrest he convinced Roland Freisler that his very unworldliness exonerated him from the death penalty.

Unable for political reasons to get a university teaching post after his doctorate, Gerstenmaier became an official in the foreign affairs department of the Evangelical Church in Berlin and then worked in the Information Section of the Foreign Office. He was in close contact with the Ecumenical Council in Geneva, and with the World Council of Churches and its president, W. A. Visser't Hooft, both of which organisations provided channels of communication to the outside world. He was one of the earliest members of the Church to recognise the necessity of killing Hitler, and in 1940 worked out a plan, with Fritz-Dietlof von der Schulenburg, either to arrest Hitler or shoot him at a victory parade in Paris on 20 July 1940. Hitler did not, however, take part in that parade, making only a single brief visit to the French capital in the early hours of one morning. Exactly four years later, in the confusion and disappointment that reigned in the Armed Forces administrative headquarters in Bendlerstrasse as it became clear that the coup had failed, Gerstenmaier pushed the participating Army officers hard to see it through, carrying a Bible in one hand and a pistol in the other.

Schulenburg also belonged to the Kreisau Circle, though he regarded its 'discussion group' mentality with scepticism. His view was
that Hitler should be removed and an interim military government set
up; then the work of constructing a new administration could begin.
He was right, in that the long political-philosophical papers produced
by the Circle look very like 'escape into theory', using up energy and
intellect that might have been better employed developing concrete
plans. Even Moltke, at the centre of the Circle, wrote to his wife in
August 1942 that a ninety-minute speech by the liberal former head of
the State Committee of German Youth Organisations (now subsumed
within the Hitler Youth), Hermann Maass, had sent several of his
listeners to sleep – though he added that Maass had shown what a
firm understanding he had of the workers' movement. In fairness to
the Circle, they saw themselves, at least initially, less as a Resistance
group than as an underground political Opposition. In any case under
Nazi law they were committing high treason.

Schulenburg's early attraction to the Nazi Party had been born
of disaffection with the shambling and ineffective Weimar Republic,
whose dying days he experienced when he was in his late twenties. But
he quickly saw what lurked behind the Nazi mask, and by 1937 he had
joined Wartenburg's 'Counts' Group'. Wartenburg was godfather to
Schulenburg's only son.

Schulenburg was police vice-president of Berlin from 1937 to
1939, and in 1940 he joined the famous Infantry Regiment 9 in
Potsdam. Near the Front in the east in 1940 and 1941, he witnessed
Jews being killed wholesale in the little Polish town of Brest-Kujawsk,
and noted dead Jews lying in the gutters of Białystok. A year later
he was on Manstein's staff in the Crimea, when, during the assault
on Sebastopol, he heard a report of the mass machine-gunning of
Jews behind the lines. He complained to Manstein about it, and the
Field Marshal replied irritably, 'Schulenburg, I'm in the middle of
a major artillery battle – these matters must wait.' In the context it
is interesting to remember that Manstein was an adopted child. His
own family name was Lewinski, and a tradition persists that he was
the great-grandchild of a rabbi. In an Order of the Day posted as late
as 11 November 1944 he stressed the need to 'suppress the Jews, the
spiritual carriers of the Bolshevik terror' as harshly as possible.

Schulenburg subsequently served in various administrative departments in Berlin, and was thus able to serve the Resistance as an

information gatherer and go-between. One of his most significant achievements in Infantry Regiment 9 was the recruitment of young officers to the cause: at least three of them, Ludwig von Hammerstein (son of Kurt), Ewald Heinrich von Kleist (son of Ewald von Kleist-Schmenzin) and Axel von dem Bussche, were to play highly significant roles later on. He also established close links with the commander of 23 Division in Potsdam, Walter von Brockdorff-Ahlefeldt, who as we have already seen was involved with the Resistance under Witzleben. Schulenburg's friend Cäsar von Hofacker, who was also a cousin of Wartenburg and Stauffenberg, later became the contact man between the Resistance in Berlin and the Army Group in Paris under Stülpnagel. A very large number of contacts within the Resistance at this level was based on family ties and friendships formed at school, cadet school or university.

'The social structure of the active Opposition was comparatively homogenous,' notes the German historian Hans Mommsen.

> Its members were predominantly upper class and regarded them-
> selves – unlike the 'dilettante regime' which they combated –
> as personally qualified to assume a leading role. There was no
> significant distinction between bourgeois and socialist. Reichwein,
> Mierendorff and Haubach were not merely typical Social Democrat
> intellectuals, Leber was the complete opposite of a socialist official,
> and Leuschner and Maass had succeeded in discarding inhibitions
> of class as a result of their political activities and their experience
> under National Socialism . . . With the exception of Leuschner,
> there was no one in the Opposition who could be regarded as a
> typical representative of the Weimar Republic.

One forward-looking younger member of the Resistance who significantly held himself aloof from the Kreisau Circle was Hans von Dohnanyi. He held that Goerdeler's and Moltke's constitutional plans were illusory, unhistorical and not remotely realistic for the future. Fear of democracy on account of the failure of the Weimar Republic made for ultra-theoretical and impracticable plans.

Kreisau itself was a small village, but the locals, who were surprised that their 'squire' (Moltke) and his family were not Nazis, would never have dreamt of betraying them. The only thing Freya ever got when she said 'Good Morning' rather than 'Heil Hitler', was a crisp and admonitory 'Heil Hitler' in return. The long flow of letters from Moltke – though he was always careful not to mention Resistance matters even obliquely – was equally easy to watch over and protect from informers or spies. The postmistress in Kreisau was dependable and, both at Berlin and Kreisau, the recipients of letters knew exactly when the post would arrive. (Despite the vengeful bombing strategy of Sir Arthur 'Bomber' Harris, which involved the selection of civilian targets, the German postal service operated with miraculous efficiency until 1945, when central Berlin was reduced to a pile of rubble.)

The first of the three major meetings at Kreisau took place in May 1942. Among those present was the thirty-nine-year-old clergyman Harald Poelchau, who was later to fulfil a role which was sad and ironical – as chaplain in Tegel Prison and Plötzensee Prison, Berlin, where most of the principal conspirators were either beheaded or hanged between August 1944 and April 1945. In a letter to Freya written in May 1943, Moltke arranges for a hundredweight of peas to be sent from his little estate to Poelchau, to help him feed his flock of 'U-boats' (Jewish and political fugitives in hiding).

The meeting discussed such important matters as rebuilding the constitution, reform of the education system, and the relationship between Church and State. It begat a number of essays and, ultimately, a series of draft constitutions, based on a pyramid of power sharing by elected representatives in a one-party state. Despite the left-wing sympathies of several members of the Circle, the voices of the Social Democrat politicians who joined the Circle later, and the relative youthfulness of the participants, there was no time here for a democracy along multi-party lines. It is curious now to read the constitutional plans of the Kreisau Circle – they seem to come from a distant age. However, such plans were theoretical, and would have been adapted if faced with the possibility of implementation. No doubt if the 20 July 1944 coup had succeeded, and Julius Leber become Chancellor with Stauffenberg's backing, a more hardheaded democratic process would have emerged.

Though succeeding Mierendorff as the political conscience of the Circle, the practical working-class Leber had little time for their theorising and suspected them of being fundamentally undemocratic. He attended meetings only occasionally and one suspects that very shrewdly he was using contacts in the Circle for his own ends – much, one suspects, as the equally practical Stauffenberg would when he 'joined' the group later in the war.

The second session was held that October, following intensive individual discussions between the socialists Mierendorff, Leuschner and Maass, and the Jesuits Rösch and Delp, which touched on finding common ground between Christian and socialist trade unions. Fundamental state and social questions were discussed. It was followed by the third and final major discussion at Whitsun, 1943, which tackled the themes of foreign policy and the punishment of war crimes. By that time, the war was clearly lost, and the thoughts of the Kreisauers were turning more towards the idea, already mooted by Goerdeler and Beck, of a European Community which might possibly have Germany as its centre.

Earlier in the year, in January, there had been a famous confrontation at Wartenburg's Berlin apartment in Hortensienstrasse between the 'young' conspirators of the Kreisau Circle, and the 'old' members grouped around Goerdeler, including Hassell and Jens Jessen.

Beck chaired the meeting, which lasted until 1a.m., and became heated. Moltke even accused Goerdeler of trying to find a solution along the lines of Kerensky, the Russian revolutionary who paved the way for, and was then deposed by, Bolshevism. Essentially the Goerdeler group supported the restoration of traditional trade unions (Goerdeler and Leuschner were great friends) whereas the Kreisauers, disaffected by what they perceived as worker/manager divisiveness, favoured co-operative works councils. Both sides agreed in the matter of individual responsibility, but the Kreisauers laid greater emphasis on the importance of the community. The Kreisauers were less nationalistic than the Goerdeler group, and more realistic about what kind of frontiers Germany might expect to have to make do with in the event of any peace settlement. The Kerensky jibe stemmed from fear that Goerdeler, if put in power, might not be radical enough. It may also be that he was regarded as too old, and too rooted in nineteenth-century thinking, by the younger Kreisauers.

The two sides parted friends, sitting down to pea soup and cold meat when the arguments were over, though Gerstenmaier remembered that Goerdeler had been condescending, and that Moltke had been prickly with Trott zu Solz and himself, the original engineers of the meeting. The fact was that both sides shared a common disadvantage: they were locked inside the Reich. Men like Gisevius, living in Switzerland, had a much clearer view of the march of world events.

Colonel-General Friedrich Fromm, commander of the Reserve Army, might have played a crucial role in the Resistance. In the end he betrayed it; but his final reward was to be executed by Hitler for cowardice.

Werner von Blomberg, for a time Hitler's War Minister and nicknamed 'The Rubber Lion', with, on his right, Werner Freiherr von Fritsch, and left, the Nazi Admiral Erich Raeder, in 1934.

Field-Marshal Walther
von Brauchitsch,
Commander-in-Chief of
the Army, 1938–1941.

Hitler in conference with his generals in June 1941. On his
left is Franz Halder, Chief of the General Staff, 1938–1942.
Brauchitsch is on his right, and on the far right stands Field-
Marshal Wilhelm Keitel.

Martin Niemöller, the former U-Boat captain who, as a Protestant pastor, became one of the most prominent members of the Church's Resistance, and endured many years in concentration camps.

Dietrich Bonhoeffer, the young theologian who came to represent, perhaps more than anyone else, the Church's Resistance, following Niemöller's incarceration.

Clemens August Graf von Galen – Bishop of Münster, and known as 'The Lion of Münster'. He preached an influential series of sermons against the Nazi 'euthanasia' programme.

Bartolomäus (Bartel) Schink – a sixteen-year-old leader of the Cologne Edelweisspiraten, and one of the regime's youngest victims: he was hanged at Ehrenfeld on 10th November 1944.

Helmuth Graf von Moltke
at his trial in Berlin,
thirteen days before his
execution on 23rd January
1945.

Peter Graf Yorck von
Wartenburg, who with
Moltke led the influential
Kreisau Circle, which
provided a forum for
discussing Germany's
constitution after the fall
of Nazism.

Sophie Scholl, with two fellow members of the White Rose –
her brother Hans on her right, and Christoph Probst.

Sophie Scholl in happier
times. Her anti-Nazi
pamphleteering as a
student at Munich
University would lead to
her arrest and execution
there in February 1943,
aged 21.

The diminutive Admiral Wilhelm Canaris, head of the Abwehr, was one of the leaders of the Resistance; his key role was to liaise between the Secret Service, the Army and the Foreign Office. He also protected the activities of Oster and Dohnanyi.

Hans von Dohnanyi, the incisive young lawyer who compiled a vast dossier of Nazi crimes, in anticipation of a successful coup. He worked closely with Oster, and his arrest in 1943 robbed the Resistance of one of its most brilliant lights.

Perhaps the most important member of the Resistance, General Hans Oster – who disdained to wear a uniform he considered besmirched by its association with Nazism – worked tirelessly against the regime from his department in the Secret Service: a lonely and highly dangerous task.

Adam von Trott zu Solz, the lawyer and diplomat who sought throughout the war to maintain and develop links with contacts abroad for the Resistance, using his own highly placed British connections, and his position at the German Foreign Ministry.

Ewald von Kleist-Schmenzin, one of the leaders of the conservative Resistance to Hitler. Executed in the wake of the failure of the 20th July Plot, he had advised his son Heinrich to make the suicide-bomb attempt on Hitler.

Ewald-Heinrich von Kleist-Schmenzin, right, who volunteered to kill Hitler by carrying armed bombs in his own greatcoat pockets and at the critical moment grasping the Führer in a deadly embrace, talking to a fellow member of the Resistance, Kunrat Freiherr von Hammerstein-Equord.

Colonel-General Kurt Freiherr von Hammerstein-Equord, an early member of the Resistance within the Army, and Commander-in-Chief, 1930–1934, in his Berlin garden in 1940 with his son Kunrat and a Japanese guest.

Fritz-Dietlof von der Schulenburg with his wife and four of his children. Schulenburg was a disabused Party member who was able to use his position as Deputy Police President of Berlin to act as a highly effective liaison officer for the Resistance.

The mayor of Leipzig,
Carl Goerdeler, worked in
Hitler's 1934 cabinet
before joining the
opposition to him. Never
losing his belief in the
power of words, he
worked with Ludwig Beck
on two major treatises,
and led the Civilian
Resistance until the very
end.

Julius Leber, the journalist and Social Democrat politician, at
his trial in Berlin following the failure of the 20th July Plot.
Leber was Stauffenberg's candidate for Chancellor in the
event of a successful coup, and arguably one of the great
politicians lost to postwar Germany. He was executed on 5th
January 1945.

Colonel-General Ludwig Beck, Chief of the Army General Staff, 1935–1938. After a forty-year career as a professional soldier, this scholarly, ascetic man became in retirement the leader of the military Resistance to Hitler.

An unlikely-looking hero? Lieutenant Ludwig Freiherr von Hammerstein-Equord was in the forefront of the plot against Hitler and was Beck's ADC-elect in the event of a successful coup. His intimate knowledge of the geography of the Bendlerblock enabled him to avoid capture after the debacle of 20th July 1944.

Field-Marshal Günther von Kluge – 'Clever Jack' – photographed here before his promotion in the uniform of a Colonel-General. Kluge never found the courage to join the Resistance, nor could he refuse Hitler's bribes. His support might have been crucial. In disgrace as France fell, he committed suicide in August, 1944.

Field-Marshal Erwin von Witzleben, Commander-in-Chief-elect and after Beck the leading senior officer in the military Resistance. Surrounded by policemen at his trial, he was hanged on 8th August 1944.

Erich Hoepner at the Volksgericht on 7th August 1944. Members of the Resistance were often dressed in deliberately demeaning clothes for their trials, but even Hitler's remorseless hanging judge, Roland Freisler, considered it too much that Colonel-General Hoepner should be obliged to appear in court in a hand-me-down cardigan.

Hitler greets General Fromm at the Wolfsschanze on 15th July 1944, five days before the most famous attempt on his life. Its perpetrator, Graf Stauffenberg, stands to attention next to Fromm, while to Hitler's left Keitel, with folder, looks on.

Henning von Tresckow, fourth from right, at a conference
with officers of his staff. On the extreme right, with
spectacles, is Fabian von Schlabrendorff.

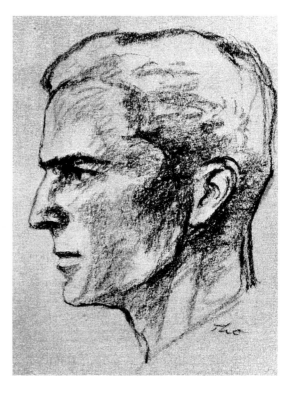

Claus Graf Schenk von
Stauffenberg, prime mover
of the German Resistance
from late 1943, and its
most famous member.

The devastated conference room at the Wolfsschanze after
the bomb attempt on Hitler's life on 20th July 1944.

Hitler shows Mussolini the damage caused by Stauffenberg's
bomb. Immediately after the attempt, Hitler was said to be
euphoric with relief. He was virtually uninjured and
continued with his day's schedule as planned.

In 1941, Beck and Goerdeler had produced a massive essay called 'The Goal'. A statement of their belief and their view of the function of a State, it began with a long analysis of German history and German political development, culminating in Bismarck's 'Golden Age', as they saw it. It looked to Britain with admiration for the way it had developed and run its Empire, and suggested that this was because the English, living within the scope of the Gulf Stream, were a people more blessed by nature than the Germans. At the same time, 'The Goal' looked forward to a federation of European nations under German leadership 'within ten or twenty years'. This idea might not have appealed to the Allies in 1941.

Eleven points followed, pleading the case for the restoration of German colonies and 1914 frontiers, requesting agreement on multilateral disarmament, and warning against the Japanese as potentially 'dangerous competitors'. International agreement was called for on the establishment of a Jewish state, possibly in Canada or South America. Clearly from this and other provisos it was desirable from Goerdeler's point of view to remove Jews from Germany; but on the other hand the authors made no attempt to duck responsibility for the atrocities which had already been carried out against the Jews by Hitler. Otherwise, as far as domestic politics were concerned, a plan was laid out by which human rights and freedoms would be guaranteed. Certain restrictions, such as quite a mature age, are laid on the right to vote, and some of Goerdeler's references to the innate superiority of what he calls 'the white race' strike a modern ear as odd, but, taking such points in their historical context, the document is a fundamentally good blueprint for a benign, conservative rule.

Moltke's first constitutional draft, also composed in 1941, was far more historical and theoretical than Goerdeler's, which is couched in very urgent language. Indeed, what is most striking about Moltke's work is that he does not seem to have been motivated by circumstances to take a more urgent line. He seems detached, even fatalistic. But this would concur with the Kreisau Circle's initial line of *laisser aller*, something which Moltke clung to longer than his associates. He was never wholly persuaded that the assassination of Hitler was the only solution. Nor, interestingly, was Goerdeler. Another Kreisauer, Hans-Bernd von Haeften, a Foreign Office official, took the severest line in opposing an attempt on Hitler's life. He succeeded in dissuading his younger brother Werner from making an attempt himself – on

religious grounds. The headstrong Werner, who was Stauffenberg's
ADC, did however accompany and abet Stauffenberg in the attempt
on 20 July 1944.

A later essay by Beck and Goerdeler, 'The Way', appeared in
1944. Significantly, their fellow contributors included Julius Leber,
Wilhelm Leuschner, and the Catholic trade unionist Jakob Kaiser.
This was a historical review in three parts, Imperial Germany, Repub-
lican Germany, and Totalitarian Germany, which attempted to trace
what had gone wrong. It offered more generous explanations for the
failure of the Weimar Republic, blaming the French for too harsh an
interpretation of the Treaty of Versailles and the crippling burden of
reparation payments; but in one sense 'The Way' is an indication of
how hard the Resistance was still trying to justify its own existence
to itself.

By 1943 Moltke was living with the Wartenburgs, his own flat having been bombed. He may have reflected sadly on this. In December
1940 he'd read in *The Times* of London (the Abwehr got all foreign
papers) that the Inner Temple law courts where he had studied as a
young man had been bombed: 'The bomb hit the dining hall where I
used to eat . . . In the photograph I even recognised one of the Inner
Temple waiters . . .'[8]

The war weighed deeply on this sensitive and intelligent man.
Two extracts from his letters written in the autumn and early winter
of 1941 indicate both his state of mind and what induced it:

> In one place in Serbia two villages have been reduced to ashes,
> 1700 men and 240 women from amongst the inhabitants have been
> executed. That is the 'punishment' for a [partisan] attack on three
> German soldiers . . . [he goes on to list further atrocities in France
> and Greece] and that is child's play compared with what is happening
> in Poland and Russia. How can I learn of such things and still sit at
> table in my warm flat, drinking tea? Am I not making myself an
> accessory by doing so? What would I say if someone asked me later:
> And what did you do during that time? . . . Since Saturday they've
> been rounding up the Berlin Jews; they're picked up at 9.15p.m. and
> locked in a synagogue overnight. Then they're sent, with only what
> they can carry, to Litzmannstadt [Łódz] and Smolensk. A female
> acquaintance of [Karl Otto] Kiep saw a Jew collapse on the street.
> As she went to help him, a policeman stopped her, gave the prone
> body a kick, so that he rolled into the gutter, then he turned to the
> lady with what appeared to be the vestiges of shame and explained:
> 'We're only obeying orders, ma'am.'

In the second extract he mentions 'a nerve clinic where SS men are cared for whose minds have collapsed through having to shoot women and children', and Bishop Preysing later remembered Moltke telling him of an incident on a tram. There was a nurse on the tram and she was very drunk. Moltke helped her off at her stop. She said to him, 'I expect it horrifies you to see me like this.'

He replied, 'No, not horrified; but I'm sorry to see someone like you in such a state.'

She told him, 'I work in an SS hospital, and there the sick, the men who cannot shut out what they have done and seen, cry out all the time, "I can't do it any more! I can't do it any more!" If you have to listen to that all day, you reach for the bottle at night.'

1941 was the year when the European War became a World War. Hitler invaded the Soviet Union on 22 June 1941 and later, in December, after the Japanese bombed the American fleet anchored at Pearl Harbor, he also declared war on the United States. He had been rebuffed by Churchill, underestimated the strength of the Royal Navy and the Royal Air Force, and been forced to withdraw Operation Sealion the previous autumn. But by the end of 1940 the dictator was supervising preliminary plans for Operation Barbarossa – the conquest of Russia. Never mind that this was where Napoleon had come unstuck; Napoleon had neither the technology of a modern army at his disposal, nor Hitler's genius. The technique of Blitzkrieg which had served him so well so far would do so again. He would knock out Leningrad (St Petersberg), make a quick advance to Moscow and take it, and neutralise major industrial centres such as Stalingrad (Volgograd). The country would be paralysed, all her vast natural resources would be in his power, and he would be invincible. Besides, his own ideology taught that the Russians were mere sub-humans with no fight in them. His agrarian scientists were already planning how the rich wheatfields of the Ukraine could be better utilised and farmed by a whole new generation of German colonists.

Before he could move, however, he suffered setbacks at home. Mussolini made disastrous attempts at taking Greece and Egypt, and had to be bailed out by the terms of their treaty. Hitler could not afford to lose Italian support yet, however useless it was turning out to be. To make matters worse, Yugoslavia refused to allow German troops transit through to Greece, so the Yugoslavs had to be taken over too, thereby using up more valuable manpower. Nevertheless, four panzer groups, commanded by Guderian, Hoepner, Hoth and Kleist, were ready to roll by June. Either Stalin's Intelligence had been seriously faulty or he refused to heed warnings; either way, the surprise element of the attack was entirely successful.

The Russian campaign was the most bloody and bitterly fought of the war. The Soviets lost 20 million men – a tenth of the entire population of the Soviet Union – and hundreds of villages and towns were razed to the ground. Almost from the start the very landscape was against the Germans – Hoepner's advance on Leningrad failed in part because this was not the terrain for tanks, and to the south Hoth's advance on Minsk was similarly impaired by sandy tracts of land and dense forests. In the end, Hoepner's tanks were withdrawn, and German and Finnish infantry settled in for the long siege of Leningrad. Minsk was taken, and Guderian and Kleist drove into the Ukraine, but, as autumn brought torrential rain, more problems began. The Germans were now faced with the difficulty of maintaining a front of nearly 1500 miles, from Leningrad to Rostov-on-Don, which in places was up to 600 miles deep. Seventy-five per cent of the German Army was committed here, comprising its best divisions. This was a very big gamble.

That the Germans held on at all is a testimony to their doggedness and courage. They were not equipped for the severity of a Russian winter, with temperatures of well below −25° Celsius. Hitler, who had run the campaign personally from the first, almost without consultation, would not hear of retreat. When Guderian and Hoepner withdrew their troops for sound humane and tactical reasons, both were dismissed in disgrace. An attack ordered on Moscow in the depths of winter ground to a halt in the suburbs of the city on 5 December. The city never fell to Hitler.

Guderian was subsequently recalled; Hoepner was not. Already allied to the Resistance, Hoepner had never had any faith in the assault on the USSR, telling his ADC: 'This can't be true: it'll be our hara-kiri.'

His Number 4 Tank Group was ordered away from the Leningrad Front in mid-September 1941 to join the attack on Moscow. After fighting his way south-eastwards, by November he could see no chance of a successful conclusion of the campaign that winter and requested permission to retreat, secure winter quarters and batten down. This was refused, and Hoepner could see that if he continued to follow the Führer's orders he would be cut off by the Russians coming behind him at Borovsk, Kaluga, near Moscow. He struggled with his conscience for a long time before deciding that his duty to his men took precedence over his obedience to Hitler. On 8 January 1942 he gave the order to withdraw. He was relieved of his command the following day. By now the diktat of the Führer-order was in place: Hitler's word was absolute law, in accordance with the Führer-principle. The dictator saw himself as nothing less than god on earth. It is strange that so few people stood up to such a manifest lunatic; but the nation was now firmly locked into war, and many of the generals were torn between fighting for their country and the attendant obligation of fighting for Hitler. More and more of them closed their minds to the implications of defending Nazism along with Germany. Unified action by the generals could have stopped the war at any time; but any hope of creating the necessary unity – if it had ever truly been possible – was vain by now.

In his farewell address to his troops Hoepner said, 'I have been in the Army since my youth and as I have learnt a sacred duty to the German soldier, I feel that my obedience is owed to a higher authority than any on earth. At any time I would repeat the action which has led to my dismissal.'

This dismissal was another smack in the face for the Army, for Hoepner was summarily dismissed, without benefit of a hearing or a court martial. He was deprived of his right to wear uniform – a singular dishonour – and of his pension (though the latter punishment was later rescinded). He retired to Berlin, now a confirmed and dangerous enemy of the Reich. Immediately he took up contact with the military Resistance there, and became a regular attender at Wednesday Club meetings. Beck briefed him to take over the Reserve Army in the event of a successful coup.

Hoepner's commanding officers did not stand up for him against Hitler, who by now had added the title of Commander-in-Chief of the Army to his other titles. On 6 December von Brauchitsch, who had suffered a series of heart attacks, tendered his resignation. Hitler's response was that he was too busy to pay attention to such petty matters at that moment; but on the 19th Brauchitsch's retirement was duly announced. Hitler told Halder that although he would remain as Chief of Staff, all administrative functions relating to Army High Command would be transferred to Keitel. Halder's job therefore had no meaning any more. He did not resign, however, but continued to attend strategy meetings, and courageously kept up his criticism of Hitler's increasingly erratic plans. Finally Hitler had had enough. On 24 September 1942 Halder was dismissed in one of Hitler's not infrequent High Command reshuffles. His nerves were shattered, but he had managed to be a thorn in the flesh of the Führer, and also something of a restraining influence. In the round-up following 20 July 1944, he was arrested and interrogated, but sent to a VIP barrack in a concentration camp. He survived the war.

The winter of 1941–42 saw a change in Army High Command following the departure of Brauchitsch. Two generals who had long been a source of irritation to Hitler, von Leeb and Witzleben, were retired – the latter on grounds of ill health which had plagued the ageing soldier for years, but which did not prevent him from continuing to be of service to the Resistance.

Despite Stalin's counter-attacks – he had hoped that 'General Winter' would help drive the Germans out of Russia as it had the French in 1812 – the German Army held its line, and in June 1942 could even launch a new campaign of its own. Hitler's purpose was to secure the Baku oilfields in the Caucasus, as those of Romania were no longer supplying enough for him. The idea was that Hoth's panzer army would drive the Russians back to the line Voronezh-Stalingrad and hold them there, while Kleist drove south-east down to Baku, occupying the land between the Black and Caspian Seas. Throughout the summer the campaign went well, but, ominously, by the end of August 1942 it had become bogged down. Stalingrad proved almost impossible to take. The city straddled the River Volga and the Russians could send reinforcements across every night: they were never driven back to the east bank completely. But Hitler was determined to hold on to what he had of the city, even though Kleist's advance had ground to a halt to the south as a result. More and more troops were poured into the Stalingrad cauldron, to no avail, and, as not enough German divisions were available, weaker units of Hungarians, Italians and Romanians were used. The Russians counter-attacked in mid-November, stronger both on land and in the air, as well as being used to, and fully equipped for, fighting in conditions of deep snow and freezing cold. The Romanian armies protecting either side of the city crumbled immediately and the Russians had the city surrounded within three days, encircling twenty-two divisions – 250,000 men – of the German 6th Army. Hitler ordered them to stand firm, and told Hoth to break through to relieve them. This was a mistake because Hoth could not organise a relieving action until mid-December, by which time the Russians had the city firmly in their grip. Soon afterwards they smashed the remaining Italian and Romanian armies in the area. A plan by Göring to relieve the city by air proved to be as vainglorious as its proposer, marking the end of Göring's already shaky career. At last, Hitler ordered Hoth and Kleist to retreat to lines they could defend. The 6th Army was left to its fate but ordered to fight to the last man. On 2 February 1943 its commander, Field Marshal Friedrich von Paulus, finally surrendered. There were only 90,000 survivors. Nazi propaganda gave it out that *all* had died in a glorious action on behalf of the Fatherland.

Before Stalingrad, Hitler had been at the peak of his power, his dominion stretching from the Atlantic to the Black Sea, and from the Baltic to the Mediterranean. The orders to Hoth and Kleist to retreat were the first such orders he had ever given. On 30 January 1943 he celebrated the tenth anniversary of his seizure of power, but it was the beginning of the end now, as everyone but the Führer and his most fanatical acolytes realised. The Resistance, however, still felt a moral duty to try to bring him down. Perhaps Germany might yet be saved from the wreck of the Third Reich.

Since 1939, when the pact between Stalin and Hitler was concluded, the Communist Resistance in Germany had been in abeyance. Hard-line ideologues held that anything the Soviet Union did must ultimately be in the interests of world Communism, but ordinary workers with serious socialist views could not go along with such a blinkered point of view. After the outbreak of war with the USSR, issues once again became clearer, though efforts to make reasonable contact (as Trott tried to in 1943) with such extravagant revolutionary figures as Alexandra Kollontai, Russia's ambassadress in Stockholm, whose taste for high living was notorious, came to nothing.

At home, several groups made their presence felt. A many-branched organisation had centred itself since the late thirties on the Berliner Robert Uhrig, who succeeded in making Berlin a core of Communist Resistance until the early forties. His contacts spread not only to workers' underground organisations in Hamburg, the Ruhr and the

industrial south, but also to the group run by Beppo Römer and even
to the Goerdeler group. Their activities involved the distribution
of anti-Nazi literature and industrial disruption, especially in the
armaments industry. Uhrig himself, a lifelong Communist born in
1903, worked in the radio-valve testing department of the Osram
Company, and was clearly a master organiser, though the ultimate
effectiveness of his network in denting the Nazi machinery must be
doubted. It did establish a great sense of solidarity among disparate
groups however. But, because of its sprawling nature, it was relatively
easy for the Gestapo to infiltrate the Uhrig group. Uhrig was executed
in August 1944. He had been arrested in 1942 with Römer, who was
killed immediately. Their ultimate plan had been to establish a Soviet
state after the collapse of National Socialism.

The other group which stemmed from the workers' movement
and which gave Hitler pause during the war years was that led by
a young Jewish electrician called Herbert Baum. Most of the group
were Jewish skilled workers employed in the Jews Only sector of the
Elmo factory in Berlin. Baum worked there from 1941.

The main function of the group, once again, was the dissemination
of anti-Nazi literature, a dangerous and expensive business, especially
in wartime. The group financed itself through burglary. As Jews and
Communists, the Baum group were taking quite extraordinary risks.
Their finest hour, however, was yet to come.

After the outbreak of hostilities with the Soviet Union, the German
Propaganda Ministry was not slow to set about slandering the image of
the USSR in every way possible. In spring 1942, in the Lustgarten,
a large square in central Berlin, the Nazis set up an exhibition called
'Soviet Paradise', at which life in Russia was held up to sarcastic
criticism. (They had done the same with the 'Degenerate Art' of
banned painters in Munich in 1937 – unfortunately for them, that
was the most popular exhibition the Nazis ever staged.)

On 17 May, following a meeting at which a leaflet campaign
to coincide with the planned 'action' was organised, Baum and
several friends visited the exhibition, managed to distribute small
bottles of inflammable liquid in corners, and set the place on fire.
The fire, which was seen by the group as of symbolic significance
– they wanted to demonstrate disapproval, not involve innocent visitors in a conflagration – was quickly put out, but the plan had been
betrayed to the Gestapo and most of the group were arrested during

the following week. Baum himself, in order to avoid the torture which might compel him to betray more of his friends, committed suicide in Moabit Prison on 11 June. He was just over thirty years old. Five hundred Jews were arrested in Berlin. One hundred and fifty of them, together with another hundred already in Sachsenhausen concentration camp, were shot out of hand as part of the 'vengeance' exacted for the assassination of the SS leader Reinhard Heydrich in Prague, which had recently been carried out by Czech partisans. The rest were sent either to Sachsenhausen or to another camp at Theresienstadt (Terezín) near Prague.

There was a third Communist group working in Berlin in the early forties. It was associated with the leaflet campaign planned by the Baum group to coincide with the firesetting at the Soviet Paradise exhibition. This third group was the most important, and its base was in the heart of Göring's Air Ministry. Its main function was to process secret military information and relay it to the Russians. For this reason, a long controversy has existed about whether its members were indeed members of the Resistance to Hitler, or simply Soviet spies and traitors to their country.

The group, which later came to be known by the nickname the Gestapo gave it, the 'Red Orchestra', was run by two married couples, Arvid Harnack (who was related to the Bonhoeffers) and his American wife Mildred; and Harro and Libertas Schulze-Boysen.

The 'Red Orchestra' in fact had two wings. One fed information to the Russians, but the other was a very widespread Resistance organisation, involved with pamphleteering and discussion groups. It had a high and disparate membership. One typically detailed Gestapo report, discussing the 118 arrests which followed the breaking up of the group in 1942, spoke of '20 per cent professional soldiers and civil servants, 21 per cent artists, writers and journalists, 29 per cent academics and students, and 13 per cent workers' among them. The group produced a regular magazine, *Inner Front*, and established contacts both abroad and with foreign forced labour in Germany.

Boysen, whose volatile marriage to Libertas Haas-Heye was the subject of much gossip, had always been an opponent of Nazism. In the early thirties he worked for an important national revolutionary magazine called *Gegner* (Opponent), which occupation landed him in a concentration camp as early as April 1933. He was well connected, however, being an indirect descendant of Admiral Tirpitz and related to the von Hassell family, so he was soon released, and thereafter joined the Air Force. He knew that Hitler was bent on war and embarked on a pamphlet campaign against it, but through artist friends with Communist sympathies he also contacted the Russian Trade Delegation, which he was able to supply with information about 'illegal' German Air Force activities in the Spanish Civil War. This activity in turn attracted the interest of the Russian Secret Service. In 1939 the headstrong Boysen met the Harnacks, who were both left-wing radicals. Arvid came from a family of eminent academics. He had met his wife at the University of Wisconsin. Mildred had by now been in Germany, her adopted country, for many years, and taught at the university in Berlin.

The two couples found they had much in common, and were convinced that only a total military defeat could bring about the end of National Socialism. Like Boysen, Harnack was sensitively placed in the Nazi hierarchy. He was a senior civil servant in the Ministry of Economics and had even joined the Party in 1937 to further the interests of his secret cause.

Boysen, who had the rank of lieutenant, had been working for the Press Office of the Air Force, but now transferred to the department dealing with reports sent in by German air attachés abroad. He passed information contained in the reports on to the Russians via the Trade Delegation, which gave his organisation three radio transmitters early in 1941, foreseeing the need for other means of communication after hostilities had broken out between the USSR and Germany. The Red Orchestra had only one radio operator, however, and he was not skilled; nor were the transmitters very reliable.

The Security Service soon picked up their signals, but it took another nine months to break their code. By the end of August 1942 the Gestapo was ready to close in, and made a clean sweep. Fifty-five members of the group, including nineteen women, were executed. At no time do the Harnacks or the Boysens seem to have hesitated about the nature of their role as spies for the Russians. Emotionally and intellectually they were committed to the Communist cause, and their aim was to bring down the Nazi regime and replace it with a German Soviet. They never accepted any payment from the Russians for their work. Harnack envisaged, even before Hitler came to power, that Germany would have to choose between East and West, and that in every respect – social, political and ethical – the East offered the right solutions, and Mildred shared this point of view. In the death cell at Plötzensee he wrote in a letter of farewell: 'I believe in the rise of mankind!' Boysen's most important pamphlet, written soon after the beginning of the war with Russia, was headed: 'The Care for Germany's Future is in the Hands of the People'. It was signed 'Agis' – the name of the son of a king of Sparta who tried to deliver Greece from the Macedonians with the aid of the Persians.

The Boysens were executed in December 1942, the Harnacks in January 1943. The large number of executions was insisted upon by Göring, who was furious that such a conspiracy should have been based in the Air Ministry. Manfred Roeder, the prosecuting counsel, refused to hand over the bodies of the Boysens at the request of Harro's mother.[9]

Meanwhile, with their entry into the war, the Americans had set up a bureau of the Office of Strategic Services in Berne, Switzerland, under Allen Dulles. An English colleague remembers his arrival:

> He was a man of extraordinary personality and panache. When he arrived in Berne he announced publicly: 'I've been sent here by the President to find out what the fucking Krauts are up to, and so if anyone knows what the fucking Krauts are up to they had better call on me at 23 Dufortstrasse. They'll be assured of a warm welcome . . .' The Swiss hated him, but he got away with it, and they collected very important information.

Dulles kept his door open not only to Gisevius and other representatives of the Resistance, but also to SS agents representing Himmler, who from 1942 was sending out peace feelers on his own account.

The official American line, however, was to close its doors, and this was a stumbling block to the Resistance in Berlin. When it became clear that America would enter the war soon, they approached the head of the Associated Press Bureau, Louis P. Lochner. Lochner had known Hermann Maass for years. He was also friendly with Prince Louis Ferdinand. During his time in the USA, Louis Ferdinand had become friends with President Roosevelt, and Lochner also knew Roosevelt personally. Lochner therefore seemed an ideal and sympathetic ambassador to represent the Resistance to Roosevelt.

One evening in November 1941, Lochner was invited, under

conditions of great secrecy, to meet a selection of leading figures of
the Resistance. Among them were Jakob Kaiser, Klaus Bonhoeffer,
Otto John and Justus Delbrück, a member of the Abwehr and another
brother-in-law of the Bonhoeffers. Lochner was due to return to the
States soon anyway, and the ad hoc committee which he met asked
him to convey to Roosevelt the character, make-up and aims of the
Resistance as soon as he possibly could. They also sought Roosevelt's
opinion on what form of government he would like to see take shape
in Germany after the fall of Hitler. A secret radio link was arranged.

Lochner was happy to take on this mission but, before he could
leave, hostilities between the USA and Germany broke out officially
and he was interned. He did not get back to America until June 1942,
by which time the fortunes of the war had changed dramatically, and
the Allies were beginning to sense the tide turning. He still tried to
fulfil his promise, but without success; Roosevelt would not see him.
After several unsuccessful attempts to gain an audience, he was finally
told that the information he had was not wanted and that he had better
stop trying to push it.

The USA already had a good deal of intelligence about the
Resistance as a result of Adam von Trott's visit in 1939. Dulles's
Berne office was set up in November 1942 and subsequently pro-
vided a rich supply of information. But these sources were unofficial.
Roosevelt may well have been interested in doing a side deal with the
Resistance, but his hands were tied. The official Allied line was that
the Germans, having started a second war of world domination within
twenty-five years of the first, had to be put squarely in their place.
Most importantly, if Stalin had learnt of any deal being done between
the Americans and the Resistance, he might well have exposed it to
Hitler and concluded a separate peace with the Führer. The Germans
were not yet conclusively beaten in Russia but, even if they had been,
Roosevelt still needed Stalin on his side in the battle against Japan.
The atom bomb was in the future.

Contact was also being maintained with other interested parties
abroad by the members of the central Resistance. Von Trott, together with Eugen Gerstenmaier and Hans Schönfeld, an official of
the Ecumenical Council in Geneva, drafted a memorandum addressed
to Sir Stafford Cripps, the British Lord Privy Seal, whom Trott knew
through his son, a contemporary at Oxford.

The memorandum pointed out the huge waste of life and resources represented by the war, repeated that the only way to avert absolute catastrophe was to get rid of the Nazi regime, and on behalf of the Resistance within Germany, appealed for the solidarity of the rest of the world. The message was relayed to Britain via the World Council of Churches, and found favour with Cripps, but it cut no ice with Churchill or his Foreign Secretary, Anthony Eden. Germany was still powerful at the time, and not yet losing. The Resistance had never shown itself capable of undermining the regime.

Nevertheless, representations continued to be made wherever a sympathetic ear could be found. In April 1942 Dietrich Bonhoeffer and Helmuth von Moltke had travelled to Norway under the auspices of Abwehr work. By now Bonhoeffer was forbidden to publish, but the Security Service still allowed him to travel. Their purpose was to effect the release of Bishop Eivind Berggrav, who had managed to persuade Norwegian priests to resign *en masse* in protest at the German occupation and Nazi activities. Bonhoeffer and Moltke persuaded the local authorities that Berggrav's imprisonment would lead only to greater discontent among the population, making it harder to control. The Bishop was released, and the two Germans were able to give him secret encouragement in continuing his fight. Bonhoeffer, particularly, saw that the Church in Norway had committed itself to the very fight he had hoped the Confessing Church would have engaged in.

Following this excursion, Bonhoeffer determined to meet the English Bishop of Chichester, George Bell. He knew Bell from his own English days, and the Abwehr had long been aware that a visit to Sweden by the Bishop, to renew his contacts with the Church there, was scheduled for May. Also hastening to meet Bell was Dr Schönfeld, who did so in Stockholm on 26 May, when he reconfirmed the content of the memorandum sent to Cripps and stressed the need for British support of the Resistance. He gave Bell a written report to take home. A few days later, Bonhoeffer – again travelling under the protection of the Abwehr – managed to meet Bell in Sigtuna. The two independent approaches made a strong impression on Bell, who was already sympathetic to the cause of the Resistance. He persuaded Bonhoeffer to give him a list of the names of the leaders of the Resistance movement, and as soon as he returned home he used Schönfeld's note and Bonhoeffer's information to draw up a report for Eden.

The resulting memorandum was a very full summary of the position and aims of the Resistance, together with a note of the peace terms they proposed. The Resistance had added the warning that, if the Allies refused to enter into negotiations at all, the Army would fight to the bitter end in defence of Germany, if not of the regime. Bell also passed on information he had received about a secret plan for a coup being considered by Himmler, which, if effected before the Resistance could act, might nevertheless be used as a stepping stone by the Resistance: there was no question of Himmler's being allowed to remain in power any more than Hitler.

This was delivered in mid-June. In the course of the next month Eden consulted Stafford Cripps, who remained positive and enthusiastic. Bell also saw Cripps, but the two men could not move Eden. On 17 July the Foreign Secretary sent a note to Bell in which he said, 'I have no doubt that it would be contrary to the interest of our nation to provide either of them [Schönfeld and Bonhoeffer] with any answer whatsoever.' Eden was still suspicious of the clergymen's true motivation; but he was also seriously blinkered, and his unimaginative stubbornness was a contributory factor in the extension of the war.

Bell did not give up the fight. He invoked Churchill's own speech of 13 May 1940, in which he had spoken of Hitler's regime as a 'monstrous tyranny' – surely Britain's duty was to support those who opposed it? Eden replied that no one could believe in the Resistance until it had taken active steps to remove Hitler. So far the Resistance had given 'little proof of its existence'. The Bishop then pointed out that, after all, the German Resistance faced a fight of rather a different quality from that of the French or the Yugoslavs, for example. Their liberation as Germans was not guaranteed. The Anglo-American Atlantic Charter of 1941 had implied that Germany and its allies would be crushed along with the Nazis. This was a far cry from the earlier stance of Chamberlain, that the fight was not with all Germans, but with the Nazi Party and its followers.

Although Bell carried the fight as far as the House of Lords, he did not succeed in changing the government's stance. The Resistance once again had to face its problems alone.

NINE

Protest of Youth

Today, the main square outside the University of Munich is called Geschwister-Scholl-Platz. The name commemorates a small group of students who, operating independently, managed to create one of the few single protests of great significance outside the main body of the Resistance, in the town which had, throughout the mid-thirties, advertised itself on tourist brochures as 'The Birthplace of the Party'.

Hans and Sophie Scholl were the second and fourth of the five children of Robert Scholl, the liberal and independent mayor of the little town of Forchtenberg on the River Kocher to the east of Heilbronn. He was a big, warm-hearted man, rarely without a cigar smoking away below his luxuriant moustache. Hans and Sophie were born in 1918 and 1921, and in those days Forchtenberg's only contact with the outside world was a yellow post-coach that connected it with the nearest railway station. The children loved it, but Robert had ambitions for his town. He managed to get the railway extended to Forchtenberg, and had a community sports centre and a warehouse built. These improvements were not without their critics: Robert was far too progressive for some, and in 1930 he was voted out of office. The family moved first to Ludwigsburg and then to Ulm, where they settled. Robert, who had a tendency to live beyond his means, rented a large apartment for his family on the Cathedral Square. He set himself up as a business and tax consultant.

The five children, Inge, Hans, Elisabeth, Sophie and Werner, were free to enjoy, as compensation for the loss of the countryside, the large palace park nearby. Hans, according to his brother-in-law, was more like his father – impulsive, generous and extrovert. Sophie, no less strong a personality, had her mother's quiet sensitivity. What she shared with Hans was an absolute sense of human rights, something which all the children had inherited from their father, who exerted a strong but benign influence on them. Sophie also developed a mystical feeling for nature. She loved dancing. She was a good pianist and she could have become a professional artist – her drawings for *Peter Pan*, for example, glow with life; but when she went to university in Munich she opted to read the unusual combination of biology and philosophy.

The happy family life did not end with Hitler's seizure of power. The arrival of National Socialism was the first impact of politics on the children's thought. Hans was fifteen, Sophie, twelve.

Inge Aicher-Scholl was sixteen. She remembers that on 30 January 1933 the radio and the newspapers were full of the news, 'Now everything will be better in Germany. Hitler is at the tiller.'[1]

> We heard a great deal spoken about the Fatherland, of comradeship, the union of the Germanic people and love of the homeland. It impressed us, and we listened eagerly when such things were talked about on the streets or in school – for indeed we loved our homeland . . . And everywhere we heard that Hitler wanted to help the homeland back to greatness, happiness and security. He would see to it that everyone had a job to go to and enough to eat. He wouldn't rest until every single German enjoyed independence, freedom and happiness . . .

The children were keen to join the Hitler Youth, and their parents, though they had given them a liberal upbringing, did not forbid it. But never for an instant had Robert been fooled by Hitler, and he said to them, 'Have you considered how he's going to manage it? He's expanding the armaments industry, and building barracks. Do you know where that's all going to end?' The children argued that Hitler had solved the problem of unemployment, and pointed to the new motorways being built throughout the land. Robert wondered aloud if material security would ever make happy a people which had been robbed of its right to free speech.

At first his arguments fell on deaf ears. His children were enthusiastic members of the Hitler Youth and its female branch, the League of German Girls. They became group leaders. Only Sophie was a little less enthusiastic than the others. She was already worried by the fact that her Jewish schoolfriends could not join. She listened more attentively to her father's arguments. He and Hans, on the other hand, were barely on speaking terms some of the time.

But then Hans attended the 1935 Party Rally at Nuremberg. He had been selected to carry the flag of Ulm-Standort at the Rally – a great honour. But he came back a changed man. He did not say much at first, but gradually new ideas emerged. The endless, senseless drilling, the hate-filled aggressive speeches, the stupid conversation, the vulgar jokes – a concentration of all this at Nuremberg had finally focused his mind on what Nazism really meant.

There had been signs of Hans's disaffection before this. He was annoyed when he was told that the Hitler Youth was not interested in his collection of international folksongs – foreign, especially Russian, songs were strictly forbidden. And the special flag of his group was forbidden too – all groups were expected to carry a swastika banner. When finally his twelve-year-old standard bearer was threatened by a senior Hitler Youth official for refusing to give up the group flag, Hans hit the official. That was the end of the Hitler Youth for him. Soon afterwards he heard that a young schoolteacher had been picked up by a gang of SA and spat upon *to order*; the schoolteacher's crime was failure to join the Party. Gradually, news of the concentration camps seeped through.

Sophie was quick to pick up his mood. The first cracks had appeared in the cement which bound their allegiance to Hitler. Hans began to show more of an interest in another kind of youth group – the dj.1.11, so-called because it had been founded as *Deutsche Jugend* on 1 November 1929. The dj.1.11 was now illegal – all youth groups and organisations had been banned under the Nazis or amalgamated with the Hitler Youth – but it still existed underground. Its spirit was the open-minded, liberal, easy-going one of the Weimar Republic at its best. Its members would organise hitch-hiking expeditions as far as Finland and Sweden, or travel south to Calabria and Sicily. It represented cosmopolitanism, not nationalism. Its members did not wear uniforms or salute each other. They read 'illegal' books – works by George Bernard Shaw (who the Nazis thought was a Jew on account of his red hair), Stefan Zweig and Paul Claudel. It was for culture and against militarism, for the individual and not the mob. Sophie might have joined it too, but for the fact that it was open only to boys from

the age of twelve upwards. Nevertheless, she and her oldest sister
Inge caught its mood.

One day in late November 1937 there was a ring at the door of the
Scholls' apartment and two men from the Gestapo stood there. The
secret police had had the dj.1.11 group under observation for some
time and now they were ready to pounce. The men said they were
there to search the flat and arrest the children. With great presence
of mind, Frau Scholl told them that they could do so by all means,
but that, if the gentlemen would excuse her, she had to go to the
baker's. The policemen didn't object – women in the Third Reich
were consigned to three areas of life: church, kitchen and children.
Even female Nazi leaders were never given much status or publicity
by the regime.

Frau Scholl left the flat and went up to the attic floor where
Hans's and Werner's – the younger brother was also a determined
anti-Nazi – bedrooms were to be found. Quickly she packed any
potentially incriminating literature into a basket and took it round
the corner to trusted friends. The Gestapo search turned nothing
up, and the officials took Inge, Sophie and Werner – the three
children who were at home at the time – away with them. Sophie
was released almost immediately, but Inge and Werner were taken to
Stuttgart and detained for a week, interrogated about what they might
know of Ernst Niekisch and his *Widerstand* (Resistance) magazine,
and about dj.1.11. They managed to play dumb, and were finally
released. Hans, who had been arrested subsequently, was held for
five weeks. Luckily for him he had been conscripted by then, and
his sympathetic commanding officer had him released, telling the
Gestapo that as Hans was a soldier, he was in the Army's jurisdiction,
not theirs.

The Scholls – who were a well-known family in the smallish
town of Ulm – failed to stay out of trouble. Werner had taken
an early decision to leave the Hitler Youth. It was a gesture of
solidarity towards his friend Otl Aicher (who later married Inge
Scholl), who had refused to join it and as a result was not allowed
to take his final school examinations, thus cutting off any hope of
university. Aicher later remembered how Werner had tied a swastika
scarf round the eyes of the bust of Justice in front of the Ulm Law
Courts.

Werner was a keen photographer, and most of the surviving

pictures of Sophie were taken by him. He died on the Russian Front, aged twenty-one.

At a meeting of the League of German Girls to discuss suitable material for home reading, Sophie suggested Heinrich Heine, the brilliant nineteenth-century revolutionary German poet who was also a Jew. Replying to appalled objections at her suggestion, she said, 'The person who doesn't know Heine, doesn't know German literature.' Robert Scholl himself was later arrested and imprisoned briefly for anti-Nazi activities.

The children read a great deal: Socrates, Aristotle, St Augustine, Pascal; Maritain and Bernanos. The influence of these thinkers went deep, strengthening their resolve against the regime. The question was what to do, and how to do it? Meanwhile, for Sophie, school continued. She met Fritz Hartnagel, a career soldier four years her senior, and they went for tours in the country occasionally in his father's car, together with her older sister Elisabeth. For the innocent Sophie friendship with Hartnagel began to turn into something more. But it never quite became love. After the war Hartnagel married Elisabeth. They still live in Stuttgart, where before his retirement he was a judge.

If she was moving away from Nazism through the late thirties, Sophie Scholl turned actively against it as a result of two experiences: *Kristallnacht*, which she lived through in Ulm, and the outbreak of war on 1 September 1939. She extracted a promise from each of her male friends that they would never fire their guns, but she was well aware of how unrealistic such a promise was. She wrote to Hartnagel with uncharacteristic bitterness:

> You'll have your hands full from now on. I just can't accept that now people will be in peril of their lives because of other people. I can't accept it and I find it horrifying. Never tell me that it's for the sake of the Fatherland.

Her subsequent letters express increasing disgust and anger at the war. 'I think I know you and that you're not much in favour of this war,' she wrote to him later. 'So how can you spend your time training people for it?' And in September 1940 she wrote a letter of which Beck and Oster would have approved:

> For me the relationship between a soldier and his people is roughly

like that of a son who swears to stand by his father and his family through thick and thin. If it turns out that the father harms another family and then gets hurt as a consequence, must the son still stick by him? I can't accept it. Justice is more important than sentimental loyalty.

Hartnagel himself remembers:

> It was striking to see with what incisiveness and logic Sophie saw how things would develop, for she was warm-hearted and full of feeling, not cold and calculating. Here is an example: in winter 1941–42 there was a big propaganda campaign in Germany to get the people to give sweaters and other warm woollen clothing to the Army. German soldiers were at the gates of Leningrad and Moscow in the middle of a winter war for which they weren't prepared . . . Sophie said, 'We're not giving anything.' I had just got back from the Russian Front . . . I tried to describe to her how conditions were for the men, with no gloves, pullovers or warm socks. She stuck to her viewpoint relentlessly and justified it by saying, 'It doesn't matter if it's German soldiers who are freezing to death or Russians, the case is equally terrible. But we must lose the war. If we contribute warm clothes, we'll be extending it.'[2]

After matriculation from school in 1940 she took a one-year course in kindergarten supervision, in the hope of avoiding State Work Duty – a kind of civil national service which all would-be students had to fulfil. But not only did the authorities refuse to accept the kindergarten training as a replacement for the State Duty, but with the acceleration of the war in 1941 they added to it State War Work. For another year, therefore, Sophie endured barrack life and manual labour before she could finally start her course at Munich University. She travelled there from Ulm early in May 1942. It was just before her twenty-first birthday – her last.

Hans was at the station to meet her. He was reading medicine at the university – the semesters alternating with service at the Front. Through him she quickly gained an entrée to university life. Among the first people she met was Professor Carl Muth, whose library Hans had been cataloguing. Muth was a pillar of the literary Resistance. His Roman Catholic magazine *High Land* had been banned finally in June 1941, having managed for eight years never once to mention Hitler's name. By now Hans had read the sermons of Bishop Galen. He had not given up his own ideas of making some kind of stand against the regime, and had become markedly politicised. From his writing it is clear that had he lived he would have chosen politics, not medicine, as his career.

He was already at the centre of a group of young medical students – Willi Graf, Christoph Probst and Alexander Schmorell – who had decided to launch a leaflet campaign against the war, encouraging passive Resistance to the regime. They were joined by the popular philosophy lecturer Kurt Huber, who had already attracted the suspicion of the Nazis. He was considerably older than the others, but had no wish to lead the group. He guided his younger comrades' thoughts, and edited the last two of the six leaflets they produced. His lectures were always packed, because he managed to introduce veiled criticism of the regime into them.

The group had no wish to throw bombs, or to cause any injury to human life. They wanted to influence people's minds against Nazism and militarism. Already a sympathetic architect had lent them his studio in a rear courtyard for their clandestine activities, and the relatively well-off Schmorell had been able to buy a typewriter and a duplicating machine. They called their group the 'White Rose'. Sophie was not brought into it initially, but she had a shrewd idea of what her brother was up to from early on. She would find books in his rooms – which smelt of jasmine and cigarettes – with significant passages marked.

The choice of the name 'White Rose' is not easily explained. The rose as a symbol of secrecy might have occurred to them, and 'white' might have reflected the fact that their leaflets were not inspired by any colour of political thought, but by broad humanism.[3] It's also possible that the name was taken from B. Traven's eponymous novel, in which a Mexican farmer fights a tyrannical oil company. Whatever the reason, the symbol is still a powerful one in Germany.

The first four leaflets of the White Rose appeared in quick succession in June and July 1942. They were written jointly by Hans Scholl with Alexander Schmorell and Christoph Probst, who was the only married member of the group apart from Huber and who was already, at twenty-three, the father of two children (a third, whom he would never see, was born after his arrest).

The first leaflet begins uncompromisingly: 'Nothing is less worthy of a cultivated people than to allow itself to be governed by a clique of irresponsible bandits of dark ambition, without Resistance.' The four issues, each covering two sides of the paper, draw on Goethe, Schiller and Aristotle, among others, to make their point, which is contained effectively in the sentence quoted. They refer to the murder of Jews in Poland, encourage the idea of sabotage in the armaments industry, and criticise the anti-Christian and anti-social nature of the war. 'We are all guilty . . . We will not be silenced. We are your bad conscience. The White Rose will not leave you in peace!'

Sophie soon joined. Fear for the safety of her family was overridden by her desire to do something to fight Hitler. It was hard for them all: hard to swim against the current, and harder still to wish defeat upon their own country. Worst of all was the isolation in which they worked.

Tirelessly the group distributed the leaflets by the suitcaseload throughout towns in southern Germany, either travelling with them (a very dangerous undertaking) and delivering them by hand at night, or using the mail. They were so successful that the movement spread, notably to Hamburg, where a branch of the White Rose was set up which survived its originator.

The White Rose went into temporary abeyance during the summer of 1942 as Hans, Willi and Alexander were ordered to the Russian Front, but they returned to Munich in October. The period had been of special significance to Schmorell. His mother, whom he had lost in infancy, was Russian. Meanwhile Sophie had spent the vacation working in an arms factory, and Robert Scholl had been in a Gestapo prison.

Hans had seen the maltreatment of Jews and Russian prisoners at first hand. One day he gave his tobacco to an old man, and his iron rations to a girl. The girl had thrown the rations back at him, but he had picked them up, plucked a daisy, placed it on the pile of rations, and laid them at her feet. After a moment's hesitation, she had accepted them, and put the flower in her hair.

The group returned from the Front more determined than ever to carry on the work of Resistance, and to make the White Rose into a permanent Resistance cell. Hans and Alexander even managed to arrange a meeting with Falk Harnack, the younger brother of Arvid Harnack of the Red Orchestra, with the intention of making contact with the main Resistance in Berlin, though death was to prevent this ever happening. In the meantime, postage and paper cost money. Fritz Hartnagel gave Sophie 1000 Reichsmark, for what she told him was 'a good purpose'. A generous source of support was the Stuttgart tax consultant Eugen Grimminger, who was married to a Jewess and had looked after Robert Scholl's business while he was in prison. A schoolfriend of Sophie remembers a meeting in Stuttgart in December 1942, when she told her, 'If I had a pistol and I were to meet Hitler here in the street, I'd shoot him down. If men can't manage it, then a woman should.' She replied, 'But then he'd be replaced by Himmler, and after Himmler, another.' Sophie retorted: 'One's got to do something to get rid of the guilt.'

They bought a new, less noisy, duplicating machine. On trains, they took suitcases full of leaflets. If the police searched the train, they would leave the suitcase on the rack and hide in the lavatory, or spend the journey in another compartment. They became used to living on their nerves, but they never considered that they had a choice. Sophie and Hans took adjoining rooms in Franz-Josef-Strasse 13. In January 1943 a new White Rose leaflet appeared, this time written in a more popular style. Several thousand copies were made. Addresses were painstakingly copied out of telephone directories. The conspirators had to ensure that the Gestapo could not trace the source to Munich. Once again by train journeys, the group had to run the police gauntlet and post their leaflets from neighbouring towns.

On 13 January, to mark the 470th anniversary of the university, the Nazi *Gauleiter* – District Leader – of the city, Paul Giesler, gave a speech in the course of which he told the female students that it would be better for them to get on with giving the Führer a child than wasting time on books; he even offered to put his henchmen at their service. Several girls immediately left the hall in protest, only to be arrested at the exit. This led to a demonstration, in the course of which the Nazi Student Leader was dragged from the podium, beaten up, and declared a hostage against the release of the girls. The Nazis telephoned the police, who promptly arrived and broke up the meeting. This was the first student demonstration against the Nazis in Munich, and it stimulated the Gestapo to redouble its efforts to find the originators of the White Rose.

Elisabeth Scholl spent a week at the end of January and the beginning of February with her brother and sister in Munich. She found a Russian blouse in a wardrobe and Sophie told her that Alexander liked to put it on when he went to visit the Russian forced-labourers in their barracks. Christoph Probst dropped in on his way between postings during a period of military duty and, though he only stopped for an hour and a half, Elisabeth was struck by the fact that he changed into civilian clothes. On 3 February news of the defeat at Stalingrad (where Fritz Hartnagel was fighting) came through on the radio. One evening soon after, Alexander and Hans said they were going over to the Women's Hospital. Later on Willi Graf arrived and when Elisabeth told him where his friends were, he laughed and said they would hardly go there without him. All that evening Sophie was nervous, and kept talking about the need to write anti-Nazi graffiti on walls. 'You'd need to use something that was hard to get off,' she said, 'like bitumous paint.'

The following morning Hans, Sophie and Elisabeth went to the university to attend a lecture by Huber on Leibniz. On a wall by the entrance the word 'Freedom' had been written in huge letters. 'What bastard did that?' snarled an older student. A large group of people were watching a handful of Russian women labourers trying to clean it off. 'They'll have a hard job,' said Sophie. 'That's bitumous paint.' Another friend, Traute Lafrenz, who was one of the leaders of the Hamburg White Rose, and now works as a doctor in Illinois, was in Munich too that day and saw Hans Scholl. 'I remember he was smiling to himself. Some outraged student or other came up to him and said, "Have you seen what's happened?" "No," said Hans. "What?" But his smile broadened. From that moment on I began to be terribly afraid for him.'

The significance of the defeat at Stalingrad, in whatever light Goebbels presented it, could not be concealed from the German people, and the group around Hans Scholl realised that they should follow up with another leaflet immediately. This, the last from the White Rose, was quickly prepared and addressed to their 'Fellow Students'. It was more strongly and directly expressed than any of its predecessors.

> The day of reckoning is come, the reckoning of German youth with the most appalling tyranny that our people has ever endured. In the name of the entire German people we demand from Adolf Hitler the return of our personal freedom, the most valuable possession of the Germans . . .

Hans and Sophie decided to distribute it in the university personally.

On Thursday 18 February 1943 the weather was springlike. They hurried to the university at 10a.m. before the first morning lectures were over, carrying copies of the new leaflet in a small suitcase. They hurried to spread them wherever they could – on windowsills, shelves, the tops of walls – until their supply was almost exhausted.

They had already left the main building when they decided to go back and get rid of the rest. They ran up the main staircase of the university's central hall and emptied the remaining contents of the case from a parapet into the courtyard. They were just in time. Immediately afterwards the doors of the lecture halls opened and students poured out. But the Scholls had been seen. The university's caretaker, Jakob Schmid, charged towards them as they raced back down the staircase, seized them each by the arm and bellowed, 'You're under arrest!'

Both the young people stayed calm. They remained quiet and dignified as they were taken first to the bursar and then to the rector, SS Oberführer Dr Walter Wüst, lecturer in Aryan language and culture. The doors of the university were sealed and all the students remaining inside had to assemble in the courtyard. Those who had picked up leaflets had to surrender them. The Scholls were taken to Gestapo Headquarters in handcuffs. Secret police went immediately to the rooms at Franz-Josef-Strasse, where they found several hundred new red 8-pfennig stamps. Very soon afterwards, the Gestapo was on the trail of the rest of the group, though the Scholls betrayed no one. Christoph Probst was arrested the following day and the others soon after.

The Scholls had known the risk that they were running. Sophie had even said shortly before: 'So many people have already died for this regime that it's time someone died against it.' There had been plenty of indications that the Gestapo investigation had been getting closer to them every day. They failed to receive a warning at the eleventh hour: the previous day, 17 February, Otl Aicher, who had been wounded on active service, was staying with Carl Muth. He was in Munich with the intention of seeing Hans and Sophie, but before he could make contact he received an urgent coded message from Ulm by telephone, to the effect that Hans should be told personally that the 'book called *Totalitarian State and Utopia* was out of print'. He had rung Hans and told him that he had important news. They made a date for the following day – 18 February – at 11a.m. But when

Aicher reached Franz-Josef-Strasse, it was too late. The Gestapo were already there, and he, too, was arrested – luckily to be released soon afterwards.

Hans and Sophie were not tortured, but they were interrogated intensively for four days in Gestapo Headquarters at Wittelsbach Palace in Munich. Otl Aicher and Traute Lafrenz took the bad news to their parents, who tried to see if anything could be done to secure their release. It was in vain. Throughout their ordeal, the brother and sister, who each shared cells with one other political prisoner of their own sex, remained calm and fatalistic. Neither of them was broken by the experience. The trial was set for 22 February. Roland Freisler, Hitler's hanging judge, flew down from Berlin specially to preside. This was an indication of the importance the Nazi leadership considered the White Rose to have. The war was lost; the Allies were already bombing Munich; but protestors still had to be smashed.

The hearing started at 9a.m. and lasted until 4p.m. It was a closed trial, and those without passes, including Hans's and Sophie's parents, were not admitted, though Robert was able to force an entrance briefly. The Scholls were tried together with Christoph Probst. None of them flinched under the sarcastic, hectoring onslaught of the judge. The verdict was a foregone conclusion: death by the guillotine. They were taken from the court to Stadelheim Prison immediately after judgement had been passed.

By a miracle the parents had a last opportunity to see their children. They saw Hans first. Robert embraced him saying, 'You will go down in history. There is another justice than this.' Hans asked them to say farewell to his friends, and only when he mentioned one name very special to him did he weep, bowing his head so that no one should see. Sophie, when her turn came, accepted some little cakes that her brother had refused, saying, 'Lovely. I didn't get anything to eat at lunchtime.' She looked wonderful, fresh and full of life. Her mother said, 'I'll never see you come through the door again.' 'Oh mother,' she answered, 'after all, it's only a few years' more life I'll miss.' She was pleased and proud that they had betrayed no one, that they had taken all the responsibility on themselves. Her main concern was that her mother should be able to withstand the deaths of two children at the same time. But, for herself, she was completely composed.

The parents left and returned to Ulm, thinking that something might still be done to help – at least to get the sentence commuted.

But in the Nazi State, punishment normally followed sentence with terrifying speed. By 6p.m. Sophie and Hans were dead.

The following day, Inge Scholl was able to visit the flat in Franz-Josef-Strasse and there she found Sophie's diary, which had been overlooked by the Gestapo. Inge saw it as a gift from heaven. The family, in accordance with Nazi custom, was placed under arrest for being related to the malefactors. Kurt Huber, Willi Graf and Alexander Schmorell, who were arrested later, were sentenced to death on 19 April.

Hans and Sophie were buried in Perlach Cemetery in south Munich on 24 February. In the town, graffiti appeared on walls: 'Their spirit lives.'

Germany in the late nineteenth and early twentieth centuries had more youth movements, clubs and organisations than any other country. They were attached to the various sects of the church, to political parties, to health and fitness societies, sporting groups and trade unions. Their basic philosophy centred around a healthy open-air existence, self-sufficiency bolstered by a sense of community spirit, and the singing of folksongs. All of them were made illegal by Hitler, who replaced them with the Hitler Youth and the League of German Girls (there were similar organisations for children below the age of fourteen), to which every boy under eighteen and every girl under twenty-one was supposed to belong. The Hitler Youth was founded in 1923, but by 1932 it still had by far the lowest membership of all its rival organisations – 40,000, compared with 2 million members of the other young sports clubs. Many Hitler Youth members were members in name only anyway, and the old youth organisations flourished underground. But new groups sprang up as well, as a direct protest to Nazism. They went by various umbrella names, such as 'Swing Youth' and 'Jazz Youth'. Sometimes their protest went no further than listening to 'decadent' western music and especially jazz, frowned on by the Nazis because it was the product of Negro culture. Nazi accusations against the non-conformist youth groups ranged from homosexuality to 'cosmo-politanism'! Himmler was quick to suggest sending all 'unregenerate' members to the concentration camps and there, boys and girls alike, should be 'beaten, given the severest exercise, and then put to hard labour'.

A broadly based youth organisation which grew out of the working class and flourished in the industrial west went by the name of
'Edelweiss Pirates'.

They evolved partly as a reaction to the underground Communist
Party. In exile in the USSR, under such men as Walter Ulbricht and
Wilhelm Pieck, the Party flourished; but at home, after some success
in Resistance work before the war, it fell into a no-man's-land because
of the pact with Stalin. That Stalin could come to terms with a man like
Hitler, who had made the Communist Party illegal, was a testimony to
the cynical contempt both men showed for their own so-called ideals
and for the people who were forcibly governed by them. Officially,
German Communists were bidden to regard the Ribbentrop–Molotov
Pact as a stroke of genius by Stalin in protecting the Motherland from
the Nazi threat. Communist Resistance virtually ceased until 1941. By
then, the war was well under way, and the deprivations it brought in
its wake encouraged moods of passivity, apathy and resignation in
all but the strongest; the typical Communist of the Resistance in the
last years before the war was about thirty, a skilled worker used to
many years' unemployment. Now such men were an important four
or five years older, and most had been called up. Youth groups had
formed already in rivalry to the Hitler Youth, but now, especially
in the Rhineland, the Edelweiss Pirates emerged as an expression of
spontaneous protest.

The groups grew as the Allies destroyed more and more sports
facilities and youth clubs as part of their policy of bombing civilian
targets, and as the leaders of the Hitler Youth grew up and were
conscripted. Their centres were the towns of Cologne, Duisberg,
Düsseldorf, Essen and Wuppertal. The groups were not coherent
and had no ideology. They were united in enmity to the regime
and to the regimentation of the Hitler Youth in particular. They
did not want to be cannon fodder and they could see which way the
war was going. They avoided uniforms, but they had a mode of dress
by which they could recognise each other – usually (for boys) shorts,
white socks, check shirts and a neckscarf. They would also wear an
Edelweiss or an Edelweiss badge if possible, usually attached under
the lapel. Girls wore white pullovers, white socks and windcheaters.
The police drew up detailed sartorial lists by which Pirates could be
recognised. Their songs were the old prewar international folksongs,
and the guitarist of any group was protected like a standard bearer.

Most of them were male, and aged between fourteen and seventeen. Many members of the Hitler Youth were closet Edelweiss Pirates, though the Pirates concentrated on damaging Nazi property – especially public bulletin and notice boards – and pitched battles with Hitler Youth groups were not unusual. To begin with the authorities contented themselves with keeping the groups under observation, and took no action beyond the occasional raid when the activities of the Pirates became too bold for comfort. But towards the end of the war, when the bands of boys were joined by young German deserters and fugitive foreign forced-labourers, the Gestapo laid a heavier hand on them.

Where a group took what could be construed as specific action against the regime, they would be merciless. The youngest member of the Resistance to be beheaded at Plötzensee – the familiar red Notice of Execution appeared on the Berlin streets on 27 October 1942 – was only seventeen years old. His name was Helmuth Hübener. He was a member of the Mormon sect, and his crime was to organise a small group which wrote down the details of BBC broadcasts, then duplicated and distributed them. The court found that he was of above average intelligence and maturity for his age. Because of his alleged precocity and his political essay, 'The War of the Plutocrats' (written for his final school examination before he went on to become an administration trainee) it was considered correct to try and punish him as if he were an adult.

The loose structure of Edelweiss Pirate groups meant that it was easy to classify them officially as criminals, and only recently have they come to be regarded as part of the Resistance. A further muddying of the water was caused by confusion of them at the very end of the war with the so-called Werewolves. These were groups of fanatical Nazi adolescents, who at the very end of the war, and even after it had ended, fought on, sabotaging Allied equipment and executing 'traitors'.

Some joined the Edelweiss Pirates after becoming disaffected with the Hitler Youth. Fritz Theilen's first protest was to shit in his Hitler Youth leader's briefcase – an imposing-looking bag which he found to contain nothing but a newspaper and a sandwich. He got away with that, but he was expelled from the Hitler Youth for refusing to do punishment exercises when his group's flag was found to be less than perfectly presented.[4] Theilen then joined a group of older boys who were waiting to be called up, but who met at the local sports ground on Saturday mornings. Through them he joined the Navajos – an offshoot of Edelweiss Pirates – which used to meet in Blücher Park, Cologne. They were occasionally harassed by Nazi groups, because they sang forbidden songs quite openly, but if there were no police to back the Nazis up, it was usually possible to fight them off. But heavy restrictions were placed on young people in Nazi Germany. By a police decree of 9 March 1940, those under eighteen years old were forbidden to be on the streets during the hours of darkness, and banned from bars, cinemas, cabarets or clubs after 9 o'clock at night. They were also prohibited from smoking or drinking in any public place, and they were not allowed to go to dances or use sports facilities or shooting galleries. Members of the Party, Party organisations, or the Armed Forces were exempted from these rules. Punishments for infraction of them ranged from up to either 50 Reichsmark or three weeks in prison for young offenders, to 150 Reichsmark or six weeks in gaol for adults encouraging or permitting them to indulge in such activities.[5]

As the war progressed, so did the popularity of the Hitler Youth wane. The police and the Hitler Youth's own 'police' units – origi-nally developed to seek out and punish misdemeanours within the ranks of the Hitler Youth – found it increasingly difficult to control the growing ranks of unofficial youth groups, which began to hold meetings numbering several hundred. There was safety in numbers, and the guitar player would always be especially protected. Two rings would be formed around him or her – the first of girls, the outer one of boys. Hitler Youth attackers would aim to carry the guitar player off or at least smash the guitar. They rarely succeeded.

The Edelweiss Pirates were not without a sense of duty, however. In the massive Allied air raids on Cologne at the end of May and begin-ning of June 1942, which wrecked the old town completely, Pirates formed themselves into auxiliaries of the police and the fire brigade in order to help in firefighting and rescue work. These young people, born around 1925, had experienced nothing but the repression and dreariness of National Socialism all their lives, and they were simply fed up with it. The horror of the war was brought home to them in the regular bombing raids on the industrial west from 1942 on. The spontaneous reaction was the healthy and natural one of young crea-tures to throw off the bungling, destructive management of the old.

Girls, not always able to express Resistance as aggressively as boys, were courageous in acts of disobedience. The girls of one branch of the Düsseldorf League of German Girls so hated having to belong to it that they simply turned left when told to turn right at square bashing exercises and their leaders could do nothing but rant in the face of such unassailable solidarity.

The Pirates used the air raids – when everyone else was sheltering in bunkers – as cover for their meetings as they became better organised. Older, more politically orientated leaders appeared among them – renegade schoolteachers and former youth workers. The police made a show of stepping up their activities against them, but in fact the Gestapo chased them only when they were sure they would not be outnumbered. When Pirates were arrested, however, they could count on a beating and interrogation. By 1944, they began to be in danger of their lives.

By 1944 too it became imperative to go underground in order to avoid being drafted into the Army – or even the SS, for by now you had no choice where you were sent. About this time Fritz Theilen came into contact with Bartholomäus 'Bartel' Schink. Bartel was sixteen and ran a group in the Ehrenfeld district of Cologne. They engaged in political activity: fly-posting anti-Nazi leaflets (when the flour for flour-and-water glue ran out they used powdered plaster from bombed-out houses, though fish glue was best for permanence), graffiti mocking Nazi slogans ('One People, One State, One Heap of Rubble' instead of 'One People, One State, One Leader') and the spreading of news from the BBC. Their headquarters was a shed on an allotment owned by the parents of one of the gang, and by May their main activity was pillaging the supply trains in the Cologne goods yards in order to pass on the food to Russian prisoners-of-war. They also carried out these activities under the dangerous cover of air raids. By now Allied bombers had reduced Ehrenfeld to a wasteland, inhabited by the homeless, deserters, escaped POWs, draft-dodgers and Resistance fighters. In this atmosphere the Pirates found themselves blamed for the crimes of looters and black-marketeers, and for the looting of private property that never took place (citizens invented stories in order to claim extra supplies for themselves). The police also took part in this kind of thing: Fritz Theilen was once sent into a burning tobacconist's to rescue cigarettes and cigars for the benefit of the police.

During a raid on the goods yards in August, they were surprised by a Gestapo patrol. Bartel fired at the Nazis – all the boys had pistols – but most of the group were arrested soon afterwards. The majority were sent to hard labour camps for dissident youth behind the crumbling West Front, but thirteen Pirates were publicly hanged in Hüttenstrasse in Ehrenfeld on 10 November, on charges of helping deserters and forced labourers. Bartel Schink was one of them.

TEN

Resistance in the East

As Germany became ever more embroiled in the conflict she had started but could never win, and as Germans grimly accustomed themselves to the new idea of 'total war', so an increasing number of senior officers took refuge from moral responsibility in their military duty. This tendency was heightened by the joint declaration from Churchill and Roosevelt following a conference at Casablanca in January 1943 that Germany would now be coerced into unconditional surrender. The Allies would also begin a systematic bombing campaign on Germany.

At the same time, Stalingrad was falling. In the Resistance, Beck's group knew Paulus to be a weak character, but hoped nevertheless that he would have defied Hitler by now, given the inhumanity of the Supreme Commander's order to hold on. Beck even wrote to Manstein, under whose overall command the 6th Army was, but neither he nor Paulus rose to the occasion.

This and the Casablanca decision were further serious blows to the Resistance. Now that it became clear that it would be a fight to the finish, many officers sincerely felt that their duty lay in protecting Germany as far as possible. Only those clearsighted enough to see that the best way of averting ruin was to stop Hitler in his tracks, and who had the courage to believe that the removal of the Führer was still an imperative moral action, continued to work with absolute determination towards killing him.

The job of doing so was getting more difficult. Hitler, faced with setbacks for the first time, and suspicious even of constructive criticism, was following the textbook progress of a megalomaniac tyrant.

Here already were the signs of that complete madness which would lead him to order the destruction of Germany itself – its factories, towns and ports – when it finally became clear to him at the very end that he had lost. The German people had failed him; the only glorious Germans were dead; the rest he would take down with him in an unholy Viking funeral.

He became increasingly reclusive, rarely leaving the Berghof in Berchtesgaden, or his bunker-like headquarters in the depths of East Prussia, the so-called Wolf's Lair (*Wolfsschanze*) near Rastenburg (now Kętrzyn). His security measures, however, increased with his paranoia, and he had eyes everywhere. Hitler had never been under any illusions that his people loved him; it is unlikely that he wanted love. He had always prided himself on his sixth sense for danger – Goebbels had created a myth around it – but it did not always work and he backed it up with complex and rigorous security arrangements.[1]

By 1923, the Führer already had a bodyguard of 100 men – the 'Shock Troop Hitler'. As Chancellor, he was provided with protection at the expense of the State. Inherited from the Weimar Republic, it was not very substantial – just a few policemen drummed up as bodyguards on important public occasions. Hitler added to this force from the ranks of the SS and the Security Service. He never used a foreign car, and the German make he preferred was Mercedes. He had a Mercedes 770 G4 W31, a 770 KW 150 II and a 7.7 litre W150. Each had a reinforced bodywork and bulletproof glass. Holsters were built into the doors. When travelling by car, he always did so in a large convoy to confuse possible assassins.

He had two personal aeroplanes. The first was built in 1937, a Focke-Wulf FW 200 Condor V3 – the 'Führermaschine Immelmann III'; the second, built in 1942, was an FW 200 Condor C-4/U-1. Both had a reinforced bulkhead between the part where Hitler sat and the other passengers. His armchair in the second aeroplane at least could be ejected, and had its own built-in parachute.

Hitler preferred to travel by car or plane, but when he needed to use it, the 'Führer-train' was at his disposal. It was made up of eleven coaches, including a saloon, a dining car, a conference car, a baggage waggon, a coach for his bodyguards and another for the press.

His greatest security measure, however, remained his own temperament. He instinctively liked to keep people guessing about what he would do, and to catch them wrong-footed. He was the supreme exponent of divide and rule, to the extent of living in an atmosphere of senior management confusion. He always made his mind up about when and how to travel at the last moment, and he would frequently decide not to go at all. When he appeared at meetings, he was always surrounded by SS men, though curiously it was not until very late in the war that attenders at meetings had to leave their pistols outside, and briefcases were not searched. General security at Berchtesgaden and the *Wolfsschanze*, however, was very tight.

The Führer did not often visit the East Front. The activities of the SS and the *Einsatzgruppen* caused outrage and disgust among many Regular Army officers, but they could salve their consciences if they so wished with the consideration that they, at least, had nothing to do with the atrocities. However, in early June 1941, before the order was ever given to attack Russia, Hitler, with his usual contempt for Brauchitsch and Halder (who in any case gave in), issued instructions regarding the treatment of captured Soviet political commissars. The written order included this: 'You are requested to limit distribution to the Commanders of Armies or Air Fleets . . . and to arrange for further communication [of this order] to lower commands by word of mouth . . .' and, as if that were not indication enough of the criminal intent to follow, it continued: 'in the struggle against Bolshevism, we must not assume that the enemy's conduct will be based on principles of humanity or international law.' In view of the Germans' behaviour in Poland already, such sentiments are sickening, but now came the meat of the order:

> Political commissars have initiated barbaric, Asiatic methods of warfare. Consequently they will be dealt with immediately and with maximum severity. As a matter of principle they will be shot at once, whether captured during operations or otherwise showing resistance. The following regulations will apply: . . . on capture they will be immediately segregated from other prisoners on the field of battle . . . After they have been segregated they will be liquidated.[2]

This so-called Commissar Order was countersigned by Keitel, the chief of the Overall High Command of the Armed Forces. All Brauchitsch and Halder could do – and to be fair to them they did this – was pass the order on with the rider that, as the duty of soldiers was fighting, there would be little time for such 'mopping up' operations.

The implication of the order was clear though: Hitler wanted to force the Army's direct involvement in his crimes. It was another way of trying to demonstrate his power over it. In fact he failed. The order was barely carried out at all by members of the Regular Army, and his action in trying to impose it had, if anything, a stiffening effect on the Resistance in Army Group Centre – the Army on the East Front.

The senior operations officer on the Staff of Army Group Centre was Lieutenant-Colonel Henning von Tresckow.

Tresckow was born in 1901, the son of an old Prussian-Brandenburg military family. He followed in the family tradition, and in 1918 he became the youngest lieutenant of 1st Infantry Guard Regiment. He was a brave, intelligent soldier, but after the war he found the Army too restricting and left it to join a bank. In 1924 he travelled with the military historian Kurt Hesse through England, France and South America. Returning in 1926, he married Erika von Falkenhayn, the daughter of the former Prussian Minister for War, and rejoined the Army as a lieutenant in the prestigious Infantry Regiment 9. His thinking and ideas remained broader than the Army could contain, however. He conceived Germany's future, ideally, along the lines of a British constitutional monarchy. His sympathies were broadly liberal and he supported the dismantling of class barriers. Like many of his brother officers, he was disappointed at the Weimar Republic's inability to establish order and stability in Germany, and initially welcomed the arrival of Hitler, but the murders of 30 June 1934 disenchanted him. From 1936 onwards he remained consistently opposed to the regime. He realised that the Russian campaign was as good as lost from the moment it started. Nevertheless, the great successes scored at Białystok, Minsk, Smolensk and Vjasma were largely his work. His aim was to keep the Army intact, not to help Hitler; and though the latter effect was the inevitable by-product of the former, he hoped it would be possible to preserve the Army for the period after Hitler had been toppled, as a means of defending German integrity, if need be. He constantly badgered his commanding officers – first Bock, later Kluge – with complaints about SS atrocities committed behind the lines, and was tireless in his attempts to 'turn' any generals he could contact in the eastern theatre of war.

When he realised that the generals were not going to take any action, he decided on a plan of assassination himself. At first he recoiled at the idea of using a bomb – his traditional Army upbringing caused him to consider such a method ungentlemanly. To begin with he thought about using several officers to shoot Hitler down simultaneously. Such a means would also avoid the risk of causing the death of innocent people. But the plan proved to be impracticable, and once Tresckow had decided to use explosives, he set about looking for the most effective ones.

He had been building up a Resistance group within Army Group Centre since the beginning of the Russian campaign. Its members included the Intelligence officer, Rudolf von Gersdorff, and Tresckow's own aide, Fabian von Schlabrendorff. Hammerstein's contact with British diplomats in Berlin just after war broke out and a lawyer by profession, Schlabrendorff was already a veteran of the Resistance. Oster had sent him to London in 1939 before the outbreak of war to try to intercede with the British. As a great-grandson of Queen Victoria's adviser, Baron Stockmar, he was able to make the visit to Britain a private one, ostensibly to consult family papers kept in an archive at Windsor. Another important member of the group was Carl-Hans Graf von Hardenberg, who was ADC to the Army Group's commander from the end of 1941, Field Marshal Günther von Kluge. Also associated with the conspiracy were the brothers Freiherrn Philipp, and the highly decorated Georg von Boeselager. This purposeful group of younger men, who had Kluge's tacit backing if not his wholehearted support, formed the strongest and most closely knit action unit the Resistance had yet known. Tresckow was an intelligent tactician and a determined man. The only missing prerequisite was access to Hitler, though their resolve was strengthened by Hardenberg's witnessing of an action against Jews at Borisov, where he saw several thousand slaughtered by Latvian SS. Tresckow forwarded a complaint, but there was no reaction to it.

Although the group had no formal link with the centre of Resistance in Berlin, Schlabrendorff frequently travelled between Army Group Headquarters at Smolensk and the capital, and had maintained contact with Oster, who in turn, through fellow conspirators like Hassell and Trott, sounded out likely Allied responses to a coup in the east. Schlabrendorff also made contact with Beck, Goerdeler, Otto John, Dohnanyi and Guttenberg, and in the course of time Tresckow's group was welded to the main Resistance.

Tresckow himself counts among the most notable of all the conspirators. His attempt on Hitler's life was to be the most important since Elser's in 1939 – and it came as close to success. Through Schwerin von Schwanenfeld, Field Marshal Erwin Witzleben, still at this stage commanding in the west, was also kept *au fait* with Tresckow's plans. But this was still early days. Witzleben retired owing to ill health on 15 March 1942.

Günther von Kluge took over command of Army Group Centre in December 1941. He was a gifted commander but a weak man, one who would have doubtless gone along with a successful coup but who could not bring himself to join one in advance. When Hitler sent him a gift of 250,000 Reichsmark for his sixtieth birthday, for improvements to his estate, Kluge accepted it. Tresckow tried to persuade him that the only way he could justify so doing – for it was clearly a bribe – was to make a firm commitment to the Resistance. But once again 'Clever Jack', as he was privately nicknamed, prevaricated.[3] Meanwhile, after the fall of Stalingrad and Goebbels' speech invoking 'total war' at the Berlin Sports Palace on 18 February 1943, ordinary soldiers at the Front had lost faith and openly wrote disillusioned letters home: 'The only thing I'd like to know', wrote Heinrich Roth to his wife in May, 'is how these idiots think they're going to win now . . . None of us soldiers think there'll be good times after the war. On the contrary, none of us think we'll even be able to bring the war to a good end . . .'

One key general was, however, brought into the conspiracy in the winter of 1942–43. He was Friedrich Olbricht, head of the General Army Office (Allgemeines Heeresamt – AHA), though he, too, needed constant prodding to keep him up to the mark. Schlabrendorff made the contact with him through Captain Hermann Kaiser, who in turn was on the staff of the head of the Reserve Army, General Friedrich Fromm. Fromm was also targeted by the conspirators. As has been mentioned, the Reserve Army would be a vital tool in securing Germany's domestic infrastructure in the event of a coup. Fromm turned out to be a good deal less tractable than Olbricht, but he betrayed nobody to the Gestapo. Whatever else the vacillating generals did, they did not betray their brother officers to the Nazis.

In summer 1942 Tresckow asked Gersdorff to organise the necessary explosives and fuses for an assassination attempt. The explosives had to be compact and the fuses silent. This was not an easy commission, but as an Intelligence officer, Gersdorff had access to the Abwehr, and in Section II, the one which dealt, among other things, with sabotage, he found what he was looking for. His excuse for requisitioning it was that he wished to equip White Russians serving in an anti-partisan unit, the 'Boeselager Brigade' (in fact created as a back-up force in the event of a coup) to be formed under Georg Boeselager. Section II gave him a plastic explosive from stock captured from the British. A small amount was very effective. He was also given British fuses. These were silent and much more sophisticated than German types, which could be set for much shorter times, but which betrayed their presence by a loud hissing sound. The model chosen by Gersdorff operated by the action of acid released from a capsule when the fuse was activated, which ate through a wire in a given amount of time, which in turn released the spring driving the firing pin on to the detonator. Fuses were set with delays at ten-minute intervals, the precise time determined by a fixed temperature. The colder it was, for example, the longer the fuse took to detonate.

This was important, and over the next few months Gersdorff obtained a supply of the explosive and the fuses, which Tresckow and Schlabrendorff secretly tested in fields at the Front. In the course of these experiments during the second half of 1942, the conspirators were introduced to a little British bomb not much bigger than a prayer-book and known as a 'clam', because it was designed to adhere to a target by magnets. Filled with plastic tetryl and TNT, it packed enough punch to drive through a 2cm steel plate. The conspirators knew, however, that for such a bomb to have a fatal effect on a man, it would have to be discharged in a confined space to maximise the blanketing effect of the enclosed shock wave. Tresckow decided that his best bet would be to smuggle such a bomb, with a time fuse of appropriate length, into either Hitler's car or his aeroplane.

While Tresckow was planning his attempt, the Resistance in Berlin was busy organising ways of securing the country after Hitler's fall. Olbricht, aided by Gisevius, who worked over the old 1938 plans once more, was engaged in working out means of taking major cities for the Resistance. Of these, Berlin was the most important. Providentially, the Brandenburg Division of the Army, which was under the Abwehr's control, was undergoing reorganisation and needed a new commanding officer. Canaris and Oster were able to place Colonel Alexander von Pfuhlstein in this position in spring 1943. Pfuhlstein was on good terms with Olbricht and Oster. The Brandenburg Division would be able to cut off the large SS division stationed at Jüterbog to the south of Berlin, and isolate the city from Rastenburg to the east.

In the meantime, the 'Boeselager Brigade' was provided with the best possible equipment, thanks to the efforts of another conspirator, Helmuth Stieff, head of Organisation in the Army General Staff. There remained the problem of cutting off telecommunications to and from Hitler's Wolf's Lair HQ; but although the head of Signals, General Erich Fellgiebel, was in the conspiracy and prepared to do this as best he could, complete segregation would depend upon the occupation of signal stations and key telephone exchanges as soon as Hitler was dead.

Every detail of the plot was arranged, though it would be difficult to co-ordinate each element to the day. The other maverick factor was Hitler's own unpredictability – he was growing ever more suspicious, and had yet to accept an invitation to visit Smolensk. However, the failing fortunes of war had made the Führer anxious, and he did agree to come on 13 March 1943 for a briefing meeting. He arrived in a flight of three Condors, accompanied by Jodl and Colonel-General Kurt Zeitzler, Halder's youngish replacement as Chief of the General Staff, whom Canaris referred to rather unfairly as 'that fat Nazi'. The party landed at Smolensk airport but was driven from there to Army Group Centre HQ in Hitler's own convoy of cars which had been driven over from Vinnitsa specially. He was, as always these days, surrounded by machine-gun toting SS men.

'Operation Flash', as this attempt to kill Hitler was coded, was ready to be launched. The action itself was almost casual in its simplicity, given the complexity of the arrangement surrounding it.

The headquarters of the Overall High Command of the Armed Forces, Mauerwald, was not far from Hitler's Wolf's Lair, and several OKW members had travelled with the Führer from there for this briefing meeting. One of them, travelling on the same aeroplane, was an Operations Staff officer called Heinz Brandt, a former Olympic rider. Tresckow asked him if he would take back a couple of bottles of Cointreau as a present for Helmuth Stieff. The package, whose squarish shape suggested two small bottles of the liqueur, was in fact two pairs of 'clam' bombs, held together by their magnets and tightly wrapped. They were accompanied by a thirty-minute fuse.

That same afternoon after lunch, Hitler embarked on his Condor once more, and Schlabrendorff gave the package to the unsuspecting Brandt. Just before doing so, he activated the fuse. Soon afterwards the Condor took off. Tresckow, Schlabrendorff and Kluge (who was a party to the conspiracy) watched it disappear with bated breath. Four 'clams' should be more than enough to do the trick, and Hitler's death would look like the result of an air crash, especially if Artur Nebe ran the investigation and could cover up any incriminating evidence. The Army could legitimately take control of the country in the interests of national security, and Goerdeler and Beck could set about the business of negotiating a peace with the Allies.

Schlabrendorff telephoned Ludwig Gehre, a contact in Dohnanyi's office, to give him the signal that Operation Flash was on. They calculated that the Condor would explode just before it reached Minsk, some 130 miles to the west.

They passed the rest of the afternoon in a state of unbearable tension, waiting for confirmation of the Führer's death. Then came the news that he had landed safely at Rastenburg aerodrome.

It barely seemed possible, but there was no time to be lost in reflection. Schlabrendorff rang Gehre again to give him the codeword for the failure of Flash, while Tresckow rang Brandt to ask him to hang on to the 'Cointreau'. There had been a mix-up, he said, but Schlabrendorff would be arriving the following day to collect the package and give Brandt the parcel really destined for Stieff. Then there was nothing they could do but wait. Stieff had not been told of the ploy, as a security measure; all they could hope for was that Brandt would not become curious, and that the bomb would now not explode after all.

The following morning Schlabrendorff took the normal courier flight to Rastenburg, taking with him a package which really contained two bottles of Cointreau. He immediately sought out Brandt and swapped the parcels with him, his heart in his mouth at the casual way the innocent Brandt manhandled the explosive packet. He took this with him to the sleeping car in a railway siding which served as overnight accommodation for visitors to Mauerwald, and there in his compartment he carefully slit open the package and examined the bomb. The detonator had worked, but the 'clams' had not ignited. He could only conclude that despite the high tolerance of the explosive, it had simply been too cold for it to go off.

Fighting the stress which was affecting them all, he took the bombs with him to Berlin the following day, and told Oster the whole story. Their disappointment was great, but they still had the bombs, and they immediately cast about for another opportunity to use them.

It so happened that the annual Heroes' Memorial Day had been postponed by Hitler by a week that year. Normally, it would have fallen on 15 March, the day Schlabrendorff arrived in Berlin, but the Führer had put it off until 21 March in the hope that the German Army might score some counter-victory against the Russians in the meantime which he could exploit for propaganda purposes. In fact an SS division retook Kharkov just in time. The delay also gave the Resistance time to organise another attempt, and once again Fate seemed to be helping them, for part of the ceremony was to involve a visit by Hitler to an exhibition of Russian war material captured by Army Group Centre and set up by Rudolf Gersdorff's Intelligence section. The exhibition would be in a hall of the Old Arsenal Museum in central Berlin, where the Heroes' Memorial Day ceremony normally took place, with the playing of classical music and a speech by Hitler.

At first the Resistance considered the possibility of concealing the bomb somewhere in the exhibition, but there was no opportunity to do so undetected before Hitler's visit, and in any case no guarantee that he could be induced to stand near enough any given spot for long enough for the bombs to go off. Gersdorff, who had no dependents since the death of his wife the previous year, volunteered to carry the bombs with him in the pockets of his greatcoat. If he could stay close enough to Hitler – as his guide to the exhibition – he should be able to blow the dictator up at the cost of his own life. Tresckow accepted this brave proposal, but then Hitler's Army ADC, Rudolf Schmundt, though an old friend of Tresckow's (they had been in Infantry Regiment 9 together), became vaguely suspicious and would not allow Gersdorff's name on the list of those to be admitted to the exhibition with Hitler. Finally he was persuaded that Gersdorff was the only man able to explain the exhibits properly to the Führer.

There were other difficulties. Normally, this rare annual public appearance by Hitler followed a set timetable. This year, matters were not fixed according to the usual schedule, nor was the schedule published in advance. What did seem certain was that Hitler would spend at least ten minutes viewing Gersdorff's exhibition. That, however, entailed another problem. The shortest duration of time-fuses available of the silent British type was ten minutes. German grenade fuses might have been used as they only took four or five seconds, but they hissed noisily and in any case could not be adapted to fit the 'clams'. Gersdorff would have to judge the moment when he activated the fuses to the second. Another problem was that Hitler was acutely sensitive to mood. If Gersdorff showed tension or fear, Hitler would know it.

The day dawned and the hour approached for Hitler to visit the exhibition. As a senior officer with special responsibilities, Gersdorff was able to avoid the SS body searches, but he was aware of much tighter security than there had ever been hitherto. Had Hitler somehow got an inkling of Operation Flash? It was too late now for reflection. Hitler was approaching the spot where Gersdorff was waiting with other dignitaries at the entrance to the museum. Gersdorff had two of the little bombs in each greatcoat pocket. He gave the Hitler salute and then quickly set the fuse in his left pocket. He dared not put his hand in his right pocket immediately afterwards for fear of arousing suspicion. Everywhere around them were alert young SS men.

There was another shock in store for Gersdorff. Unexpectedly at the last minute Hitler asked that Field Marshal von Bock, Kluge's predecessor in command of Army Group Centre, should accompany the visit with his ADC, Graf von Hardenberg. Hardenberg was innocent of this assassination attempt, but he was in the conspiracy and he was also a close friend of Gersdorff. But the die was cast.

Hitler entered the exhibition hall with his entourage, and Gersdorff at his elbow. Then, taking everyone aback, he flew through it. He paused nowhere, took no interest in anything, and firmly avoided any attempt by anyone in his entourage, including Göring, to delay or detain him. He was outside again in two minutes, throwing the organisers of the day into momentary confusion. Gersdorff, breathing hard and too shocked to analyse what could have gone wrong, quickly and unobtrusively made his way to a lavatory where he defused the armed bomb in his left pocket.

There could be little doubt that Hitler's sixth sense had saved him this time. Goerdeler wrote an extremely long secret memorandum to the generals on 26 March, in which he discussed sixteen points which argued the absolute necessity of an immediate coup. He tried to rally them by recalling to their minds Hitler's outrages against their own colleagues – referring to the dictator ripping the epaulettes from senior officers' shoulders after the first defeats in Russia, and describing the collapse of the German internal infrastructure as the war effort made ever increasing demands on the nation and the Allies' air raids smashed ever more German factories. Goerdeler finally proposed his old solution of making a deal with the western Allies against Russia, which was an indication of how out of touch he had become with enemy thinking.

Tresckow was not defeated, but he had shot his main bolt. Stauffenberg had made his entrance, but his role was yet to develop. The Kreisau Circle continued their moral and ethical reflections. It was a time when the Resistance needed all the strength and the courage of their convictions; and precisely now, within a month of the failure of Operation Flash, they were to suffer another, all but mortal, setback.

ELEVEN

Breaking Point

On 5 April 1943 Hans Oster was removed from office and Hans von Dohnanyi was arrested. His wife was also arrested, as were Dietrich Bonhoeffer and Josef Müller, the lawyer and diplomat whom the Resistance used as their contact with the Vatican. Neglect of a tiny crack had brought down a whole wall.

This was one of a series of disasters. Beck's cancer had grown so bad that in March 1943 he had to undergo major surgery and, although he recovered, he was out of action for a time. In March, the Resistance approached Kurt von Hammerstein in the hope that he would go to see General Fromm and persuade him to change sides; but Hammerstein also had cancer, and was by now seriously ill. He could not help and said so, but added, showing his old fighting spirit, 'If I only had a division, I'd go and fetch that devil [Hitler] out of hell.' Captain Hermann Kaiser wrote sorrowfully in his diary in February: '[Olbricht] wants to act when he gets the order, and [Fromm] wants to give the order when someone else has acted.' In March, Moltke wrote bitterly to an English friend:

> The main mistake was to leave such an attempt to the generals. It was a vain hope from the start, but it was hard to convince most people of that in time. The French generals couldn't get rid of Napoleon. It's exactly the same with the Germans today.

Witzleben, too, was ill: in July he entered a hospital with a gastric ulcer. The fall of Mussolini in the same month, and the failure of the Kursk summer offensive, leading to counter-attacks from the

Russians, were of some comfort to the Resistance, but it was remote.

In April 1943, Kurt von Hammerstein died. The family had to go to enormous lengths to have the funeral service held at the Dahlem Church where he had worshipped – the incumbent pastor would not agree to officiate at first – and to avoid having the coffin wrapped in the swastika flag: it was deliberately abandoned in a brown paper parcel at Thielplatz underground station. They had to accept a wreath from the Führer, however, which was laid by General Joachim von Kortzfleisch, now commander of the Army division covering Berlin and the surrounding district. The city commander of Berlin, Paul von Hase, who was Dietrich Bonhoeffer's uncle, and Wilhelm-Friedrich, Graf zu Lynar, Witzleben's ADC, lent their support to the family. Both were members of the conspiracy.

Tresckow was tireless in his efforts to keep the momentum of the Resistance going and, pleading sick leave on account of Front fatigue, managed to spend several months in Berlin in the course of 1943, during which he tried with every means at his disposal to get a posting to a position where he could be of some service to the central Resistance, but to no avail. He was finally ordered back to a command on the east Front, far from the action he so desperately wanted to be a part of. The Resistance considered making an approach to Guderian, but Schlabrendorff considered him 'the incarnation of characterlessness', and Tresckow had no faith in him either. In late October 1943 the vacillating but generally sympathetic Kluge had a serious car accident and was replaced as commander of Army Group Centre by Ernst Busch, a rigorously pro-Hitler officer.

The arrest of the Scholls in Munich had put the Gestapo on its toes and even Schulenburg was arrested briefly and interrogated about his attempts to recruit young officers from Infantry Regiment 9 to the cause, but he was able to exonerate himself. That was on 2 April. The night before he had collapsed on the Berlin S-train, almost certainly from nervous exhaustion. Most principal members of the central Resistance were under observation. Himmler stayed his hand in case they could be useful to him in a coup of his own against Hitler – and Schulenburg was changing lodgings frequently to minimise Security Service observation.

Three days after his arrest the great blow fell. The Nazi Security Service had long been looking for an opportunity to take over the Abwehr, and now it thought it had seen an opening. The Abwehr

office in Munich had become involved in a private currency exchange
racket going on in Prague, and the culprit, a Portuguese honorary
consul called Wilhelm Schmidhuber who also worked as an agent
of the Abwehr, was arrested in October 1942 by the local Gestapo.[1]
Schmidhuber was not a pleasant or terribly trustworthy character, but
he was useful. He was very much Dohnanyi's man. After the arrest,
the steps the Abwehr took to protect him were not sufficient, and it
allowed itself to be outmanoeuvred by the Gestapo. When the Abwehr
then found itself unable to bail Schmidhuber out without becoming
compromised, the consul saw this as betrayal, and decided to tell the
Security Service everything he knew. Fortunately it was not much;
but it was enough.

Through Schmidhuber's interrogation it was discovered that
Dohnanyi had been using large amounts of foreign currency,
of which the Abwehr had the disposal, to help Jews by illegally
compensating them for their confiscated property or businesses in
Germany. The matter was not helped by the fact that Dohnanyi was
of distant Jewish extraction himself, and had been allowed to continue
his Abwehr work only by special dispensation of the Führer. A third
weapon the Security Service was able to use against the Abwehr was
that they had been using Jews as agents for a long time. Moltke had
a tip-off that the Gestapo was about to strike but his warning came
too late.

On the morning of 5 April Manfred Roeder, the Nazi pros-
ecutor, presented himself at Abwehr headquarters on Tirpitzufer.
Roeder was forty-three years old, and had made his mark as an 'ice
cold' investigator by breaking the Red Orchestra ring. He informed
Canaris that an investigation was being held, and then asked Oster
to accompany him to Dohnanyi's office, as he had a warrant for
his arrest. Oster immediately insisted that, as Dohnanyi's senior
officer, he would take full responsibility and should be arrested
instead. Roeder retorted that the offence was a private criminal one
of unauthorised currency exchange and that therefore only Dohnanyi
could answer the charges. They went down the narrow corridor to
Dohnanyi's office. There had been no time to warn him, and he was
anxious to conceal certain papers and files on his desk, dealing with a
new mission to Rome for Dietrich Bonhoeffer, and containing a draft
report to Josef Müller about the failure of 'Flash'. The file with the
key papers was marked with an 'O' – the significance of which is in

doubt. The papers were apparently destined for Beck, but Oster took the symbol to mean himself.

While Roeder was searching the safe, Dohnanyi tried to indicate the incriminating papers to Oster. He wanted Oster to pass them off as fiction – misinformation to be fed to the enemy as part of the Abwehr's routine work. Oster, however, misunderstood, panicked and tried to conceal them. His action was noticed by Roeder's assistant, a glacial Nazi police captain called Franz Xaver Sonderegger. Oster thus drew suspicion on himself, though he was not immediately arrested. However it took months of coded messages smuggled out of Dohnanyi's prison cell to persuade him to change his attitude to the 'O' papers and treat them as official misinformation. By then Oster himself had been suspended. Later in the year he was placed on the Reserve list. By the end of 1943 he was forbidden by Keitel to have anything to do with the Abwehr, and the following spring he was retired. He left Berlin and went to live on the estate of his sister and her husband at Schnaditz. From then until his arrest immediately after 20 July 1944 he was permanently under Gestapo surveillance. Dohnanyi, who never left prison again and who was later transferred to Sachsenhausen concentration camp, also moved heaven and earth to get the 'Zossen documents' – his huge archive of Nazi war crimes – destroyed; but this the Resistance was still unwilling to do, to their ultimate cost.

The immediate reaction of the Resistance was to put every plan on ice for the summer months of 1943 at least. Gisevius was sent to convey a warning to the Pope, who was still interested in the principle of peace brokerage. Canaris was in more immediate danger than Beck, but he not only managed to hold on to his position but to hit out actively at the unpleasant and unwelcome Roeder. Roeder had said scornfully that the Brandenburg Division was a gang of layabouts and that he would soon be throwing some light on them. This boast reached the ears of Canaris, who made sure that the division's commander, Alexander von Pfuhlstein, heard about it. Pfuhlstein leapt to the defence of his men, went to Roeder and slapped his face. This was in January 1944, by which time Roeder had become very dangerous indeed. Keitel gave Pfuhlstein a mild punishment, however: seven days confined to quarters. By April, though, Pfuhlstein's 'defeatist' attitude led to his being relieved of the command – another blow to the Resistance, though Schwerin von Schwanenfeld managed to transfer from his staff job with the division to an administrative position with Army High Command only a few minutes' walk away from the offices of Olbricht and Stauffenberg in Bendlerstrasse. His new post had the advantage of giving him the authority to issue passes and IDs. In Pfuhlstein, however, Oster lost a close supporter and friend, and Pfuhlstein's ingenuous answers to Gestapo questions damaged Oster's case seriously.

Meanwhile, the arrogant Roeder had become involved in litigation with a colleague, Ernst Kanter, following a complaint by the latter about the former's failure to observe confidentiality. After a row, Roeder requested a transfer. The damage by then, however, had been done. Canaris managed to hold on until February 1944, but then the defection of an Abwehr agent, Erich Vermehren, in Istanbul to the British gave the Security Service the final handle it needed to pull the 'little Admiral' from office. The British regarded the defection as a minor triumph, though unbeknownst to them it had robbed them of one of their best allies.

Vermehren had defected in panic when he heard the news of the arrest of his friend Otto Kiep, along with other members of the Solf Circle. Vermehren had also met Trott in Istanbul on one of the latter's peace-feeler missions. He had never been pro-Nazi, and his own freedom of movement had been limited by his marriage to Countess Elisabeth von Plettenberg, a devout Roman Catholic several years his senior, who was related to Bishop Galen and former Chancellor von Papen. Trott had been instrumental in getting Elisabeth to Istanbul to join her husband, on von Papen's guarantee (Papen was German ambassador to Turkey by now) – upon which Vermehren contacted the British agent in place there, Nicholas Elliott, who got the couple out. The immediate result was imprisonment for their families at home, and interrogations for Trott and Vermehren's boss in Istanbul, Paul Leverkühn. To be fair to the Vermehrens, they defected only after much heart-searching; they were aware of the possible effect their action would have on their families and friends. Hitler, beside himself with rage because he believed the Vermehrens to have left with more important information than they actually had, made travel for German nationals much more difficult after this incident, and even Papen told the neutral Turks that failure to hand the couple over was a *casus belli*. The increased Nazi security which resulted from their defection was another unwelcome blow to the Resistance. The Vermehrens are still alive; they have changed their name and live in Switzerland.

Over the years, the strain of leading a double existence had told increasingly on Canaris. He grew ever more mistrustful and bitter. His consolation was the company of his dachshund, Seppl; when the dog died, there was uproar in the household until he was replaced. But Canaris fought to the last, and was even able to have Colonel Georg Hansen, a fellow conspirator and head of Abwehr I, placed as his successor. However, the days of the Abwehr were numbered; the young and ambitious head of Security Service Department VI (Foreign Affairs), Walter Schellenberg, had it subordinated to his department after 20 July 1944. This was the same Schellenberg who had distinguished himself by arresting the British spies at Venlo in 1939, and who now ran peace-feeler errands for Himmler in Sweden. Canaris himself was given a meaningless job as head of the Department for Economic Warfare at Eiche, near Potsdam – he was thus effectively marginalised. In the days following 20 July 1944 he was arrested by Schellenberg personally.

Dietrich Bonhoeffer can have had no idea that his arrest was so imminent. 1943 had started well for him with his engagement to Maria von Wedemeyer in Pomerania on 17 January. It is unlikely that he knew how closely his brother-in-law Hans von Dohnanyi was involved with Operation Flash – members of the Resistance confided in nobody: everyone knew how effective Gestapo methods were at extracting information from suspects. Towards midday on 5 April he telephoned his sister Christine Dohnanyi from his parents' house in Marienburger Allee in Berlin and was surprised to hear the phone answered by a man. Instantly he realised what had happened. He did not disturb his elderly parents, who were enjoying their after-lunch nap, but went straight upstairs to his own room to check that there were no incriminating documents in his desk. Then he went next door, where another sister, Ursula Schleicher, lived, to await events. At about 4p.m. his father came over to tell him that two men wanted to speak to him in his room. The two men were Roeder and Sonderegger. Soon afterwards they drove off with him.

His parents received a reassuring letter from him on 14 April – how quickly, he remarked, one could adapt to going without creature comforts: he barely even missed his cigarettes. The truth was that he had been placed in solitary confinement, given stinking blankets, and was denied access to soap and water or clean linen. The warders were forbidden to talk to him. He was fed on dry bread thrown on to the

cell floor through a slit in the door. Nevertheless in May he managed
to smuggle out a speech to be read at the baptism of his godson – the
child of Bonhoeffer's niece and her husband Eberhard Bethge. In it
he quoted Proverbs 4, 18: 'But the path of the righteous is like the
light of dawn, which shines brighter and brighter until full day.'

There was no reason to give up hope. Many of the conspirators
thought that the end of the war could be only weeks away, and they
went on believing it, clinging to the thought, as 1943 gave way to 1944
and the months passed. Karl Sack, the General Staff judge who had
always been on the fringes of the conspiracy, did all in his power to
get the investigations dragged out and the trials delayed. As late as
June 1944, Dohnanyi deliberately infected himself with diphtheria so
as to be too unwell for investigations against him to proceed. While he
was still in office, Canaris did what he could to frustrate the Gestapo,
as did Guttenberg and Justus Delbrück, who were still working at
the Abwehr. The determination of the surviving Resistance was not
dented even by the conference at Tehran at the end of the year, at
which Churchill and Roosevelt agreed the division of Germany with
Stalin, and drew up plans to move Poland's frontiers some 150 miles
westwards, thereby robbing Germany of all her rich agricultural
eastern provinces, including East Prussia. Perhaps the Resistance
had little or no intelligence of the decisions the most powerful Allies
were making about the future of their country. Certainly Goerdeler and
even Stauffenberg continued to entertain hopes of retaining the 1914
frontiers as well as the German-speaking lands occupied by Hitler
until the very end – a quite unrealistic ambition by any standards.
Hope of quarter from the Allies by now must have been illusion. In
July 1943 the Allies launched 'Operation Gomorrah', a bombing raid
which destroyed 277,000 homes in Hamburg and left 3000 civilian
dead. This brought the population of Berlin to the verge of hysteria, as
one of the conspirators wrote to his wife. It was a foretaste of what was
yet to come to Leipzig, Dresden and the capital itself.

Meanwhile in the East, as the Russians slowly but surely pushed
the German armies back, a new Resistance movement was growing
in the POW camps of the Soviet Union. In 1943 the National Committee for Free Germany was established as an anti-Fascist movement
to overthrow Hitler.

It was not exclusively Communist, though it had the absolute
backing and encouragement of the Soviet authorities, who no doubt

saw it as a potential force through which to establish a post-war regime in Germany that would be loyal, and possibly subservient, to Moscow. In terms of the administration of what was until 1990 the German Democratic Republic (East Germany) this policy was a complete success.

Leading German Communists in exile in Russia suffered the agony of split loyalties after the German invasion in 1941, because they were natives of the country invading the one which was offering them asylum. In that year, the Bulgarian Communist leader Georgi Dimitroff (also an exile at the time) convened a meeting in Moscow to remind them of their supra-national political loyalties, to call to mind the crimes of the Nazi state, and to map out the future duties of German Communists at home. Meanwhile, the USSR should be given every possible aid and support in its hour of need. The Russians kept a low profile at the meeting, which was dominated by former leading politicians like Wilhelm Pieck and Walter Ulbricht, and intellectuals and artists like Johannes R. Becher and Erich Weinert. Most of these men had been out of Germany for eight years, and at their first contact with young German working-class POWs, they were horrified at the enthusiasm for Hitler they encountered. By the winter of 1941, however, the German Communists had already experienced some success in converting these men, as Hitler's campaign foundered and they began to realise the sacrifices Germany was making in pursuit of merely the realisation of one man's ambition.

Among the new converts was Captain Ernst Hadermann, a former socialist teacher who had won the Iron Cross First Class in the First World War. He was articulate and intelligent, and his patriotism could not be in doubt. He was an ideal proselytiser. In May 1942 he gave a memorable speech to his fellow prisoners in Camp 95 at Yelabuga near the River Kama. In it he described the 'nefarious effects of National Socialist rule upon Germany's peasantry, youth, education and culture'. Warning of the inevitable defeat of National Socialism, Hadermann called for the overthrow of Adolf Hitler, the restoration of freedom to the German people, and the signing of an honourable and timely peace treaty.[2]

The speech had a profound effect, and it was published in an edition of 500,000 with an introduction by Erich Weinert under the title 'An Honest Word by a German Captain'. Copies were dropped over the German lines, and even found their way into Germany itself.

Propaganda leaflets were increasingly dropped over the lines from aircraft (as the war progressed the Russians had little or nothing to fear from the Luftwaffe), or even fired from guns.

Hadermann's work resulted in the formation of the First Anti-Fascist Officers' Group. There were twenty-one of them, not all of them by any means Communists or even Socialists. They cast themselves in the role of the German officers who had defied their king in order to help Russia defeat Napoleon and thereby free Prussia from the French yoke – Boyen, Gneisenau and Scharnhorst, Clausewitz and Wartenburg.

A newspaper soon followed, *The Free Word*, which appeared from August 1942. A Central Anti-Fascist School for German POWs was founded in Oranki, and German Communists canvassed the camps. Their reception was not unsympathetic, not least because the Russians treated their prisoners relatively well – certainly not in the brutal manner depicted by Goebbels (and actually practised on Russian prisoners by the Germans in defiance of the Geneva Convention); but it was at the defeat at Stalingrad that the process of conversion found real success. Ulbricht, Weinert and the novelist Willi Bredel travelled to Stalingrad in January 1943 to assist propaganda efforts and interview new German POWs there. Most felt then that Hitler would rescue them yet. So, to disabuse them, a concentrated campaign of leaflets and loudspeaker broadcasts encouraging surrender was aimed at the German Front. Essentially they gave the lie to the Nazi statement that the Soviets 'took no prisoners'.

The campaign worked. The soldiers were disillusioned by Hitler's broken promises of a rescue, and came to see that the Führer still expected them to give their lives to the last man even after continued defence had become meaningless. The final insult to the 90,000 survivors came when they realised that they had indeed been written off at home. In order to make heroic capital out of the defeat, Goebbels' Propaganda Ministry was giving it out that the 6th Army had defended Stalingrad to the death, drawing a shameless analogy with Thermopylae.

The Soviets were careful not to push Communist ideology too hard and were rewarded with thousands of converts. They had less success with senior officers captured at Stalingrad and during the defeats which followed it, but it was out of the Officers' Group that the National Committee for Free Germany was founded on 27 July

1943 at Krasnogorsk. Erich Weinert became its president. He argued convincingly that as the Germans had helped Hitler to power, they could only clear themselves of guilt by being the ones to remove him. Otherwise they would deserve to share in the débâcle which would follow unconditional surrender to the Allies.

From the National Committee came the League of German Officers. The League was designed to appeal to senior officer prisoners, and this time the Russians and the German Communists had better success in recruiting them. The German campaign in the Soviet Union was over, the Nazis had brought Germany to its knees, and it was time to think of the future. General Melnikov, head of Soviet POW administration, told three key captive generals, Walther von Seydlitz-Kurzbach, Otto Korfes and Martin Lattmann, that the USSR had no designs on Germany and would agree to a unified state within the boundaries of 1937, together with the continued existence of a strong German Army. Seydlitz, who had commanded 51st Army Corps at Stalingrad, and had tried to persuade Field Marshal Paulus to surrender as early as November 1942, was a descendant of the General Seydlitz who had been one of the signatories of the Treaty of Tauroggen with Russia against Napoleon in 1812. He agreed to join the League on his fifty-fifth birthday in 1943 and was followed by his two colleagues. Unfortunately, in his crusading zeal, he then tried too aggressively to convert more of his colleagues at a prison camp for German generals at the Voikov Estate in Vladimir. They closed ranks against him.

The Russians did all they could to boost the kudos of the League. After its founding convention, a number of leading Soviet artistes were invited to perform, but they were outraged when they discovered that their audience was to be German. The soprano of the Nemirovich-Danchenko Theatre had lost her only brother at the Front the day before. After the performance, Seydlitz invited her to sit at his table. She said: 'Kindly wait with your invitations until the war is over.'

The League continued to grow, notwithstanding the attitude of the generals at Vladimir, and close ties were effected with the National Committee, to avoid any suspicion of elitism. The greatest coup was the conversion of Field Marshal Paulus. He joined the Free Germany Movement on 14 July 1944. The Allied attack in the west on 6 June (D-Day) had convinced him that the future of Germany no longer lay with Hitler. He brought many hitherto reluctant generals with him.

They set themselves three main goals: to persuade the German Army to leave the occupied territories, to convince the German civilian population that Hitler should be removed, and to convert POWs to the anti-Fascist cause. Time was of the essence. The Russians set up a radio station for them, and executives were introduced into every prison camp. So-called front workers conducted propaganda campaigns at the Russian front line, and the Soviets released newly captured POWs deliberately to give the lie to Nazi propaganda about Russian mercilessness. Leaflets were dropped instructing German soldiers how to surrender in Russian, a tactic which was highly successful at Cherkassy in January 1944, where the men were abandoned by their commanding officers.

The National Committee was not without its setbacks, however. A group of fanatical Nazis among the POWs joined and rose as a Fifth Column within its ranks. One of them, Hans Huber, a former SS Obersturmbannführer (Lieutenant-Colonel), sent coded messages about National Committee activities to the Nazis through his Free Germany articles and radio broadcasts. He planned to have the whole of the Committee leadership captured by a special Nazi airborne assault. In this he overreached himself, but not without creating a crisis of confidence between the Committee and the Russians at a crucial time, when the Western Allies were beginning to express doubts to Stalin about the whole Free Germany movement. The split widened when the Germans discovered that the USSR and Poland planned to take a large slice of German territory east of the rivers Oder and Neisse after the end of the war. This news especially affected the non-Communist members of the National Committee, which by now however could count its total membership in tens of thousands.

After Cherkassy, Hitler acknowledged the existence of the movement, Seydlitz was sentenced to death in absentia and his wife was forced to divorce him. Some wives did not support their husbands' anti-Fascist stance at all. The wife of Major Bernhard Bechler reported eight anonymous letters she had received in September 1943 telling her of her husband's broadcasts[3] for Radio Free Germany. She also reported a fifty-seven-year-old coalminer who came to see her to give her the same news because he thought she would be relieved to know her husband was still alive. The coalminer was arrested and executed as a result. When Bechler returned to Germany after the war and learned the truth, he divorced her.

As the war progressed, specially trained units of converted German POWs were equipped with forged German Army IDs, German and Soviet currency, ration cards and uniforms, portable printing presses, radios and megaphones. Later they were also armed. They combined propaganda with Intelligence work and finally, on German soil, engaged in combat on the Russian side. Radio Free Germany was assisted by the BBC, which publicised its broadcasts. The Free Germany Movement continued its efforts until the very end of the war, even when it was clear that Russia had no intention of honouring any of the undertakings originally promised by General Melnikov. Out of it grew the new Communist State of East Germany, which in turn has now been swallowed up by history.

Part Three

1944–1945

Göring was a keen huntsman. He also boasted that if ever foreign warplanes should fly over Germany, you could call him Meyer. When the Allies began to bomb the country, the Germans nicknamed the air raid siren 'Meyer's hunting horn'.

TWELVE

A Hero Enters Late

It was in 1943 that Stauffenberg joined the Resistance. The impetus
he gave it was such that many wished he had made his conversion
years before. He was not universally admired by the conspirators,
but he had precisely the qualities of leadership that the Resistance
so badly needed. He was young and charismatic, and he combined
a strong intellect with realistic political instincts and the qualities of
a man of action.

Claus Philipp Maria Graf Schenk von Stauffenberg[1] was born at
Jettingen, to the west of Tübingen, in 1907, of a Swabian Roman
Catholic noble family whose written records went back to 1382, but
the earliest mention of which occurs over a century earlier. Though
conservative in outlook – Stauffenberg's father was senior marshal of
the court of the King of Württemberg – there was an unconventional
streak in the family. His great-grandfather, Franz-Ludwig, was raised
from Freiherr to Graf by Ludwig II of Bavaria as a punishment (Franz-
Ludwig had supported Bismarck's unification policy against the king's
wishes) because Franz-Ludwig had formerly stated that he was against
any such form of aristocratic promotion. Claus's father, Alfred, was a
great handyman and gardener from whom Claus inherited his practical
streak. His mother, Caroline, was unworldly and artistic. From her
Claus inherited his gift for music – he was a talented cellist – and for
drawing. He had twin brothers, Alexander and Berthold, who were
two years his senior. Alexander became a historian, and Berthold a
lawyer. Berthold, in the Navy during the war, was also involved in
the Resistance. Alexander, the least worldly of the three, was never
taken into their close confidence. He was the only one to survive the

war. Claus was the leader, and was often mistaken for the oldest brother – by Moltke, for example.

During his childhood, Stauffenberg experienced the collapse of the old order and the rise of the Weimar Republic, which held little attraction for him. He had a liberal education at the 250-year-old Eberhard Ludwig Grammar School in Stuttgart, one of Germany's best. Tall and very handsome, he was nevertheless prone to illness and not physically strong. His natural disposition was for cultural pursuits. He preferred Beethoven to Wagner, whom he found bombastic, enjoyed *Lady Chatterley's Lover* which his mother gave him in English, and he appreciated wine and good food – like Moltke, he even cooked with pleasure, an unusual trait in a German male at that time.

He had great natural charm, and one of his more endearing pastimes in later life was to lie on the drawing-room floor with his wife Nina, she with a cushion under her because she was so slim, while they read an English novel together, the quicker reader waiting for the slower. He was characteristically untidy in his dress, and was careless of his uniforms. He could cat-nap to order, and he was maniacally punctual. Times for daily domestic events like luncheon had to be fixed precisely. Like Oster, he rode a bicycle to and from work. Despite being casual about clothes, he was strict about orderliness. If, for example, his boots were not lined up exactly side by side, he could become furious. He had a highly volatile temperament which he learnt to control by assuming a stony countenance. He was a heavy smoker all his life, but could stop at will if it was necessary to do so – to combat an illness, for example. Someone who did not know him once saw a bust of the twenty-one-year-old Stauffenberg by his friend Frank Mehnert, and said that the physiognomy suggested a murderer. His hero was his ancestor August Wilhelm Anton Graf Neidhardt von Gneisenau, who took part in the American War of Independence on the side of the British, but who was later a leading figure in the reform of the Prussian Army.

The sculptor Mehnert had met Stauffenberg through the George Circle – an elite group of talented young men who were disciples of the poet Stefan George. Clause was introduced to the Circle – and to George – by his older brothers when they were students at Heidelberg University in 1923. George had a profound effect on the young man's thinking. The poet published a sequence of poems in

1928 under the title, 'The New Reich', in which he evokes the vision of a new Germany which will fulfil the ideal of ancient Greece. This led to an unfortunate association with the Nazis, who exploited the work for their own ends. George himself would have nothing to do with them, and when Hitler came to power he went into voluntary exile in Switzerland, where he died later in 1933, aged sixty-five. The poem which made the greatest impression on Stauffenberg was 'The Anti-Christ', which he invoked to justify his Resistance activity. His own name for the Resistance – 'Secret Germany' – was taken from the title of another of George's poems, in the 'New Reich' sequence. It is interesting to note in passing that one of George's older disciples, the Jewish academic Friedrich Gundolf, had years earlier turned down a would-be student burning with ambition called Josef Goebbels.

Stauffenberg himself did not go to university. He scraped through his school matriculation examination – he'd lost time through ill health – and decided on a career in the Army. This surprised his family, not only because of his poor health, but because his first choice of career had always been architecture. However, there had been four other main influences during his formative years: George, the First World War, the Treaty of Versailles, and the ideal of Gneisenau, Commander-in-Chief of the Prussian Army during the Napoleonic Wars. Stauffenberg's ancestor had seen service in Poland in 1793 and 1795, and later fought at Saalberg and Jena. In 1807 he successfully defended Kolberg, and was always an advocate of resistance to Napoleon. Later Gneisenau shone alongside Scharnhorst as the greatest exponent of the democratisation of the Prussian Army. Though not temperamentally a conventional officer, Stauffenberg distinguished himself at Cadet School, becoming popular among his fellows and demonstrating effortless qualities of leadership. Among his friends were the racing-driver nephew of von Brauchitsch, Manfred, and Albrecht Mertz von Quirnheim, who would become a close associate in the Resistance. In 1926 he joined the 17th Cavalry, based in Bamberg. A legend has grown up that he led an enthusiastic pro-Nazi demonstration in the town on 30 January 1933. In fact all that happened was that a fellow officer and his troop mistakenly saluted the swastika flag that day (it did not become the state flag until 15 September 1935). Stauffenberg began as a loyal servant of the regime, but he was never either a Nazi or an active supporter of Nazi policy. He pointedly walked out of a Bamberg hall in which the Gauleiter of Nuremberg, Julius Streicher, was giving one of his obscenely anti-Semitic speeches to a gathering of the League of German Girls.

He became a lieutenant in 1930 and the same year met his future wife, Nina von Lerchenfeld, then seventeen, at a ball given by her parents. Three years later he married her in St James's Church, Bamberg. He wore full uniform with his steel helmet to the ceremony. 'Marriage is a duty,' he said. 'Therefore I will wear uniform.' The young couple took an apartment in the Lerchenfelds' Bamberg house, which was to become their permanent home, though Claus was very often absent. They had five children, the last of whom, Konstanze, was born after her father's death.

In 1936 he visited England, where he hunted as a guest of the German Embassy, and also spent time in London and at Sandhurst. He was critical of Britain, referring to the Empire as the 'embers of a dying fire'. At the same time his eclectic reading habits led him to discover not only Keynes but C. S. Forester. He devoured the 'Hornblower' books eagerly. Later that year, he went to Berlin, having passed the tough selection process for General Staff training. In 1937 the American general, Wedemeyer, met him in Berlin and later remembered him as 'a very handsome man – a fine military bearing, courteous, considerate and sensitive'.

In the summer of 1937 he distinguished himself with a prize-winning essay on defence against paratroopers. Paratroops were a new idea in warfare, and Stauffenberg's work became adopted as part of standard training. He also distinguished himself in analysis of another relatively new military science – tank warfare. A year later he was posted as Number 2 Staff Officer to General Erich Hoepner's 1st Light Division at Wuppertal – innocent of its intended use in the abortive 1938 coup attempt. That October he entered the Sudetenland with it, to be greeted with enthusiasm.

Any sympathy he might have felt towards the regime withered, however, with the experience of *Kristallnacht*. Stauffenberg's character seems to have been completely free of any racism whatsoever. He was, however, a professional soldier and he had not yet become politicised. Thoughts harboured against the National Socialist government now had to be shelved as Germany sped towards war. The 1st Light Division was in Poland at the beginning of September 1939. A six-week war had been anticipated. Stauffenberg now estimated that the war just started would take Germany ten years to win, if it could hold out that long. We have no record of how he reacted to atrocities committed behind the lines: but one occasion is indicative of his attitude. When a brother officer and a close personal friend caused two Polish women to be executed through negligence, Stauffenberg had the man court-martialled and demoted. His own career reflected others' reactions to his strong personality and individualism. Time after time, promotion within the General Staff eluded him. This was frustrating to him, though he put a bold face on it. He was proud of Germany's victories, and doubts were slow to grow in his mind. He was, after all, still only a captain at this stage.

Experience on the Russian front in the course of 1941 was to focus these doubts further, though Stauffenberg did all he could to counteract the disadvantages under which the German Army was fighting. Like Tresckow, he was caught in the cleft stick of wishing to defend his country while at the same time growing daily more disaffected with its leaders. By the end of 1941 he was beginning to appreciate the joke: 'The difference between Bismarck and Hitler is that Bismarck said what he believed, but Hitler believes what he says.' Certainly by the middle of 1942 he was convinced of the need to get rid of Hitler. Throughout the year he saw how Hitler shortchanged the Army in terms of supplies and reinforcements, to the benefit of the other services, while all the time the odds against the Russians lengthened. At the time Stauffenberg was removed from the central Resistance. He was a soldier on active service, and he was almost thirty years younger than the leaders of the Resistance. Still he continued to try to help the war effort, to keep his natural enthusiasm going; the doubts in his mind were dangerous ones. He built up units of anti-Stalinist 'turned' Russian POWs – despite Hitler's proscription of the use of what he saw as 'subhumans' alongside Aryan Germans – and even insisted on their having equal rights with German troops. In working to counteract Hitler's racist stupidity, he aided the dictator.

Halder's replacement by Zeitzler as Chief of Staff in September 1942 did not bring the hoped-for breath of fresh air. Zeitzler was, if anything, even more craven than his predecessor. The scales finally fell from Stauffenberg's eyes: the General Staff, that great institution, was irrevocably compromised by the Nazis. At a conference at Vinnitsa in October, Stauffenberg made an extempore speech in which he did not mince words. Germany was in the process of sowing such hatred in the east, he said, that 'our children will reap the reward of it one day'. This was a scandal and an insult to the sacrifice of millions of lives. Why did no senior commander have the courage to go and tell Hitler so, 'even at the risk of his life'?

He still sought escape in duty. By the spring of 1943 he had been promoted Lieutenant-Colonel. He got himself transferred to the North African theatre of war, as 1st Staff Officer to a panzer division in Tunisia. His predecessor, badly wounded, warned him to beware of strafing attacks from low-flying enemy aircraft and, once there himself, he could see how Allied air supremacy kept even the best German armoured divisions pinned down. He made a great personal impression on the men, and once, during a night manoeuvre, saved his unit from an unexpected enemy land attack. When the British started shooting, he simply bellowed the order 'Cease fire' in his impeccable English, which they did, until Stauffenberg's men were safely out of the way. Then Stauffenberg ordered the British to start shooting again, which they did, this time at each other, because they had had the Germans caught in a crossfire.

His career in North Africa did not last long. On 7 April he was badly shot up when his jeep was strafed by a British fighter. He lost his right hand, the third and fourth fingers of his left, and his left eye. He was rushed to hospital in Carthage, and thence, when he was well enough, to Munich. They saved the right eye, and conducted operations on the middle ear and one knee. With his usual determination, he learned to bathe and dress himself, and as early as August he was pressing to be returned to active service – almost as if he were eager to escape the responsibility which Fate was pressing on his conscience: to do something about Hitler. In Munich, however, he was visited by his uncle, Count Nikolaus von Üxküll, who was already involved in the Resistance and who encouraged his nephew's leanings in that direction. It was an enormous decision for Stauffenberg to make, especially in view of his background and his chosen career; but he did make it, motivated finally by his sense of honour and of what was right. The decision once made, he did not swerve from it one iota.

In October 1943, Stauffenberg was well enough to take up active duty again, but this time it was of a different kind. He went to Berlin to become Chief of Staff in the General Army Office under Friedrich Olbricht. He had arrived in the capital on 10 September, two days after the capitulation of Italy. Hitler's attitude to this had been to throw his last reserves into the fight, rather than retreat or concede a yard of conquered land. This policy ran counter to the conventional diplomatic ideas trotted out in *Mein Kampf*, where, aping Luther, he had also written that to save a state from destruction, members of that state had every right to rid it of destructive leaders. The personal Oath of Loyalty had become a complete fiction.

Stauffenberg immediately became involved in the work of the central Resistance, and soon met Henning von Tresckow, then in Berlin between his tours of duty on the East Front. The two men got on together well; though one was a Prussian Protestant and the other a Bavarian Roman Catholic, both were cultivated professional soldiers with intelligent political ideas about Germany's future.

Earlier, in the summer, he had met and spoken with Julius Leber, the man who would become his political mentor. He also talked at length with his brother Berthold, who was working in the Legal Office of the Navy, and with whom he now lodged in Berlin, in his flat in Tristanstrasse in the south-western suburb of Wannsee. He was now a man with a mission, and already he had not only a great sense of its urgency, but had caught something of its fatalism too. He cancelled the operations Ferdinand Sauerbruch had proposed to fix a replacement hand.

Tresckow's enforced departure for the Front was a personal blow, as the two men had become good friends and close confidants; but Stauffenberg was now quickly manoeuvring himself into a position of active leadership within the central Resistance. He had no rivals among the Kreisauers, who lacked his practical application and administrative ability, while backing his purpose. Beck was too old to be more than a worthy figurehead and profoundly sensible adviser, and Goerdeler, who would come to regard Stauffenberg as a rival and even a cuckoo in the nest, had no authority where it mattered for the practical purposes of a coup – within the ranks of the Army. It was, to borrow Tresckow's words, the turn of the colonels, now that the generals had failed.[2] Stauffenberg had never had any doubts about the necessity of assassinating Hitler, preferably with Göring and Himmler, so as to frustrate the succession. The problem was gaining access to the reclusive dictator.

There were two possibilities. Helmuth Stieff, as head of the Organisation Department of the General Staff, had access to Hitler's conferences, and Colonel Joachim Meichssner, head of the Organisation Department of Overall High Command under Keitel and Jodl, also had the opportunity. But Stieff lacked the fibre and Meichssner, whose nerves were shot, drank too much, so both men had to be abandoned as prospects. Three young officers, however, did present themselves as candidates for an assassination attempt between the end of 1943 and early 1944.

The first of these was Captain Axel Freiherr von dem Bussche, recruited by Fritz Schulenburg (who had also become a close friend and colleague of Stauffenberg) from Infantry Regiment 9. Bussche's own commitment to the Resistance stemmed from when he had been an involuntary witness of the slaughter of 5000 Jews, including women and children, at Dubno aerodrome by Ukrainian SS in October 1942, though he had never been a friend of the regime. Bussche was a brave soldier – he had won the Iron Cross First and Second Class by 1944 – but a lung injury early in 1942 had invalided him out of active service. Now all he wished for was an opportunity to rid Germany of the cause of its descent into evil.

Schulenburg arranged a meeting between him and Stauffenberg in Berlin in October 1943. Bussche had already offered himself as a potential assassin. After some discussion, they decided on a line of action. New winter uniforms had been developed for the continuing Russian campaign, and Hitler was due to review them. A handful of soldiers would 'model' these uniforms for the Führer, and the conspirators hoped that Bussche could be selected to talk Hitler through the exhibition, in the same way as Gersdorff had earlier in the year. Like Gersdorff, Bussche would be equipped with a bomb, and he would embark on a similar suicide mission.

Bussche was an ideal candidate. He was a 'Nordic' type, he was much decorated and he had seen service right across the east front. With great difficulty Stieff procured the necessary explosives and fuses, and Bussche was indeed selected to conduct the proposed demonstration. He held himself in readiness from late November, and then there followed a month of agonising tension for him. Time and again a date for the showing of the new uniforms was fixed, and time and again Hitler cancelled it. Finally the prototype new uniforms were destroyed in an enemy air raid. Bussche was obliged to rejoin his regiment – by now he was back on active duty as a battalion commander. When a fresh opportunity occurred for Bussche to kill

Hitler, Stauffenberg telephoned his commanding officer and asked that he be released to come to Berlin to conduct the demonstration, but the CO refused to give Bussche leave – he was too valuable where he was. Days later Bussche was so severely wounded that he lost a leg. His chance was gone.

There followed a similar plan involving Ewald Heinrich von Kleist, also an officer in Infantry Regiment 9, and the son of Ewald von Kleist-Schmenzin. When approached by Stauffenberg, Kleist first sought his father's advice, who immediately and firmly told the young man that it was his duty to perform the suicide mission. Stauffenberg, he remembers

> was an exceptional man. He took his time in sizing people up, and he himself didn't exactly make an overwhelming first impression; but he had a great inner strength and a really glowing personality. He was absolutely devoted to the task he had set himself and nothing would deflect him from it. He was greatly sympathetic. He combined the qualities of high idealism with absolute realism: a rare combination of visionary and man of action. But he was also approachable, very nice, and had a lively sense of humour. I discussed the idea [of the assassination] with him and he didn't push me, he said he knew that this was a very hard decision and that I should reflect on it for 24 hours . . . I had no problems or psychological inhibitions about killing Hitler. Equally I had no difficulties about the oath sworn to Hitler. For me it never had any meaning, it was fundamentally valueless, and I never had any intention of either keeping it or using it as an excuse for inaction. How could one take an oath sworn to a criminal under duress seriously? Our actions were firmly grounded on moral certainty.

Though he went on to play a part in the attempt on 20 July 1944, Kleist's bid failed like Bussche's and for the same reason. A third attempt, by Witzleben's former ADC, Eberhard von Breitenbuch, who favoured using a pistol (he was a crack shot and Stauffenberg agreed to let the executor choose the means), was arranged for March 1944. Breitenbuch was now aide to the pro-Nazi Field Marshal Ernst Busch. He was due to accompany Busch to a meeting with Hitler at the Berghof, and there he would try to shoot the Führer down with a Browning 7.65 which he intended to conceal in his briefcase. At the very last minute, however, one of Hitler's SS guards announced that aides would not be permitted into the meeting and forcibly held Breitenbuch back despite Busch's objections. Breitenbuch then had to sit for an hour sweating it out under the eye of the SS bodyguards until the meeting ended and he could make his exit. He admitted freely that he could not summon up the courage for a second attempt.

A completely stillborn attempt was that of Stauffenberg's own aide, Werner von Haeften, who was dissuaded from trying to kill Hitler on religious grounds by his older brother Hans-Bernd, a prominent member of the Kreisau Circle. Hans-Bernd himself was executed by the Nazis, who had no such qualms, on 15 August 1944. His brother died with his adored chief.

Although Werner von Haeften's complete loyalty to Stauffenberg was never in doubt, the young man's mercurial character and loose tongue were sometimes a security risk. As early as November 1943 he told a girlfriend, Philippa von Bredow, that he was going to kill Hitler. When she brought this up later, he snapped at her nervously to 'keep her trap shut'. Stauffenberg would have been horrified. Apart from Berthold and his closest associates, he had not breathed even an opinion critical of the Führer. He played his hand very close to his chest, and entertained only a very small group of intimates, including Tresckow, Schulenburg and Trott, who became his adviser on foreign affairs.

In the meantime, however, Stauffenberg had put backs up in the civilian Resistance, by demanding from Goerdeler a list of those scheduled to take office in the post-Nazi government. Several people objected to this on grounds of security, but Stauffenberg was adamant: either he had the list or he would not co-operate. It was simple blackmail: he was the only hope of getting rid of Hitler now. He was given the list, learned its contents and destroyed it. Neither in Bamberg nor Berlin did the Gestapo find a shred of written evidence in their investigations after 20 July 1944. But a rift was beginning to form between Stauffenberg and Goerdeler; Stauffenberg did not want to see the former mayor of Leipzig as Chancellor after Hitler; he preferred Leber's candidacy. There were fundamental differences of principle between the socialist Leber and the conservative Goerdeler. For himself, Stauffenberg had no personal political ambition, but his political instinct told him that Leber, not Goerdeler, was the man of the future. He also understood fairly quickly that there could be no separate deals struck with either Stalin or the Western Allies.

On 1 July 1944, Stauffenberg became Chief of Staff to General Fromm, head of the Reserve Army. This placed him not only in a position from which he would have direct access to Hitler himself – Fromm frequently had to attend conferences at the Wolf's Lair – but he was close to the Reserve Army, in which the hopes of the Resistance lay. For a coup to work, this Army would have to be activated. A secret official plan – codenamed 'Valkyrie' – already existed, to be implemented in the event of a coup against the Nazi regime. If the plan could be used in conjunction with Army groups in Paris, Prague and Vienna to work *for* the coup, the country would be secured for the conspirators, who could seize power through their leaders in the national interest after Hitler had been assassinated: they could claim that Hitler had fallen victim to an attempted SS coup. Military and civil district commanders were selected and briefed for the takeover of power. Proclamations and drafts of radio broadcasts were composed and typed with the assistance of Frau von Tresckow, Countess Charlotte von der Schulenburg and Margarete von Oven, who had been secretary successively to Generals von Hammerstein and Fritsch. They typed in gloves to avoid leaving fingerprints, using typewriters which were hidden when not in use. Frau von Oven remembered one occasion in late 1943, walking down Trabenerstrasse in Berlin with Stauffenberg and Tresckow, with drafts of the coup 'Valkyrie' orders under her arm, when a black car suddenly drew up and disgorged a number of SS men. Among the papers she had with her was the draft of an announcement to be broadcast by Beck, beginning with the words, 'The Führer Adolf Hitler is dead . . .' The three of them stood stock still, but the SS men ran past them into a nearby house. 'Even Stauffenberg and Tresckow, two tough officers, were white as sheets,' Frau Oven remembered. As the headquarters building where they worked was centrally heated, it was difficult to dispose of large quantities of papers. Nina von Stauffenberg once took a rucksack full of old conspiracy drafts back to Bamberg by train for burning – a journey of twelve hours.

With Tresckow away at the Front, it became clear to Stauffenberg that he would have not only to lead the coup in Berlin, but make the assassination attempt on Hitler at Rastenburg personally. It would be possible with the use of a fast aeroplane, but timing would be crucial.

Still a doubt remained. The Russians were pressing ever closer from the East. In the West, the Allies had established a bridgehead in France, and hundreds of thousands of fresh, well-fed and well-equipped American troops were bearing down on the exhausted and tattered German units trying to hold them off. The war was as good as over. Was it still worth staging a coup? Stauffenberg contacted Tresckow for advice, and received the reply:

> The assassination must take place *coûte que coûte*. Even if it does not succeed, the Berlin action must go forward. The point now is not whether the coup has any practical purpose, but to prove to the world and before history that German Resistance is ready to stake its all. Compared to this, everything else is a side issue.

THIRTEEN

20 July 1944

Colonel-General Friedrich Fromm was still an unknown quantity. He would not join the Resistance, but he did not oppose or betray it either. He does not emerge with great credit from this story; like so many of his colleagues, he was a man who wanted to run with the hare and hunt with the hounds. His appointment of Stauffenberg as his Chief of Staff was a purely military matter. He had had his eye on the young officer for some time, and at his request Stauffenberg had written a report on the possible conduct of the Reserve Army in Total War which had so impressed Fromm that he had passed it on to Hitler, who remarked, 'Finally, a General Staff Officer with imagination and integrity!' In many ways, Stauffenberg was Hitler's ideal. Though not obviously 'Nordic', he was handsome, young, and, above all, had been badly (and in Hitler's eyes, romantically) wounded for the good of the cause. It is difficult to say whether the appointment to Fromm finalised Stauffenberg's decision to attempt the assassination of the Führer, or whether he went after the posting as a means to that end. In any case, the effect was the same.

Stauffenberg's first meeting with Hitler was at the Berghof on 7 June – the day after D-Day. He travelled there from Bamberg where he had been spending a week's leave with his family prior to taking up his appointment with Fromm. At the meeting were Himmler, Göring and Speer: it is a pity the bomb could not have been planted then and there. He noted that, contrary to rumours, it was perfectly possible to get close to Hitler. It would not have been a problem to draw one's pistol and shoot the Führer. The argument against such action was the strong rumour that Hitler wore body armour. Hitler,

who habitually retired late and rose late, had not been told of the
Normandy landings until he had woken, but the military situation
was in any case quite hopeless. Supplies were all but used up, and
factories were either bombed out or operating only partially. The
German divisions were spread too thinly across all fronts and many
were unfit for full combat. It is a testament to an insane courage that
their forces held out against the enemy for so long. The paratroop
regiments and the Waffen-SS divisions showed particular resilience.

Stauffenberg returned to Berlin after another brief stay at Bamberg,
taking with him Forester's Hornblower novel *The Happy Return* to
read on the train. A few days later, he was persuading his cousin
Yorck von Wartenburg of the Kreisau Circle to enter into active
Resistance. By mid-June, Goerdeler was drawing up another of
his potential Cabinet lists, and Wilhelm Leuschner was defining
the hierarchy of a new trade union movement. Hopes, at least,
were high. But on 16 June there was an unhappy meeting of the
civilian Resistance at the Hotel Esplanade in Berlin. Leber, who had
turned down Stauffenberg's proposal that he be Chancellor in place
of Goerdeler, and who was now in line for Interior Minister, attacked
Goerdeler for his unrealistic foreign policy ideas – which still embraced
a demand for Germany to retain her 1914 frontiers. Leber thought that
East Prussia, the Sudetenland and Elsass-Lohringen (Alsace-Lorraine)
would have to go. His homeland was Alsace, and there was no question
of his patriotism, but he was still shouted down by the others.

Shortly afterwards, the Resistance was to suffer another cruel
blow. Julius Leber and his close associate, Adolf Reichwein, had
entered into negotiations with a view to Resistance and postwar
co-operation with a Communist group led by three veteran freedom fighters, Bernhard Bästlein, Franz Jakob and Anton Saefkow.
Leber knew the first two personally, having spent five years in the
concentration camps with them before the outbreak of war. A series
of exploratory meetings followed, but the Gestapo already had the
group under observation, and Bästlein had been arrested on 30 May.
Now the net closed, and early in July the Security Service raided a
meeting at which the others were seized. Stauffenberg was appalled
when he heard the news, and promised Leber's wife Annedore that
they would get her husband out of prison, whatever else happened.

One should remember that during these preparations, Berlin was
being subjected to merciless air raids day and night. The battering had

the effect of stiffening the resolve of the fanatical Nazis, who were in any case fighting to protect their own backs now. That such a man as Roland Freisler could continue to conduct trials in the name of a 'law' that had no value and had even lost the backing of power is evidence of this, and invites interesting psychological reflection. The members of the Resistance themselves knew that they had at the very most a 50 per cent chance of success, but the profound sense of Tresckow's advice to fight for it whatever the cost went home to all of them. As late as the end of June, Adam von Trott zu Solz embarked on yet another journey to Sweden, in the faint hope of renewing contact with the British. In fact there was no hope at all.

Organisation was always a great problem for the Resistance. The arrangement of meetings was a matter of difficulty, since neither the telephone nor the post could be used. Fixed meetings often had to be aborted because of air raids and the resulting disruption of transport in Berlin. Often the conspirators used the Grünewald – the vast park in the west of the city – to meet, as houses were not always considered secure. Plans, too, had to be changed continually to keep up with the progress of the war. Schulenburg commented drily, 'We'd have got further if Stauffenberg had made up his mind [to join us] sooner.'

At the end of June, Kurt Zeitzler, the Chief of Staff, had a nervous breakdown. He was replaced by Heinz Guderian. By now, Stauffenberg had taken up residence in his office near Fromm's in the Bendlerblock on Bendlerstrasse, the massive building – the size of a small estate – which housed Armed Forces administration. Fromm was astonished at the number of unfamiliar officers he saw coming and going, but he did not ask what they were doing, contenting himself with passing the remark to Count Helldorf, still chief of the Berlin police, that 'it'd be best if Hitler committed suicide'. Like many officers, he would doubtless have considered himself released from the Oath of Loyalty by Hitler's death, which he hoped for, without wishing to work for it actively.

Early in July Trott returned empty-handed from Stockholm, but with news of the efforts of the National Committee for Free Germany. Stauffenberg was chary of this. 'I don't think much of proclamations made from behind barbed wire,' he remarked.

Meanwhile, complicated arrangements were in train to obtain the correct English explosives and fuses for the attempt on Hitler. Once again, Stieff was in the forefront of this dangerous undertaking. At the same time, arrangements were being made for the takeover of power. For a time Rommel, a very popular general at home who had also earned the respect of the Allies, was considered for the position of head of state. Rommel, however, was never more than on the fringes of the conspiracy. Although he was sympathetic, he was put out of action when his heavy unmanoeuvrable open-topped Horch staff car was strafed by British fighters on 17 July and he was seriously wounded. After the 20 July attempt, however, the ever-suspicious Hitler obliged this best of his generals to commit suicide in order to spare his family the concentration camps and himself disgrace. The Führer then gave him a state funeral, but everyone knew what had really happened.

The position of post-Nazi President, therefore, reverted to Beck. Goerdeler would be Chancellor. Erwin von Witzleben would take over the Army and Erich Hoepner the Reserve Army. Wherever possible conspirators would be placed in the various Army districts around Germany and in the occupied territories, but otherwise commands from Berlin would have to have the authority of Fromm's signature initially to implement 'Valkyrie'. If Fromm would not agree at the eleventh hour, Hoepner would have to announce that he had taken over and issue the orders, hoping that the regional commanders would still obey. SS divisions and units would have to be neutralised and then subsumed within the Army. In co-ordination with 'Valkyrie', Helldorf, Nebe and Gisevius (who travelled to Berlin from Zurich for the coup) would use the regular police to take over the Security Service and seize its files. They would also arrest all Nazi leaders then in Berlin, such as Josef Goebbels and Robert Ley. There were plans to take over all radio stations, for a broadcast to the nation would have to be made immediately after the coup to establish the *bona fides* of the conspirators. Also, telecommunications at the Wolf's Lair would have to be neutralised for as long as possible. This daunting task was entrusted to the Army head of Signals, General Erich Fellgiebel.[1]

The Resistance had not yet given up all hope of making peace with the West first in order at least to stall Stalin in the East, and they were especially well prepared in France. The weak Günther von Kluge had taken over general command in the West on 2 July, and he might still be swayed. The military commander was General Karl-Heinrich von Stülpnagel, a veteran of the Resistance, and he was backed up by other convinced conspirators like Lieutenant-General Hans Speidel.

A reminiscence of Philipp Freiherr von Boeselager is an indication of the almost surreal circumstances of the time. Shortly before the 20 July attempt, Tresckow sent Philipp's brother Georg (of the old 'Boeselager Brigade') to Paris with a message for Kluge. But Georg needed an excuse for the journey. Fortunately a good one presented itself: the Boeselagers owned a racehorse, Lord Wagram, due to run at Longchamps. Accompanying it provided the perfect cover; but, as Philipp remarks, it is astonishing that such things were still possible in mid-1944!

The whole plan was rickety and riddled with risk, but it offered the only possibility, and time was running out fast for a coup of any sort to be effected.

Stauffenberg attended a further meeting at Berchtesgaden on 6 July, and another on the 11th. On this second occasion, when he travelled with his adjutant and confidant Captain Friedrich Karl Klausing, he was prepared to make the attempt, the explosives packed in a briefcase, and equipped with a pair of pliers to set the fuse whose handles had been specially adapted so that he could manipulate them with his remaining crippled hand. However, Himmler was not present at the meeting and so, after a telephone call to Olbricht, Stauffenberg decided to abort the attempt. As no plans seem to have been laid to set 'Valkyrie' in motion on this occasion one wonders if he did indeed intend to make the attempt. It may have been a full dress rehearsal. Stauffenberg must have been aware that he would have several opportunities in the next few days to attend meetings with Hitler. Nevertheless, to take such a risk without intending action seems hard to believe.

On 15 July, Stauffenberg accompanied Fromm to another meeting with the Führer, this time at the Wolf's Lair near Rastenburg. They had received the summons at midday on the 14th, so there was just time to activate 'Valkyrie'. This was to be it. Everyone was on edge. Berthold Stauffenberg commented, 'Worst of all is to know that we'll fail; and yet we must go ahead, for the sake of our country and our children.' In the West, the SS division generals Sepp Dietrich and Hausser put themselves fully under Rommel's orders. Very few people indeed seemed to have any faith in Hitler's new wonder weapons, the V-bomb rockets.[2]

The Wolf's Lair was a complex of compounds and buildings, admission to which involved various degrees of security check. At

that time it was in a state of rebuilding. At least Stauffenberg had
the opportunity to take this in, for there was no chance to use the
bomb. Once again a last-minute change of plan by Hitler saved him.
Fortunately, although 'Valkyrie's initial stages had been set in motion
in anticipation of Stauffenberg's action, the conspirators managed to
pass these off as an exercise.

Stauffenberg was deeply depressed by this setback, and those
who saw him at that time recall his state of nervous exhaustion. On
the 16th, he telephoned his wife in Bamberg to ask her to postpone a
family visit she intended to make with the children to Lautlingen.
She objected that she had already bought the railway tickets, and
he did not press her. It was their last conversation. The same day,
Rommel transmitted a message to Hitler via Kluge that the maximum
time the West Front could continue to hold out was twenty-one days.
That evening there was a meeting of 'the young counts', as Goerdeler
called them, at the Stauffenberg brothers' flat in Wannsee. Mertz von
Quirnheim, Claus's successor as Chief of Staff to Olbricht, was there,
together with Fritz-Dietlof von der Schulenburg, Adam von Trott zu
Solz, Peter Yorck von Wartenburg, Cäsar von Hofacker, the contact
man with the Army in France, Georg Hansen, who had taken over
from Canaris at the Abwehr, and Schwerin von Schwanenfeld. They
decided that the only way to save Germany now would be to kill Hitler
at the very first opportunity and immediately thereafter enter peace
negotiations with the USSR and the Western Allies simultaneously.
They had no idea that Germany had already been divided up and
parcelled out. Events had long since overtaken them and they did
not know.

The following day, the day Rommel was shot up, the Security
Service issued a warrant for Goerdeler's arrest. Goerdeler was in
Leipzig at the time, but immediately left for Berlin, where he went
underground.

Soon after, orders came for Stauffenberg to attend a meeting
at the Wolf's Lair on 20 July to report on the recruitment of new
People's Grenadier Divisions – a kind of last-minute Home Guard.
He was calm, at least outwardly, but possibly inwardly too, all day
on the 19th. He smoked neither more nor fewer cigarettes than usual,
and he fulfilled his desk duties at the Bendlerblock with his habitual
punctiliousness. At 8p.m. he left the office for home, but stopped off
on the way to attend Mass. Once back at Tristanstrasse, he packed the

explosives in a case, concealing them under a clean shirt. His thoughts must have turned to Nina, now three months pregnant with their fifth child. He spent the evening quietly with Berthold.

Stauffenberg left the apartment at 6a.m. the following morning and drove with his brother to Rangsdorf airfield, south of Berlin.[3] There he met his ADC, Werner von Haeften, and General Stieff, who was returning to Mauerwald. The courier aircraft, a Junkers JU 52, left at 8a.m., an hour late, for the 400-mile journey. They arrived at Rastenburg aerodrome at about 10.15a.m. where Stauffenberg parted company with Haeften until noon. The meeting with Hitler was due to take place at 1p.m. Haeften took charge of the briefcase with its two 2-kilogram packages of hexogen plastic explosive.

At 11.30 Stauffenberg had a meeting at the Wolf's Lair with Keitel, who told him that the meeting with Hitler had been brought forward to 12.30. Hitler had done this in order to make room for a meeting with Mussolini at 2.30p.m. The Italian dictator had been sprung from prison in a daring raid led by SS Colonel Otto Skorzeny and was now a guest of the Führer. Haeften arrived from Mauerwald half an hour later, on schedule, but now they had only half an hour to get ready. Stauffenberg asked for a room to freshen up in before the meeting, and there, aided by Haeften, he began to repack the two bombs in his own briefcase. Before they could finish the job, however, they were interrupted by an NCO with a message from General Fellgiebel. The message turned out not to be urgent, but Stauffenberg had no time now to pack the second bomb. Nevertheless, he was confident that one would be adequate for the purpose of blowing Hitler up in a confined space.

There was, however, another problem about which he could do nothing. Owing to the building works at the Wolf's Lair headquarters, the meeting was not to be held in the usual concrete bunker (Hitler by now was very much concerned by enemy air attacks), but in a large wooden hut, where the shock waves on which the bomb depended for its main effect would have considerably less effect, since they would not be contained and reflected by unyielding walls. Still Stauffenberg thought he could bring the plan off, if he could place the bomb close enough to Hitler. Neither Göring nor Himmler was to be at the meeting, which was unfortunate, but there could be no question of deferring the attempt any more.

Punctually at 12.30, the meeting began. The room was dominated by a huge map table on two heavy oak supports. Twenty-four senior officers were in attendance, including Hitler and Keitel. Stauffenberg managed to get a place at the table very close to the Führer. He had set the ten-minute silent fuse and shoved the briefcase under the table next to Hitler, against one of the oak supports. On the excuse of making a telephone call, he left the meeting a few minutes later, leaving his cap and belt in the antechamber deliberately to indicate that he would be returning. In the meantime, Haeften had ordered a car. The two men departed at 12.42, at about the same time as the explosion. That the game was now being played for all or nothing is indicated by the fact that Haeften got rid of the redundant packet of explosive by merely throwing it from the car as they drove to the airfield. It was discovered later by Gestapo investigators.

There was total chaos in the wrecked hut, but the windows had been blown out, taking the force of the blast with them, and as the smoke cleared they found that the damage was not as great as it might have been. Neither Keitel nor Hitler was seriously wounded. Keitel embraced Hitler with the words, 'My Führer! You're alive! You're alive!' Among the severely wounded were Rudolf Schmundt, who had been so suspicious of Gersdorff's attempt, and Heinz Brandt, who had innocently carried the 'Cointreau bomb' for Operation Flash. Both died within days. Everyone present except Hitler and Keitel suffered burst eardrums. Hitler had been protected by the massive table support.

By now, Stauffenberg and Haeften were speeding towards the Rastenburg aerodrome, where a Heinkel HE 111, organised by General Eduard Wagner, was waiting to take them back to Berlin. At 12.55, five minutes after they had taken off, General Fellgiebel contacted his Chief of Staff at nearby Mauerwald: 'Something terrible has happened. The Führer's alive!' Kurt Hahn, the Chief of Staff, and also a conspirator, promised to pass the message on to the Bendlerstrasse. Fellgiebel did what he could to block telecommunications, but quickly headquarters security ordered the main switchboard to stop all outgoing calls except for those from Hitler, Keitel and Jodl. Hitler himself, who had escaped with minor cuts and burns, was euphoric with relief. His trousers had been shredded by the blast, but otherwise even his dignity was intact. While his loyal signals officers hastened to put matters back in order, he took his scheduled tea with Mussolini after only a slight delay, having shown the *Duce* the wreckage of the hut. Göring and Ribbentrop were in attendance.

By 1.30, just before the clampdown on communications, both Hahn and Fellgiebel managed to relay a message to Berlin about the failure of the assassination attempt. The call was received at the Bendlerblock by Signals officer Lieutenant-General Fritz Thiele. Thiele told Olbricht, but they took no action. Fellgiebel's message had lacked detail. They decided that they could not risk unleashing 'Valkyrie' again until they knew more. If they did, and the whole thing had aborted, they could not pass the 'Valkyrie' order off as an exercise a second time. Precipitate action now might jeopardise any future chance for the conspiracy. Their decision was based on sound reasoning; but it was a fatal error.

At 3.30p.m., Stauffenberg arrived back in Berlin, to find that no action had been taken, and 'Valkyrie' had not been set in motion. Instead, he was met by confusion and doubt at the Bendlerstrasse. Grimly insisting that Hitler was indeed dead, he took over, galvanising his fellow conspirators into action. Three crucial hours had been lost, during which the conspirators could have seized the initiative irrespective of whether Hitler was dead or not.

At 6.20p.m. Fellgiebel managed to get a frantic call through to Berlin: 'What are you up to over there? Are you all crazy? The Führer is now with the *Duce* in the tea room. What's more, there will be a radio communiqué soon.' But a mark of the chaos was that conspirators were by now being obliged through the nature of their official functions to operate against the coup in order not to give themselves away. Men like Hahn and Thiele had to help the telecommunications clampdown, and Artur Nebe, the brilliant detective, was summoned to Hitler's headquarters to investigate the assassination attempt.

Nevertheless, as soon as Stauffenberg arrived at the Bendlerblock, coded 'Valkyrie' orders were set in train and soon telephone lines and teleprinters were humming in Berlin. Mertz von Quirnheim, who had been straining at the leash since early afternoon, rushed into action. Meanwhile Fromm, still in his own office in the Bendlerblock, would not participate. At about 4p.m. he telephoned Keitel who confirmed his suspicion that the Führer was alive. From then on, Fromm refused to co-operate with the conspirators, despite anything Stauffenberg said. In a stormy scene, Fromm declared that all the conspirators were under arrest, whereupon Stauffenberg retorted that, on the contrary, they were in control and *he* was under arrest. He was relieved of his pistol and kept under guard. The conspirators constantly showed a remarkable degree of mercy to their prisoners. They would have been better advised to have shot Fromm out of hand, but such action would not have occurred to them.

In the course of the afternoon, both Hoepner and Beck arrived in civilian clothes, and so, later on, did Witzleben, who was scathing about the muddle. A group of junior officers involved in the conspiracy, Ludwig von Hammerstein, Ewald Heinrich von Kleist, Georg von Oppen and Hans Fritzsche, were summoned by Karl Klausing from the Hotel Esplanade where they were awaiting orders. Not all the conspirators knew each other, and they were operating in a vast building where there were many staff officers who had nothing to do with the coup, so the confusion continued to be great. Fritzsche mistakenly helped Hoepner on with a uniform jacket destined for Beck – an unimportant detail, but an indication of the problems the conspirators were faced with. When General Joachim von Kortzfleisch, the commander of the Berlin district, arrived in response to a summons from Olbricht, and refused to join in the conspiracy by putting his troops at their disposal, he too was arrested. He ran off, but was detained by Kleist and turned over to Hammerstein, who guarded him in an empty office. He ranted and raved for some time, but then subsided and as the hours passed wondered what they were going to do with him overnight. Hammerstein asked Beck's advice, who said bitterly, 'He can stay where he is. He's the least of our worries.' Kortzfleisch said pathetically that as far as he was concerned he would rather go home and do a bit of weeding in his garden. But by then it was clear to Hammerstein that things had gone seriously wrong.

Later in the evening, a senior SS officer, Humbert Achamer-Pifrader, arrived with an adjutant to invite Stauffenberg to accompany them to Gestapo Headquarters for an interview. News of the attempted coup had been telephoned to Berlin from Rastenburg but the Berlin Gestapo clearly had no idea of the number of men involved at the Bendlerblock. Himmler was flying from Rastenburg to Berlin to liaise with Goebbels. Pifrader and his aide were arrested but time was running out for the conspirators. Already orders countermanding those sent out to the various military districts from Berlin were being issued from the Wolf's Lair. Such was the confusion that some of these counter-orders arrived at their destination before the Berlin commands!

Meanwhile in the city, the commandant, General von Hase, had failed to take control on behalf of the Resistance. The Guard Battalion under a relatively junior officer, Major Ernst Remer, had started to carry out its orders to cordon off the government quarter, but unfortunately Remer was in personal contact with a Nazi lieutenant who worked in Goebbels' Propaganda Ministry, Hans Hagen. Hagen deduced from the troop movements in the city that a coup was in train, and persuaded Remer to accompany him to see Goebbels. Goebbels had already spoken to Hitler on the telephone and knew what was afoot. When Remer appeared, overawed but still suspicious about what precisely was going on, the Propaganda Minister saw his chance to turn the tables on the conspiracy. Having assured himself that Remer was a 'good National Socialist', he put through another call to Hitler. Remer spoke to the Führer in person, recognised his voice, and stood to attention at the telephone. Hitler told him that the future of the Third Reich was in his hands. He was directly responsible for security in Berlin until Himmler arrived, with orders to take over the Reserve Army. Remer was won over, and the coup was doomed. It was about 7p.m.

Soon the Bendlerblock was sealed off by troops who now knew that Hitler was still alive and that the orders they had been given were unauthorised. The news spread and within the building itself several officers not involved in the conspiracy began to ask awkward questions about what was going on. Stauffenberg was exhausted. He had spent hours driving the others along by the sheer force of his will, but now he knew he had not carried the day. He took off the black patch he habitually wore over his dead eye – a sign with him of fatigue and irritation.

Ludwig von Hammerstein was making his way back to the office where General Kortzfleisch was locked when he heard the first shots. He drew his own pistol but a plump staff officer who had appeared in the corridor next to him said, 'Put it away, there's no point.' Hammerstein did not know whose side the plump officer was on, or what was happening, though he noticed that the officer wore 'brain reins' on his cap – a silver chain issued as a service award by the regime.

In the event there had been a shoot-out in which Stauffenberg had been wounded. Hammerstein had taken the precaution on the advice of Kleist of removing the Infantry Regiment 9 badges from his lapels, since they would be an indication of whose side he was on. He managed to escape through back corridors and staircases. He knew the building intimately since, as the son of Kurt von Hammerstein, he had lived in his father's service flat there when Hammerstein senior had been Commander-in-Chief. But he was lucky that the counter-coup officers did not know him; had the coup succeeded, he would have become Beck's ADC. Nevertheless, he had to go underground; he had had to abandon a briefcase containing incriminating papers with his name on them and his .08 service pistol in Olbricht's office. Much later, after Berlin had been occupied by the Russians, he had to throw away the gun he had with him – 'it was a lovely little thing, a 7.65 automatic my father had given me which I'd had throughout the war.' But to have been caught by the Russians in civilian clothes with a gun could have meant instant death.

Meanwhile, Fromm had been released and had taken control. He conducted a summary court martial at which he sentenced Stauffenberg, Mertz von Quirnheim, Olbricht and Werner von Haeften to death. Hoepner, an old friend, he spared to stand further trial. Beck, also condemned, asked permission to commit suicide, and this was granted him, but he had to do it immediately while the others waited in the same room. According to Hoepner's later testimony, Beck used his own Parabellum (Luger) pistol first, but only managed to give himself a slight head wound. In a state of extreme stress, Beck asked for another gun, and an attendant staff officer offered him a Mauser. But the second shot also failed to kill him, and a sergeant then gave Beck the *coup de grâce*. He was given Beck's leather overcoat as a reward.

The others were conducted into the vast grey courtyard of the Bendlerblock and shot dead. Haeften threw himself in front of Stauffenberg as the rifles thundered. Stauffenberg cried out 'Long live Germany!' as he died.

It was about midnight.

FOURTEEN

Aftermath

Helldorf and Gisevius had waited with growing impatience at the Police Praesidium in Alexanderplatz for the order to go into action to come from Bendlerstrasse. News of the bomb at Rastenburg had come through earlier and Nebe had been summoned to Gestapo Headquarters. Finally Gisevius could stand it no longer and asked Helldorf to let him have a car to get back to the Bendlerblock, where he intended to face the music with his fellow conspirators. Helldorf told him roundly that he was out of his mind, and added bitterly, 'For years these generals have shat all over us. They promised us everything: they've kept not one of their promises. What happened today was right in line with the rest – more of their shit.'

Gisevius was one of the few to survive. He managed to go underground, and later made his escape with Nebe. After they had separated, Nebe was arrested, as was Helldorf. Both were tried by the People's Court and subsequently executed. Gisevius, with the help of forged papers supplied by the OSS in Switzerland, managed to get back to Zurich where he sat out the war.

By the time the SS arrived in force at the Bendlerstrasse, it was all over. The bodies of the chief conspirators had already been taken away to a nearby churchyard for a hasty burial – they were later exhumed and burnt, their ashes scattered to the four winds on Hitler's orders. Hammerstein has a theory that Fromm had them shot so quickly in order to spare them torture and interrogation, but in that case why did he spare Hoepner, his special friend? In the event, he saved neither Hoepner's life nor his own. Fromm was arrested later and shot on Hitler's orders, ironically for cowardice.

He died with the words 'Heil Hitler' on his lips. At least he was granted the honour of a military execution by firing squad. The other conspirators, most of whom faced death either in Plötzensee prison or in Flossenburg concentration camp, were stripped naked (in accordance with SS practice) and either guillotined or hanged. Those who were hanged suffered the worse fate: on Hitler's orders they were suspended from hooks on an iron girder (still in place in Plötzensee's execution hall) by thin cord – in consequence they died by slow strangulation. The Führer had the process filmed and for a time afterwards watched the film daily in his private cinema at the Wolf's Lair. He also had the show trials secretly filmed. Most were conducted by the vile former Communist Roland Freisler, who signed himself when writing to Hitler, 'Your political soldier'.

As the coup came to an end on the night of 20–21 July, in Mertz von Quirnheim's office, Schulenburg, Berthold von Stauffenberg, Schwerin von Schwanenfeld, Wartenburg and Gerstenmaier busied themselves by frantically destroying all the coup documents there. There was no question of escape, as they were trapped in the room by counter-coup staff officers. At last they were formally arrested by SS General Hermann Reinecke – a 'real horror', as Hammerstein remembers him. Otto Skorzeny, the brutal Austrian SS colonel whose daring rescue of Mussolini had found such favour with Hitler, arrived at 1a.m. to tear the badges of rank from the uniforms of the conspirators. Schulenburg said, 'Evidently the German people must drink this cup to the dregs. We must make a sacrifice of ourselves. Later, mankind will understand what we did.' Schwerin said to Gerstenmaier, 'After all, one can't do more than die for what one believes in.'

They were all handcuffed and taken out of the building along bloodstained corridors, down bloodstained staircases. They thought they would be shot in the courtyard too, but they were taken instead to Gestapo Headquarters in nearby Prinz-Albrecht-Strasse. There they were divested of their ties, belts, shoelaces and jackets. Kleist and Oppen had also been arrested. Kleist was beaten up and forced to spend the rest of the night standing up in his cell.

More and more people were brought in during the course of 21 July, and the Berlin prisons at Plötzensee and Lehrterstrasse filled up. Kleist, Schwerin von Schwanenfeld and Wartenburg were loaded on to a lorry. Kleist thought they were going to be executed. He watched the route the truck took with interest: a sandy track would mean they were being taken to a parade ground where he knew they would be shot by half-trained SS men. A tarred road would lead to Plötzensee and the guillotine. Better the guillotine and a quick death, he thought. Instead they were taken to Ravensbrück concentration camp, where they were interrogated, Kleist for eight and a half hours at a stretch. He remembers that Schwerin was concerned for his welfare – Schwerin was twenty years his senior. Such concern was a rare thing and shows the humanity of the men of the Resistance. Schulenburg was also taken to Ravensbrück, but not before receiving a severe beating from Humbert Achamer-Pifrader, avenging himself for his Bendlerstrasse arrest. Hammerstein and Kleist remember Pifrader as a cold bureaucrat. Obviously some passion must have stirred him on this occasion.

Four hundred Gestapo officials worked on the 'case' of 20 July 1944, and for months Ernst Kaltenbrunner, the head of the Security Service, sent daily reports to Hitler via Martin Bormann. There were twenty-eight arrests by the end of 21 July, and the total had reached fifty-six by the 24th. We will never know the final figures, though they ran into thousands, as other scores were settled under the umbrella of the investigation, or the fate of each and every member of the conspiracy. Few sought to flee; of those who did, only a handful escaped. Himmler, in an extravagant display of loyalty to the Führer whom he was plotting in his black heart to betray, invoked the ancient Teutonic custom of imprisoning the entire family of a condemned man, in order to root out the bad blood. Thus all the relatives of the Stauffenbergs, the Hammersteins, the Wartenburgs, the Schwerin von Schwanenfelds, and so on, were arrested. It is however typical of the Nazis that Schwanenfeld's four sisters who had married and therefore had different surnames were not arrested. Women who had married into the conspirators' families, on the other hand, did not escape. Forty-four children from twenty families were taken to a National Socialist children's home in Bad Sachsa. The idea was to give them new names and identities, and indoctrinate them with Nazi ideology. The elder of Schwanenfeld's two sons subjected to this treatment, Wilhelm, aged fifteen, made sure at night in the common dormitory that they all remembered their real names and what they stood for.

As soon as the coup was over, Hitler, Göring and Dönitz made radio broadcasts to the nation. Hitler referred to 'an extremely small clique of ambitious, conscienceless, and criminal and stupid officers'. Göring recounted that

> An inconceivably base attempt at the murder of our Führer was committed today by Colonel Graf von Stauffenberg on the orders of a miserable clique of one-time generals who, because of their wretched and cowardly conduct of the war, were driven from their posts.

Admiral Dönitz was even more fulsome:

> Holy wrath and immeasurable rage fill our hearts at the criminal assault which was intended to take the life of our beloved Führer. Providence wished to have it otherwise; Providence guarded and protected the Führer; thus Providence did not desert our German Fatherland in its fated hour.[1]

In Paris, the coup had gone well at first. Kluge had continued to sit on the fence, but Stülpnagel managed to arrest and imprison the entire SS force there. Later, when news of the coup's failure reached him, he was obliged to let them go again. Many would not leave prison for fear of one of their own techniques being used against them – to let prisoners go and then shoot them 'while they were trying to escape'! Stülpnagel subsequently attempted suicide by shooting himself through the temple, but succeeded only in blinding himself. He later stood trial and was executed. Kluge, realising that his shilly-shallying had not endeared him to Hitler or saved him from the Führer's wrath, wrote the dictator a letter expressing his loyalty and regret, and took poison. General Eduard Wagner shot himself at Zossen immediately after the failure of the coup.

On the east front, Fabian von Schlabrendorff took the news of the failure of the coup to Tresckow. He took it calmly and said: 'I must shoot myself. The trail will lead to me and they will try to wring other names out of me. I must avoid that likelihood.'[2] The next day, when the two men parted company, Tresckow was resolute. He said:

> Now the whole world will fall on us and curse us. But I am still of the firm opinion that we did the right thing. I hold Hitler to be not only the arch fiend of Germany, but the arch fiend of the whole world. In a few hours I will stand before God's judgement seat, to lay before Him my sins of commission and omission, and I know I will stand by my good conscience in the matter of what I undertook against Hitler. When God once told Abraham that He

would spare Sodom if he could show Him ten just men there, so I
hope that God will not destroy Germany, because we stood firm for
our country. Not one of us can complain that we must die. Everyone
who joined the conspiracy put on the Shirt of Nessus. The moral
worth of a person only shows itself when he is prepared to die for
what he believes in.

On 21 July, Tresckow visited 28 Commando Division. He explained
everything to the commander, Major Kuhn. Then he walked into no-
man's-land, where he mimicked an exchange of fire with two pistols,
so that Kuhn could report that he had died in action. Once out of
sight, he took out a rifle grenade, pulled the safety pin, and blew
his head off. Schlabrendorff took his body home to Brandenburg,
where Henning von Tresckow was buried next to his parents. He was
forty-three years old. Later the Nazis exhumed the body and burnt it.

Schlabrendorff was now on the run himself. He avoided the
first huge wave of arrests that followed 20 July, and developed a
sixth sense for danger, but he was finally taken on 17 August. He
was taken to Berlin, where he had to guide his two Gestapo escorts
through Friedrichsstrasse Station, as they did not know the city. Once
in prison there, however, his treatment became noticeably more brutal. He was tortured and taken to Sachsenhausen concentration camp
to await trial. While in prison he got to know Dietrich Bonhoeffer,
although conversation between prisoners was strictly forbidden.

He was finally brought to trial before Freisler late in the morning
on 3 February 1945. The trial was interrupted by an enemy air raid
and the court took refuge in the basement. But the court building
took a direct hit and a dislodged beam fell on Freisler's head,
breaking the judge's cranium in two places and killing him. He
had Schlabrendorff's case notes in his hand at the time. During
the same raid, Gestapo Headquarters was hit and went up in flames.
Schlabrendorff's trial was not resumed and he survived the war, one
of the very few of the conspiracy who did.

Another survivor was Gersdorff, whose career after 20 July is
of psychological interest. By that time he had become Chief of
Staff to the 7th Army in France. After the failure of the coup he
found that he was faced with three choices: suicide, 'crossing the
English Channel', or going underground in France. However, once
he had learnt that the information the Security Service had against
him was not incriminating, he tried to persuade Kluge to negotiate

with the US general, Bradley. This was one of several schemes the Resistance had to open up the west front to the Allies. Kluge would not entertain such an idea, so Gersdorff returned to his post. He never considered surrender and when he was finally taken prisoner he escaped. He rejoined the German lines, and later led his troops out of the Falaise 'pocket', where they had been surrounded. He was promoted Major-General and went on fighting until the end. He was also awarded the Knight's Cross by SS-Obergruppenführer (General) Paul Hausser. Perhaps he finally succeeded in doing what many officers attempted – a retreat into simple military duty.[3] Perhaps though he felt that his only course now was to do what he had been trained to do to the best of his ability until the end.

Freisler's death came far too late for the majority of the conspirators, whom he had sent to execution in the latter half of 1944. His hectoring tone cannot be heard in the official stenographers' reports of the trials, and these also excise his foul language, but both can still be appreciated in the surviving film of his performances. His method was so thuggish that he attracted the criticism even of his fellow Nazis, though on one occasion he was moved to comment that it was hardly appropriate for a former general (Hoepner) to appear before him in a hand-me-down cardigan. He also demanded that Witzleben be given some means of supporting his trousers in court. By such small but vicious humiliations did the Nazis drive their revenge home, so that even Freisler was moved to some sense of propriety, if not humanity. Humanity did not figure in this man's personality. At Hoepner's trial, he was as brutal and humiliating as always:

> 'You are not a Schweinehund?' Freisler stretched in his judge's seat and spitefully barked at the defendant. 'Well then, if you don't want to be a Schweinehund, tell us what zoological class you consider to be your proper category?' Hoepner hesitated briefly. With the [concealed] sound camera grinding away, Freisler pursued his point. 'Well, what are you?' 'An ass.'[4]

Witzleben had taken refuge at the estate of his aide, Graf Lynar, in Kalau, but his arrest followed almost immediately. He was tried and executed in early August along with Hoepner, Stieff, Hase, Wartenburg and Klausing. Kleist and von Oppen were released in the hope that they would lead the Gestapo to other conspirators. Neither did so, and both survived the war.

Goerdeler had hidden at the home of his friend Krafft Freiherr von Palombini in Naumberg. Palombini himself was arrested at 7.30a.m. on 21 July but Goerdeler managed to escape via the back door and the garden. The Palombinis' Polish maid quickly tidied his room to make it look as if it had been unoccupied. Goerdeler reached Berlin and found refuge with various loyal friends, changing his abode almost nightly, but still finding time to write political memoranda. His thirteen-year-old youngest daughter, Benigna, was arrested on 29 July and taken to Heilbronn Prison. On 1 August, the day after his sixtieth birthday, a reward of 1 million Reichsmark was announced for his capture. As time ran out – he did not want to imperil his family – he made a foolhardy visit to his old home town of Marienwerder to pay his respects at his parents' grave. Inevitably in such a small town he was recognised, and betrayed by a Luftwaffe woman whose family had received much kindness from Goerdeler's in the past. Once arrested, he was extremely loquacious at his interrogations, in the hope of spinning out the process until it was too late to bring him to trial.

Both he and Johannes Popitz, the former Prussian Cabinet minister, were kept alive for a long time as the Security Service milked their expertise on and even asked their advice about the problems of reconstruction after the war. Himmler was by now anxiously exploring peace possibilities through contacts in Sweden, and it is possible that Goerdeler may have exploited this in his turn. Nevertheless, his mind declined during the lonely months of his imprisonment. He was executed at last on 2 February 1945. He never lost the habit of copious writing, and his 'Thoughts of a Man Condemned to Death', a political and personal testament written in prison, runs to 200 pages.

Hans Oster was arrested on 21 July and interrogated by the SS lawyer, Walter Huppenkothen, a cold-blooded sidekick of Franz Xaver Sonderegger's. Although he was able to keep one step ahead of his gaolers, he suffered terribly from isolation in prison, and when on 22 September Sonderegger discovered the great archive of Nazi crimes compiled by Dohnanyi in a safe at Zossen, he had to draw on his last reserves of strength to fight a rearguard action, but the battle was over. After the huge American air raid on Berlin on 3 February 1945, which left 22,000 dead, plans were laid to remove important prisoners from the capital and its environs. Soon after, Oster, Canaris and others were transferred to Flossenburg concentration camp near the Czech border, where for the first time they encountered physical violence. At the beginning of April they were joined there by another 'transport' which included Dietrich Bonhoeffer.

On 5 April 1945 at his regular lunchtime meeting, Hitler decided to liquidate Canaris, Oster, Karl Sack, Ludwig Gehre, Bonhoeffer and Theodor Strünck – the last an associate of Gisevius and Goerdeler. All were prisoners at Flossenburg by then. Huppenkothen was sent to the camp to supervise the executions, though he made a detour to Sachsenhausen briefly on 6 April to 'try' and see executed Hans von Dohnanyi. On 8 April a similar trial was held at Flossenburg by SS Judge Otto Thorack, with Huppenkothen in attendance. Each defendant's hearing lasted half an hour. The sentence was death by hanging, and it was carried out at dawn in the freezing cold the next day.[5] Of Bonhoeffer, the SS doctor who witnessed the killings wrote later (in 1955): 'In nearly fifty years as a doctor I never saw another man go to his death so possessed of the spirit of God.' Canaris was not shown any physical violence and was allowed clean linen, but he was not spared lengthy interrogations. He was put in a cell next door to Colonel Hans M. Lunding of Danish Intelligence, with whom he communicated using a tapping code on the partition wall. His last message, at 2a.m. was:

> I die for my country and with a clear conscience. You, as an officer, will realise that I was only doing my duty to my country when I endeavoured to oppose Hitler and to hinder the senseless crimes by which he has dragged Germany down to ruin. I know that all I did was in vain, for Germany will be completely defeated.

Otto John managed to escape to Spain, but his brother Hans, and Klaus Bonhoeffer, Justus Perels and Rüdiger Schleicher, had all been arrested by early October 1944 and taken to Lehrterstrasse Prison. They were taken from there to a piece of waste ground by an SS squad in the night of 22–23 April 1945 and murdered by shots through the neck, together with Karl Ludwig Guttenberg and Albrecht Haushofer.

Of those who died in the courtyard of the Bendlerblock on the night of 20 July, Werner von Haeften had been engaged to be married to Bonte von Hardenberg, one of Graf Hardenberg's daughters. The circumstances of Hardenberg's own arrest at his home in Neu-Hardenberg carry elements of black comedy. The four Gestapo officers arrived as the family were finishing dinner. Hardenberg said goodbye to his wife, and went into the library, followed by one of the policemen, who was not in time, however, to prevent the count from shooting himself twice in the chest. In fact the policeman thought for a moment that Hardenberg was shooting at him and fired back, after each shot jumping for cover behind the oak door of the small inner library, missing each time; but he did hit one of his fellow policemen in the leg.

Hardenberg survived his suicide attempt, and the next morning the Gestapo men, who had stayed the night, were offered breakfast by the countess. After some hesitation they accepted. It was now the morning of Tuesday, 25 July 1944. Hardenberg was still bent on dying, and persuaded his doctor, who had been summoned, to give him an overdose of morphine. However, he survived that too. Then he tried to open up his bullet wounds, saying, 'I must die!' Meanwhile his Security Service guard slept, snoring, in the same room. Another doctor arrived and from him Hardenberg procured a large pair of scissors, which he drove into his wrists, but they were too blunt to be effective. Meanwhile, more Gestapo arrived, bound the count's wounds, and drove him off to Berlin in an SS ambulance. The journey took two and a half hours.

Hardenberg was subsequently delivered to Sachsenhausen concentration camp on a stretcher. There, one of the prison orderlies whispered to him, 'Don't talk – there are stool-pigeons everywhere.' Then he kissed Hardenberg on the forehead, saying, 'I don't know what's up but we all thank you for what you've done.' Hardenberg later recalled, 'I was very gratified – until I learnt a few days later that the man had been interned for years under Article 175!' – Article 175 was the law against male homosexuality.[6]

In the camp, Hardenberg was cured by a fellow prisoner, the eminent French surgeon, Condère. He survived the war.

The whole of the Stauffenberg family was arrested within days of 20 July. Countess Nina was held in solitary confinement, but the others were kept together and, like so many other relations of conspirators, trailed from concentration camp to concentration camp, where they were kept in special barracks. They were not mistreated, though they shared the common fate of prisoners in the camps: semi-starvation and being a prey to every louse, bedbug and illness in God's creation. Goerdeler's younger brother Fritz was with them for some of the time. He had trained as a doctor and was able to give some help, but there was no medication available. Nina's mother, Freiin von Lerchenfeld, died at Stutthof camp, near Danzig, in the winter of 1944–45. Temperatures stood at −20° Celsius.

With the Russian advance, the special prisoners were transported to camps in Germany. In Buchenwald, the guards were much more brutal. Here, Kurt von Hammerstein's wife and daughter were imprisoned. By the end of April 1945 the VIPs were taken briefly to Dachau, and thence to the Tyrol. As there wasn't enough room on the trains, the younger and fitter prisoners travelled on foot. In one such group was a nephew of Stauffenberg's. He knew the area round Dachau well. When his group was well clear of the camp their two SS guards said that they would do a deal. The American forces were breathing down their necks anyway. They would let the prisoners go in return for two outfits of civilian clothes. They were harmless little privates who might well have been forced to join the SS. A deal was struck. This Stauffenberg was the first of the family to get home.

Meanwhile the main body of special prisoners were taken to Innsbruck, and thence across the Brenner Pass to a village in the South Tyrol by bus. Among them were General Halder, the former Austrian Chancellor Schuschnigg, the French statesman Leon Blum, and another nephew of Stauffenberg, Graf Otto-Philipp, then a teenager, who is today the master of the family Castle Greifenstein, near Bamberg.

I think the Nazis were keeping us as hostages to buy their liberty or at least clemency. There were over 100 of us as we arrived at the village on about 1 May. There a rumour started that orders had been given to kill us rather than let us fall into enemy hands. Our ordinary guards were scared, but their officers were fanatics, and the SS men would have carried out their orders. Against orders, we disembarked from the buses and followed the officers who had gone into the village to sort out billets. We wanted to find out what our fate would be. Our guards didn't dare fire at us, and so they escorted us. Among us was the General Staff Colonel Bogislaw von Bonin, who had been arrested for retreating on the east front in defiance of a Führer order, but he still had his full uniform with decorations and the General Staff red stripe on his trousers. He found a German Army radio station in the village, and went there without the knowledge of the SS. The regular soldiers didn't know he was a prisoner and obeyed him when he ordered them to put him in contact with the commander-in-chief, Italy, General Vietinghoff, whom he knew well. He spoke to Vietinghoff and explained the situation candidly, requesting help. He then rejoined the rest of us in the schoolhouse where we had been billeted. That night there was a great clamour, though no shots were fired. An Army major appeared in the school and told us that his unit had arrived, disarmed the SS and sent them off in one of the buses – they were killed later by Italian partisans. The unit had been sent by Vietinghoff and we were now under the Army's protection. They took us to a hotel nearby where we were liberated by the Americans a day or two later.

By then Hitler was dead – he had committed suicide in his bunker in Berlin on 30 April, taking with him his bride, Eva Braun, and his favourite Alsatian dog, Blondi. The Russian tanks were only a few hundred yards away. On 7 May the war ended in Europe, as Jodl signed the unconditional surrender in Reims. Thirty million people had died in the carnage – far more than would have done had the war ended in the summer of 1944. A further eleven million died in the concentration camps, half of them Jews, including millions during the slaughterhouse summer of 1944.

The attempt to bring Hitler down was not understood properly by the Allies at the time. On 1 August 1944 the New York *Herald Tribune* reported: 'If Hitlerism has begun its last stand by destroying the militarist tradition it has been doing a large part of the Allies' work for them.' On 9 August it followed this up with an article which argued that the attempt on Hitler was more reminiscent of 'the atmosphere of a gangster's lurid underworld' than of what 'one would normally expect within an officers' corps and a civilised state'. The attempt had been carried out with 'a bomb, the typical weapon of the underworld'.[7] Less forgivable was the attitude of the academic and diplomat John Wheeler-Bennett, one of the first Anglo-Saxons to write a history of the German Army following the war, who wrote soon after 20 July,

It may now be said with some definiteness that we are better off with things as they are today than if the plot of 20th July had succeeded and Hitler been assassinated . . . The Gestapo and the SS have done us an appreciable service in removing a selection of those who would undoubtedly have posed as 'good' Germans after the war . . . It is to our advantage therefore that the purge should continue, since the killing of Germans by Germans will save us from future embarrassments of many kinds.[8]

Today there is greater understanding of what the men and women

of the German Resistance tried to do – even taking the exigencies of
the time into account, Wheeler-Bennett's attitude is inexcusable. But
the heroes – if heroes they were – remain unsung. Streets in Germany
are named after them, but there are no monuments. Otto-Philipp von
Stauffenberg has a room dedicated to his uncle's work at Schloss
Greifenstein, but he is not aware of any great knowledge of or
interest in the Resistance among young Germans.

What happened to those who survived? Not all can be accounted
for here. In the postwar years, Schulenburg's widow, destitute, had
to prove to the authorities that her late husband, a Nazi Party member
with an 'early' number, had been in the Resistance, before she could
qualify for a pension. Other widows, Marion Yorck von Wartenburg
and Clarita von Trott zu Solz, resumed their interrupted careers.
Countess Yorck is a lawyer and Dr von Trott a psychiatrist. Both
live in Berlin, the latter a stone's throw from St Ann's Church in
Dahlem. Two minutes' walk from the church in another direction
lives Ludwig von Hammerstein, now retired, who became a journalist
after the war and was for many years head of RIAS – Berlin's Radio
In the American Sector. His house is a few doors down from where
the Bielenbergs lived. Christabel and Peter Bielenberg have lived in
Ireland since the end of the war.

Ewald von Kleist – whose father was among those executed after
20 July – is a publisher in Munich; Georg von Oppen is a rancher
in the Argentine. Axel von dem Bussche, until his death in 1993,
lived in retirement in Bonn. Oster's surviving daughter, whose fiery
personality derives in part, one likes to think, from her father, lives
comfortably in a Hamburg suburb. Hans von Dohnanyi's son Klaus
is a prominent liberal politician and a former mayor of Hamburg.
Ludwig Beck's daughter Gertrud is a widow and lives near Munich.
In a beautiful house in a village buried deep in the Allgäu lives Inge
Scholl, now retired, but one of Germany's foremost postwar educational reformers. Otl Aicher died in 1991, but his contribution to
graphic art was immense. He designed logos for Braun, Lufthansa
and ERCO, and he was the originator of the 'geometric man' used
on road signs throughout the world. Nina von Stauffenberg lives in
Bamberg – still in the same apartment she and Claus moved into as
newlyweds in 1933. Fritz-Dietlof von der Schulenburg was born in
London in 1902 where his father was military attaché. Two of his
six children live there today.

Major Ernst Remer enjoyed a rapid series of promotions following 20 July, and after the end of the war he founded one of Germany's first neo-Nazi parties: the Socialist Reich Party. He is still a hero in neo-Nazi circles there.

That this is the story of a defeat none will doubt. Some will dispute that it was an honourable one. It is certainly not the story of a failure. Against terrible odds and in appalling circumstances a small group of people kept the spirit of German integrity alive, and with it the elusive spirit of humanity. We should all be grateful to them for that.

WHO'S WHO

Colonel-General Ludwig Beck, Chief of the Army General Staff 1935–38. Then, in retirement, the leader of the Central Military Resistance. He would have been Head of State in the event of a successful coup. Attempted suicide twice before being assisted. Died in the Bendlerstrasse on the night of 20 July 1944.

George Kennedy Allen Bell, Bishop of Chichester, and contact with Britain for Dietrich Bonhoeffer.

Field Marshal Werner von Blomberg, Hitler's first Minister of War; disgraced, 1938.

Colonel Georg Freiherr von Boselager, conspirator attached to Tresckow's group initially on the East Front. Creator of the 'Boeselager Brigade'. Hanged 27 August 1944.

Dietrich Bonhoeffer, Evangelical pastor and theologian. Worked with the Abwehr after close association with the Confessing Church. Hanged at Flossenburg concentration camp on 9 April 1945.

Klaus Bonhoeffer, lawyer at Lufthansa; conspirator. Shot dead by an SS special detail on the night of 22 April 1945.

Field Marshal Walther von Brauchitsch, Commander-in-Chief of the Army, 1938–41.

Axel Freiherr von dem Bussche, junior officer who planned an assassination attempt with Claus Stauffenberg. Survived the war.

Admiral Wilhelm Canaris, head of the Abwehr and key figure in the conspiracy axis Army/Secret Service/Foreign Office. Hanged at Flossenburg on 9 April 1945.

Dr Justus Delbrück, brother-in-law of the Bonhoeffers – his sister married Klaus. Worked for the Resistance in the Abwehr. Survived the war but died soon after in Russian POW camp.

Father Alfred Delp S.J., prominent Jesuit member of the Kreisau Circle. Executed on 2 February 1945.

Hans von Dohnanyi, senior lawyer and member of the Abwehr. Hans Oster's right-hand man, and brother-in-law of the Bonhoeffers. Hanged at Sachsenhausen concentration camp, 8 April 1945.

Allen Dulles, American head of OSS office in Berne.

Georg Elser, who made a solitary attempt on Hitler's life in November 1939.

General Fritz Erich Fellgiebel, head of Army Communications and a key figure in the 20 July 1944 attempt. Executed 4 September 1944.

Roland Freisler, Hitler's hanging judge in the People's Court.

Colonel-General Werner Freiherr von Fritsch, Commander-in-Chief of the Army, 1934–38; disgraced, sought death in action in first days of the war.

Colonel-General Friedrich Fromm, commander of the Reserve Army. Executed for cowardice by Hitler following the 20 July plot.

Clemens August Graf von Galen, Bishop of Münster who spoke out against the Nazi euthanasia programme.

Captain Ludwig Gehre, Abwehr official in the Resistance. Executed at Flossenburg, 9 April 1945.

Kurt Gerstein, SS officer responsible for delivery of poison gas to the concentration camps but also involved in individual Resistance. Committed suicide (?) in Paris, 1945.

Dr Hans Bernd Gisevius, lawyer, civil servant and former Gestapo official, involved with the police and diplomatic areas of the Resistance. Survived the war.

Dr Carl Friedrich Goerdeler, one-time Mayor of Leipzig, and Weimar and National Socialist Price Commissioner. Chief of the Conservative Civilian Resistance, and Chancellor-Designate following a successful coup. Hanged at Plötzensee Prison, 2 February 1945.

Dr Fritz Goerdeler, Carl Fredrich's younger brother. Formerly City Treasurer of Königsberg (Kaliningrad).

Lieutenant-Colonel Helmuth Groscurth, Abwehr departmental chief and go-between. Committed suicide in Russian POW camp, April 1945.

Karl Ludwig Freiherr von und zu Guttenberg, intellectual monarchist and magazine editor; also an official of the Abwehr. Shot dead by an SS special detail on the night of 22 April 1945.

Lieutenant of the Naval Reserve Hans-Bernd von Haeften, lawyer and Foreign Office official, involved in the Resistance but consistently opposed to the assassination of Hitler. Executed 15 August 1944.

Lieutenant Werner von Haeften, brother of Hans-Bernd; Claus

von Stauffenberg's ADC. Shot dead on the night of 20 July 1944.
Colonel-General Franz Halder, Chief of the Army General Staff, 1938–42.
Nikolaus von Halem, businessman and planner of independent attempt on Hitler's life. Also involved with the Abwehr. Executed 8 October 1944.
Lieutenant Ludwig Freiherr von Hammerstein, junior member of the conspiracy and Beck's ADC-Designate in the event of a successful coup. Escaped from the Bendlerblock on 20 July 1944 and survived the war.
Colonel-General Kurt Freiherr von Hammerstein-Equord, father of Ludwig, Commander-in-Chief of the Army, 1930–34, and one of the earliest opponents of Nazism. Died of cancer in 1943.
Colonel Georg Hansen, Canaris's successor as head of the Abwehr, and involved in the Resistance. Hanged at Plötzensee, 8 September 1944.
Colonel-General Paul von Hase, uncle of the Bonhoeffers and Commandant of the Berlin garrison, 1940–44. Hanged on 8 August 1944.
Ulrich von Hassell, diplomat and former ambassador to Rome. Involved in negotiations with the Vatican and also a pivotal member of the Beck–Goerdeler group. Hanged on 8 September 1944.
Dr Theodor Haubach, journalist and Social Democrat politician. Associate of Julius Leber and member of the Kreisau Circle. Hanged on 23 January 1945.
Dr Georg Albrecht Haushofer, Professor of Political Geography at Berlin University, involved in the conspiracy and enjoying some influence with Rudolf Hess. Author of a sonnet cycle written in Moabit Prison. Shot dead by an SS special detail on the night of 22 April 1945.
Wolf Heinrich Graf von Helldorf, Senior SA official and President of Police, Berlin, 1935–44. Involved with Nebe and Gisevius especially in the conspiracy. Hanged on 5 August 1944.
Colonel-General Erich Hoepner, tank commander sacked and disgraced by Hitler for refusing to obey stupid and inhuman commands on the Russian Front. Senior member of military Resistance; hanged 8 August, 1944.
Lieutenant-Colonel Cäsar von Hofacker, go-between of the Central Resistance in Berlin and Military Command, Paris. Executed on 20 December, 1944.
Dr Peter Jens Jessen, conservative economist and academic; leading member of civilian Resistance. Executed on 20 November 1944.

Otto John, lawyer at Lufthansa; involved with the Lufthansa Administration/Abwehr/Foreign Office axis of the Resistance. Survived the war.

Captain of the Army Reserve Dr Hermann Kaiser, go-between of Beck and Goerdeler; executed on 23 January 1945.

Field Marshal Wilhelm Keitel, head of Overall High Command of the Armed Forces, and Hitler's lackey.

Otto Kiep, diplomat and member of the Solf Circle. Hanged at Plötzensee, 26 August 1944.

Captain Friedrich Karl Klausing, Claus Stauffenberg's adjutant; hanged at Plötzensee, 8 August 1944.

Ewald von Kleist-Schmenzin, estate owner and conservative opponent to Hitler. Executed 16 April, 1945.

Ewald Heinrich von Kleist, son of the above; junior officer who planned an assassination attempt with Claus Stauffenberg. Survived the war.

Field Marshal Günther von Kluge, senior officer who could never wholly commit himself to the Resistance, finally committing suicide in the wake of the 20 July Plot.

Dr Carl Langbehn, lawyer and associate of Popitz, who attempted to suborn Himmler. Executed 12 October 1944.

Dr Julius Leber, journalist and Social Democrat politician; Claus Stauffenberg's favoured Chancellor-Designate. Arrested after an abortive attempt to liaise with the Communist Party underground, and executed on 5 January 1945.

Wilhelm Leuschner, trade union leader and close associate of Leber, hanged 29 September 1944.

Major Wilhelm Friedrich Graf zu Lynar, adjutant to Witzleben, executed 29 September 1944.

Hermann Maass, Social Democrat and youth leader. Associate of Leber involved with the Kreisau Circle. Executed on 20 October 1944.

Colonel Albrecht Ritter Mertz von Quirnheim, friend of Claus Stauffenberg, and his successor as Chief of Staff to General Olbricht. Shot dead by firing squad, 20 July 1944.

Helmuth James Graf von Moltke, one of the leading lights of the Kreisau Circle, and active in the Resistance; executed 23 January 1945.

Dr Josef Müller, Catholic lawyer and Vatican contact for the Resistance. He variously worked in Bamberg and Munich.

Herbert Mumm von Schwarzenstein, associate of Nikolaus Halem and a member of the Solf Circle, executed in April 1945.

Artur Nebe, senior SS official and head of the Criminal Investigation Police. Involved with Helldorf and Gisevius in the Resistance, and executed on 3 March 1945.

Martin Niemöller, Evangelical priest and founder member of Church Resistance to Nazism; closely involved with the Confessing Church. Survived the war in concentration camps.

General Friedrich Olbricht, head of Army Central Administration Office and chief successively to Claus Stauffenberg and Mertz von Quirnheim. A senior Army officer involved in the Resistance in a key position; shot dead by firing squad on 20 July 1944.

Major-General Hans Oster, Canaris's right-hand man in the Abwehr and one of the most important men in the Resistance, an indefatigable opponent of the Nazi regime. Hanged at Flossenburg, 9 April 1945.

Dr Friedrich Justus Perels, lawyer closely involved with the Confessing Church, executed by SS special detail, April 1945.

Professor Dr Johannes Popitz, Prussian Finance Minister 1933–44. Senior member of the conservative Resistance, executed 2 February 1945.

Professor Dr Adolf Reichwein, Social Democrat, educationalist and traveller, associated closely with Julius Leber, executed 20 October 1944.

Field Marshal Erwin Rommel, who joined the conspiracy late as a potential Head of State. Forced to commit suicide by the Nazis on 14 October 1944.

Dr Karl Sack, head of Overall Army High Command Legal Department, and an undercover friend to the Resistance; executed at Flossenburg, 9 April 1945.

Anton Saefkow, leader of undercover Communist Party.

Hjalmar Schacht, politician and economist; originally pro-Nazi; survived the war.

Lieutenant Fabian von Schlabrendorff, lawyer and close associate of Tresckow. Survived the war.

Professor Dr Rüdiger Schleicher, brother-in-law of the Bonhoeffers, and an official in the Air Ministry. Shot dead by an SS special detail, on the night of 22 April 1945.

Hans Scholl, medical student in Munich, member of the White Rose student anti-Nazi group. Beheaded in February 1943.

Sophie Scholl, student of biology and philosophy, sister of Hans, member of the White Rose; beheaded with her brother.

Friedrich (Fritz) Dietlof Graf von der Schulenburg, highly connected former Nazi and deputy President of Police of Berlin, also involved with the Kreisau Circle; executed 10 August 1944.

Captain Ulrich Wilhelm Graf von Schwanenfeld, Adjutant to Witzleben and an important liaison officer in the Resistance; executed 8 September 1944.

General Walter von Seydlitz-Kurzbach, commander on the East Front and involved as a POW with the National Committee for Free Germany. Survived the war.

Berthold Graf Schenk von Stauffenberg, lawyer and naval officer, brother and adviser of Claus; hanged on 10 August 1944.

Colonel Claus Graf Schenk von Stauffenberg, leader of Resistance in its latter stages and the chief actor in the 20 July 1944 plot. Shot dead on the night of 20 July 1944.

Major-General Helmuth Stieff, head of Organisation Office, Army High Command, and involved in the procurement of explosives for 20 July Plot. Executed on 8 August 1944.

General Karl-Heinrich von Stülpnagel, Military Governor of France 1942–44, and involved with the Resistance on the West Front. Hanged on 30 August 1944.

Elisabeth von Thadden, educationalist and intellectual whose involvement with the Solf Circle led to her execution on 8 September 1944.

Lieutenant-General Fritz Thiele, commander of Overall High Command Signals Department, in liaison with Fellgiebel. Executed on 5 September 1944.

Major-General Henning von Tresckow, leader of the Resistance on the East Front and later associated with Stauffenberg. Committed suicide on 21 July 1944.

Adam von Trott zu Solz, lawyer and diplomat heavily involved in Resistance missions abroad. Executed 25 August 1944.

Sir Robert Vansittart, British Permanent Under-Secretary at the Foreign Office, removed by British Prime Minister Neville Chamberlain on account of his anti-appeasement stance.

Ernst Freiherr von Weizsäcker, State Secretary at the Foreign Office, involved in the Resistance.

Field Marshal Erwin von Witzleben, senior military figure in the Resistance after Beck, and overall Commander-in-Chief-Designate in the event of a successful coup. Hanged 8 August 1944.

Peter Graf Yorck von Wartenburg, co-leader with Moltke of the Kreisau Circle; hanged on 8 August 1944.

Colonel-General Kurt Zeitzler, Chief of the Army General Staff, 1942–44.

NOTES

FOREWORD

1. Wolfgang Venohr: *Stauffenberg, Symbol Der Deutschen Einheit, Eine Politische Biographie*. Ullstein, Frankfurt/Main, 1986, p. 15.
2. See Carl Zuckmayer's biographical play *Des Teufels General*, Fischer, Frankfurt/Main, 1976, which is dedicated to several members of the Resistance. Udet and Zuckmayer were close friends before the playwright went into exile.
3. For further information, see Matthew Cooper: *The German Army 1933–45*, Macdonald and Jane's, London, 1978, pp. 91 ff.
4. Translated by R. J. Hollingdale.

PART ONE 1933–1938

ONE: The End of the Republic

1. So-called for their brown uniforms. The Nazi mythmakers attributed earth association and symbolism to the colour. In fact, it was chosen in the early days of the Party because brown material was the cheapest available.
2. '*Du*' is the equivalent of '*tu*' in French and the old 'thou' in English. The polite form of calling someone 'you' in German is '*Sie*'. To transfer from this to '*Du*' is roughly equivalent to switching from surnames to Christian names. Younger Germans today switch quickly, but German social customs remain more conservative than ours, and in the first half of the century people were even more formal. Nevertheless, it is a mark of Hitler's reserve that he was so grudging in his use of '*Du*' – which of

course he would also have used to female intimates like Eva Braun.

3. A good guide is *Topographie des Terrors*, edited by Reinhard Rürup; Arenhövel, Berlin, 1987, revised and expanded 1989. Available in an English translation as *Topography of Terror*.

4. Gisevius was one of the few principal conspirators to survive. He wrote two books (see Bibliography), which are first-hand accounts of events, written from a personal and biased point of view. This passage is taken from the more important of the two, *To the Bitter End*, translated by Richard and Clara Winston; Greenwood, Connecticut, 1947 and 1975, pp. 63–64.

5. Prussia, the largest state in the German Federation and a bastion of social democracy, had had its government dissolved by an unconstitutional coup engineered by Hitler's predecessors as Chancellor, Kurt von Schleicher and Franz von Papen. Berlin was capital of Prussia as well as being the Federal Capital, and its Prussian police force might have been an effective deterrent to SA outrages there. But Prussia fell without putting up a fight. See Erich Eyck: *History of the Weimar Republic*, volume II, translated by Harlan P. Hanson and Robert G. L. Waite, Harvard UP, 1967.

6. Gisevius, op. cit., gives a full account, pp. 62–81.

7. Fabian von Schlabrendorff: *Offiziere gegen Hitler*, Fischer, Frankfurt/Main, 1962, p. 24.

8. ibid., p. 22.

9. Christabel Bielenberg: *The Past Is Myself*. Corgi, London, 1984, pp. 51–52.

10. Hoffmann, Peter, *The History of the German Resistance 1933–1945*, translated by Richard Berry, Macdonald and Jane's, London, 1977, pp. 15–16.

11. The long and complex story of the Jewish persecution cannot be addressed here. See especially Martin Gilbert: *The Holocaust*, Collins, London, 1986.

12. Camouflaged books and pamphlets generally had the cover, title page and first couple of paragraphs of a permitted or innocuous publication to prevent their being spotted by Nazi security services, especially if they were being smuggled in from abroad. Another technique was to print on fine India paper which could be folded small and thus easily concealed.

TWO: The Big Battalions

1. Richard Grunberger: *A Social History of the Third Reich*,

Penguin, Harmondsworth, 1979, p. 179.
2. The Hitler quotations are from *Mein Kampf*. The passage is from: Joachim Fest: *Hitler*, translated by Richard and Clara Winston, Penguin, Harmondsworth, 1983, p. 78.
3. The full story is told in Fabian von Schlabrendorff, op. cit., pp. 22–24.
4. See *Es gab nicht nur den 20. Juli*, Pressestelle des WDR, 1979, p. 21.
5. Finding the correct ranks in translation is a difficult task. For 'Generalmajor', 'Generalleutnant' and 'Generaloberst', I have used Major-General, Lieutenant-General, and Colonel-General. Some (see for example Hoffmann's translator, op. cit. p. 767) would argue for 'Brigadier', 'Major-General' and 'General' respectively. While this may be more accurate, strictly speaking, there is no consistency in translations and I have opted for a simple direct translation, especially as there are few direct equivalents anyway.

THREE: A Fortress Strong

1. See Klemens von Klemperer's contribution to *Widerstand im Dritten Reich*, ed. Hermann Graml, Fischer, Frankfurt/Main, 1984, p. 142.
2. Quoted in Michael Balfour: *Withstanding Hitler*, Routledge Kegan Paul, London, 1988, p. 213. Balfour experienced the Germany of the period at first hand and was a friend and biographer of Moltke.
3. Quoted in *The German Resistance to Hitler*, ed. Walter Schmitthenner and Hans Buchheim, translated by Peter and Betty Ross, Batsford, London, 1970, p. 214.
4. 'Bekenntniskirche' in German: 'the Church which acknowledges the Confession of Faith'.
5. Accounts of what follows vary. I have drawn most upon that of Eberhard Bethge, Dietrich Bonhoeffer's disciple and biographer, who was present, and on the account given by Mary Bosanquet: *The Life and Death of Dietrich Bonhoeffer*, Hodder and Stoughton, London, 1969.
6. Readers wishing for more information on Bonhoeffer than this sketch provides should consult Eberhard Bethge's 1200-page biography (see Bibliography for details). I am also indebted to Mary Bosanquet's clear and much shorter work.
7. See Mary Bosanquet, op. cit., pp. 196–7.
8. Quoted in ibid. pp. 211 ff.

FOUR: Lost Illusions

1. For a good account of the war from the German angle, which provides very useful background to the Resistance, see Matthew Cooper, op. cit.
2. There was a great clan of von Kleists. To differentiate between the branches they added the names of their estates or home districts. Hence Schmenzin. The same applied to the von Hammersteins; hence: Hammerstein-Equord.
3. See Hoffmann, op. cit., pp. 19–21.
4. The whole structure of the police/SS/SD/Gestapo was highly complicated. Those interested in finding out more should see Reinhard Rürup, op. cit.

FIVE: Annus Fatalis

1. Gerhard Ritter: *The German Resistance: Carl Goerdeler's Struggle Against Tyranny*, translated by R. T. Clark, Allen and Unwin, London, 1958, p. 21. An abridged English version of the long German original. Subsequent quotations in the early part of this chapter are from this book.
2. Not to be confused with Raoul Wallenberg, the Swedish diplomat and saviour of Jews.
3. One source states – I am sure erroneously – that the statue was of the philosopher Moses Mendelssohn, grandfather of the composer.
4. According to the account by Goerdeler's daughter Marianne Meyer-Krahmer: *Carl Goerdeler und Sein Weg in den Widerstand*, Herder, Freiburg i. Br., 1989, pp. 96 ff. Ritter, op. cit., p. 80, mentions the patriarchal Gustav Krupp von Bohlen und Halbach.
5. Ritter, op. cit., p. 83.
6. Gisevius, op. cit., pp. 439–42.
7. Karl Heinz Absagen: *Canaris*, translated by Alan Houghton Broderick, Hutchinson, London, 1956, p. 101.
8. Place and street names underwent rapid changes in the Third Reich.
9. Quoted in John Wheeler-Bennett: *The Nemesis of Power*, Macmillan, London, 1954, p. 401.
10. The complicated history of resistance missions abroad is dealt with in, inter alia, Hoffmann, op. cit., and Wheeler-Bennett, op. cit. See also Giles MacDonough: *A Good German: Adam von Trott zu Solz*, Quartet, London, 1989, and for relations with Britain, Patricia Meehan: *The Unnecessary War: Whitehall and the*

German Resistance to Hitler, Sinclair-Stevenson, London, 1992.
11. I am indebted to Clare Colvin's unpublished *Contacts of a Secret Nature* for much of what follows. Further information came from Ewald Heinrich von Kleist.
12. For a sympathetic but unsentimental view, see the work of Chamberlain's biographer, Professor David Dilks.

PART TWO: 1938–1944

SIX: The End of Germany
1. Hans Rothfels: *The German Opposition to Hilter*, translated by Lawrence Wilson, Oswald Wolff, London, (reprinted) 1978, p. 31.
2. Quoted in Meehan, op. cit., p. 46.
3. Gisevius, op. cit., pp. 335 ff.
4. See Hans Mommsen's essay in Schmitthenner and Buchheim, op. cit., pp. 95 ff.
5. Quoted in Cooper, op. cit., p. 186.
6. Wheeler-Bennett, op. cit., p. 445, quoting General Thomas's memoirs: *Gedenken und Ereignisse* (Thoughts and Outcomes).
7. See Gisevius, op. cit., p. 361.
8. Schlabrendorff, op. cit., p. 46.
9. Gisevius, op. cit., pp. 389–90.

SEVEN: In the Shadows
1. Anton Gill: *The Journey Back From Hell*, Grafton, London, 1988, p. 24.
2. Gisevius held very conservative views and was appalled at Stauffenberg's left-wing liberalism.
3. See biographies mentioned in the Bibliography for the full and rather tragic story of Adam von Trott zu Solz.
4. Quoted in Giles MacDonough, op. cit., p. 45.
5. Margaret Boveri, quoted in ibid., p. 53.
6. Balfour, op. cit., p. 183.
7. Romedio Galeazzo Graf von Thun-Hohenstein: *Der Verschwörer*, Severin und Siedler, Berlin, 1982, pp. 192–3.

EIGHT: Holding On
1. For a full list, which includes many which did not get past the 'planning' stage, see Peter Hoffmann: *Die Sicherheit des Diktators*, Piper, Munich, 1975.

2. See Saul Friedländer: *Counterfeit Nazi*, translated by Charles Fullman, Weidenfeld and Nicolson, London, 1969.
3. DEGESCH: DEutsche GEsellschaft für SCHädlingsbekämpfung. Managing Director: Gerhard Peters.
4. A memorial museum is in the process of being constructed there by Walter Lorang of Frankfurt/Main.
5. For more on the political ideas and plans of the Resistance, see Hoffmann: *The German Resistance to Hitler*, and also the work of Ger van Roon and Hans Mommsen.
6. The only letters Countess von Moltke has held back are the personal ones he wrote to her during his long imprisonment between January 1944 and his execution a year later.
7. Balfour, op. cit., p. 202.
8. Letter to Freya, 12.12.40.
9. At the time of writing, Roeder was still alive in Germany, a father figure of the neo-Nazi movement there.

NINE: Protest of Youth
1. Much has been written about the Scholls. They have been the subject of feature films and novels. Not everything written about them is accurate. I am grateful to Inge Aicher-Scholl for much of my material. See also her book, *Die Weisse Rose*, Fischer, Frankfurt/Main, 1953 and 1986. At the time of writing a new edition is in preparation to mark the 50th anniversary of Hans's and Sophie's death, in February 1943.
2. See Hermann Vinke: *Das Kurze Leben der Sophie Scholl*, Otto Maier, Ravensburg, 1986–1987, pp. 77–8.
3. In the language of flowers, the white rose full of buds symbolises secrecy. *Brewer's Dictionary of Phrase and Fable*.
4. Fritz Theilen, *Edelweisspiraten*, Fischer-Boot, Frankfurt/Main, 1986, pp. 17–18.
5. Ibid. p. 28.

TEN: Resistance in the East
1. There seems to be no conclusive evidence yet that he wore body armour and a lead-lined cap, as has been suggested, and as many members of the Resistance believed.
2. Hoffmann, op. cit., pp. 263 ff.
3. *Klug* means 'clever' in German.

ELEVEN: Breaking Point
1.   The full complicated story is in Thun-Hohenstein, op. cit., pp. 236 ff.
2.   Kai P. Schoenhals: *The Free Germany Movement – A Case of Patriotism or Treason?* Greenwood, Westport, Connecticut, 1989, p. 10.
3.   Listening to such broadcasts was a capital offence. Signed letters could and did lead to the arrest and execution of the sender.

PART THREE: 1944–1945

TWELVE: A Hero Enters Late
1.   Apart from personal reminiscences of the man from family and friends, I am indebted for much of what follows to the two best existing Stauffenberg biographies, by Joachim Kramarz (English Translation, 1970, see bibliography) and Wolfgang Venohr (op. cit.). A new biography has long been in preparation by Peter Hoffmann and at the time of writing was due to be published.
2.   Of 2000 German generals, only twenty-two were involved in the Resistance, and many of these were already retired.

THIRTEEN: 20 July 1944
1.   For full details of the acquisition of explosives and the problems of cutting off Hitler's telecommunications, see Hoffmann, op. cit.
2.   V stands for *Vergeltung* – retaliation. The V1 and V2 were developed using concentration camp labour by Wernher von Braun, who was comfortably set up in rocket research in the USA by September 1945. The German for 'wonder-weapon' is *Wunderwaffe*. They were promptly nicknamed 'WuWas' by the cynical Berliners.
3.   There is no standard account of these events. What follows is taken from the most recent research and from accounts given me by officers present at the time. For reasons of space, the story here is told in broad detail. See Hoffmann, Venohr, and the books by Kunrat von Hammerstein (see Bibliography) for more.

FOURTEEN: Aftermath

1. Quoted in Gisevius, op. cit., pp. 574–5.
2. Schlabrendorff, op. cit., pp. 154 ff.
3. Balfour, from whom some of this account is taken, suggests that it was Field Marshal Walter Model who awarded the Knight's Cross (op. cit. p. 74).
4. Gisevius, op. cit., p. 572.
5. Some sources give 10 April.
6. This story is in Kunrat von Hammerstein's memoir, *Flucht*, Walter, Olten, 1966.
7. Quoted in Rothfels, op. cit.
8. Quoted in Meehan, op. cit.

BIBLIOGRAPHY

Abshagen, Karl Heinz, *Canaris*, translated by Alan Houghton Broderick, Hutchinson, London, 1956.

Aicher, Otl, *Innenseiten des Kriegs*, Fischer, Frankfurt/Main, 1985.

Balfour, Michael, *Withstanding Hitler*, Routledge Kegan Paul, London, 1988.

Bethge, Eberhard (ed. with others), *Dietrich Bonhoeffer*; Kaiser, Munich, 1986.

Bethge, Eberhard, *Bonhoeffer*, Kaiser, Munich, 1967.

Bielenberg, Christabel, *The Past Is Myself*, Corgi, London, 1984.

Borchert, Wolfgang, *Draussen vor der Tür und ausgewählte Erzählungen*, Rowohlt, Reinbek, 1962.

Bosanquet, Mary, *The Life and Death of Dietrich Bonhoeffer*, Hodder and Stoughton, London, 1969.

Canarius, Ulrich (ed.), *Opposition gegen Hitler*, Siedler, Berlin, 1984.

Cooper, Matthew, *The German Army 1933–1945*, Macdonald and Jane's, London, 1978.

Elling, Hanna, *Frauen im Deutschen Widerstand*, Röderberg, Frankfurt/Main, 1981.

Fest, Joachim, *The Face of the Third Reich*, translated by Michael Bullock, Penguin, Harmondsworth, 1983.

Fitzgibbon, Constantine, *The Shirt of Nessus*, Cassell, London, 1956.

Foerster, Wolfgang, *Generaloberst Ludwig Beck*, ISAR, Munich, 1953.

Friedländer, Saul, *Counterfeit Nazi* (biography of Gerstein), translated by Charles Fullman, Weidenfeld and Nicolson, London, 1969.

Gamm, Hans-Jochen, *Der Flüsterwitz im Dritten Reich*, List, Munich and Leipzig, 1990.

Gisevius, Hans Bernd, *To the Bitter End*, translated by R. and C. Winston, Greenwood, Connecticut, 1975.

Gisevius, Hans Bernd, *Wo ist Nebe?*, Deutscher Bücherbund, Stuttgart, 1966.

Graml, Hermann (ed.), *Widerstand im Dritten Reich – Probleme, Ereignisse, Gestalten*, Fischer, Frankfurt/Main, 1984.

Grunberger, Richard, *A Social History of the Third Reich*, Penguin, Harmondsworth, 1979.

Hammerstein, Kunrat von, *Spähtrupp*, Govarts, Stuttgart, 1963.

Hammerstein, Kunrat von, *Flucht*, Walter, Olten, 1966.

Heinemann, Ulrich, *Ein konservativer Rebell* (biography of Fritz-Dietlof von der Schulenburg), Siedler, Berlin, 1990.

Hoffmann, Peter, *The History of the German Resistance 1933–1945*, translated by Richard Barry, Macdonald and Jane's, London, 1977.

Höhne, Heinz, *Canaris*, Bertelsmann, Munich, 1976.

Jacobsen, Hans-Adolf (ed.), *Spiegelbild einer Verschwörung – Die Opposition gegen Hitler und der Staatsstreich vom 20. Juli 1944 in der SD-Berichterstattung. Geheime Dokumente aus dem ehemaligen Reichssicherheitshauptamt*, Seewald, Stuttgart, 1984.

Kettenacker, Lothar (ed.), *Das andere Deutschland im zweiten Weltkrieg*, Klein, Stuttgart, 1977.

Klemperer, Klemens von, *The German Resistance to Hitler* (translation), OUP, 1992.

Kramarz, Joachim, *Stauffenberg*, translated by R. H. Barry, Mayflower, 1970.

Leber, Annedore (ed. with Willy Brandt and Karl-Dietrich Bracher), *Das Gewissen Steht Auf* and *Das Gewissen Entscheidet*, Mosaik, Berlin, 1954 and 1957.

Liddell Hart, B. H., *The Other Side of the Hill*, Cassell, London, 1948.

Malone, Henry Ozelle, *Adam von Trott zu Solz*, Ann Arbor, 1960.

MacDonough, Giles, *A Good German – Adam von Trott zu Solz*, Quartet, London, 1989.

Meding, Dorothee von, *Mit dem Mut des Herzens – die Frauen des 20. Juli*, Siedler, Berlin, 1992.

Meehan, Patricia, *The Unnecessary War*, Sinclair-Stevenson, London, 1992.

Moltke, Helmuth James von, *Briefe an Freya* (ed. Beate Ruhm von Oppen), Beck, Munich, 1988.

Müller, Klaus-Jürgen, *Der Deutsche Widerstand 1933–45*; UTB/Schöningh, Paderborn and Zurich, 1986.

Ortnert, Helmut, *Der Einzelgänger* (biography of Elser); Moewig, Rastatt, 1989.

Peukert, Detlev, *Die KPD im Widerstand*, Hammer, Wuppertal, 1980.

Rauschning, Hermann, *Hitler Speaks*, Butterworth, London, 1939.

Ritter, Gerhard, *The German Resistance – Carl Goerdeler's Struggle Against Tyranny*, translated by R. T. Clark; Allen and Unwin, London, 1958.

Roon, Ger van, *Widerstand im Dritten Reich*, Beck, Munich, 1987.

Rothfels, Hans, *The German Opposition to Hitler*, translated by Lawrence Wilson, Oswald Wolff, London, 1961 and 1978.

Rürup, Reinhard (ed.), *Topographie des Terrors*, Arenhövel, Berlin, 1987.

Scheurig, Bodo, *Deutscher Widerstand 1938–44. Fortschritt oder Reaktion?*, dtv dokumente, 1969.

Schlabrendorff, Fabian von, *Offiziere gegen Hitler*, Fischer, Frankfurt/Main, 1962.

Schmädeke und Steinbach (eds.), *Der Widerstand gegen Nationalsozialismus*, Piper, Munich, 1986.

Schmitthenner and Buchheim (eds.), *The German Resistance to Hitler*, translated by P. and B. Ross, Batsford, London, 1970.

Schoenhals, Kai P., *The Free Germany Movement*, Greenwood, Connecticut, 1989.

Scholl, Hans und Sophie, *Briefe und Aufzeichnungen* (edited by Inge Jens), Fischer, Frankfurt/Main, 1989.

Scholl, Inge Aicher, *Die Weisse Rose*, Fischer, Frankfurt/Main, 1986.

Schwerin, Detlef von, *Die Jungen des 20. Juli 1944*, Verlag der Nation, Berlin, 1991.

Theilen, Fritz, *Edelweisspiraten*, Fischer-Boot, Frankfurt/Main, 1984.

Thun-Hohenstein, Romedio Galeazzo von, *Der Verschwörer* (biography of Oster), Severin und Siedler, Berlin, 1982.

Vansittart, Robert, *Black Record*, Hamish Hamilton, London, 1941.

Vansittart, Robert, *The Mist Procession*, Hutchinson, London, 1958.

Venohr, Wolfgang, *Stauffenberg*, Ullstein, Frankfurt/Main, 1986.

Vinke, Hermann, *Das kurze Leben von Sophie Scholl*, Otto Maier, Ravensburg, 1987.

Wheeler-Bennett, John, *The Nemesis of Power*, Macmillan, London, 1954.

Zeller, Eberhard, *Der Geist der Freiheit*, Rinn, Munich, 1952.

Index

Numbers in bold denote entries in the **Who's Who**

Grateful acknowledgment is made to reprint the following illustrations:

1, 2, 3, 4, 8, 11, 17, 21, 23, 25, 27, 30, 31, 32: Ullstein Bilderdienst.
5, 9, 13, 14: Bildarchiv Preussischer Kulturbesitz.
6, 7, 22, 26, 29: AKG, Berlin.
10, 20, 28: Gedenkstätte Deutscher Widerstand.
12: Geschwister Scholl Archiv.
15: Barbara von Krauss, family collection.
16: Clarita von Trott zu Solz, family collection.
18, 19, 24: Ludwig Freiherr von Hammerstein, family collection.